The Metaphysics of Mysticism

A Commentary on the Mystical Philosophy of St. John of the Cross

By
Geoffrey K. Mondello

"In finem nostrae cognitionis Deum tamquam ignotum cognoscimus" *

Dedication: to Mary, Mother of God

*Saint Thomas Aquinas

CONTENTS

A Brief Note to the Reader

Mysticism is a phenomenon fraught with nuances, both linguistic and metaphysical. *The Metaphysics*, consequently, as a *philosophic* work, presumes to address issues of a nature less than congenial to the universe of ordinary discourse. Philosophy, to be sure, demands a rigorous language, a syntax, if you will, that is subtly antagonistic to the fluid and sometimes extremely volatile concepts intrinsic to the phenomenon of the mystical experience. The austere language that philosophy arrogates to itself is sometimes too rigid a probe to uncover, reveal, the subtle and often delicate complexities that inevitably arise in a careful examination of mysticism; hence a sometimes involuted terminology will be encountered in our fragile attempt to render *linguistic* what merely *verges* on becoming *intelligible*. I have, to the best of my ability, limited this proliferation of abstruse language applied to an already abstruse subject. I have attempted to keep neologisms to a minimal, but have not blenched from employing them when my own linguistic resources are exhausted. Notwithstanding the difficulties inevitably encountered in language, I have endeavored in this work not simply to clarify what is obscure, but to address what is unique and compelling in this type of experience, an experience that has challenged philosophy for something more than a parenthetical account, an account, more often than not, much too eager to either dismiss this phenomenon, or to relegate it to psychology through its own failure to provide it with an adequate epistemological framework. Philosophy, in a word, has not yet coherently responded to this challenge. I am not satisfied that I have done so to the extent required, and many readers will no doubt concur with my assessment. Nevertheless it is a beginning of sorts, and if it provokes more questions than it answers it will at least have served to rehabilitate the philosophical arrogance that has been too ready to dismiss what it finds uncongenial. Hence the impetus of this work.

What this Book is

... and what it is not

Although this book is subtitled a "*Commentary* on the Mystical Philosophy of St. John of the Cross" it will become immediately evident to the reader that, both in scope and purpose, it is a commentary structured around some very specific epistemological issues. In particular, it is concerned with exploring the possibility of articulating a coherent *theory of knowledge* that is implicit, or perhaps better yet, latent, in the writings of St. John. I say *latent* because the theory itself is really rather an aside to the very practical issues raised by St. John in the writing of his several treatises on mystical experience. Anyone who has read St. John will undoubtedly agree that his approach to the subject is more programmatic than analytical, at least in any contemporary sense. As such, the aperture, if you will, of our focus must go beyond the hard and fast boundaries that might otherwise define our expectations of a commentary dealing strictly with the theological complexities that inevitably arise upon a close reading of St. John of the Cross.

In one sense, of course, the works of St. John are a commentary unto themselves, and while this may simplify matters in one respect, it considerably complicates them in another. The verse by verse interpretation which St. John himself offers is, obviously, the first and most apparent level, a level where St. John provides us with an often detailed explication of the meaning behind his extremely subtle poetic utterances. This meaning, both in scope and intention, is purely theological. Our own purposes within this book, however, are not: they are, by and large, *epistemological*. And this is where the issue becomes a bit more complex.

A commentary of the type proposed, it seemed to me, must take this first level of meaning fundamentally rooted in *theology*, to the next and less apparent level of meaning radicated in *epistemology*; in other words, one that specifically emerges from an epistemological criticism of the first level. In this sense it is a striving for what might be called hypo-textual meaning, a meaning always latent within, but often suppressed by, the complexities of the text itself. At the same time it is also a striving for contextual coherence. In any critical encounter between mysticism and epistemology, it is the demand for coherence, and not credence, which inevitably predominates. The often attenuated and sometimes conflicting principles that have largely become part and parcel of mystical theology remain no more than mere speculations until coherence is demonstrated to obtain not merely between the principles themselves within their own legitimate province (theology), but more importantly, between these principles and the canons of reason to which epistemology presumes to hold them accountable. Questions likely to emerge from such an encounter are of the following sort: "Do the implications of St. John's often abstruse statements actually hold up under epistemological criticism?" "Does a fully explicated meaning which accords with accepted theological principles, *also* accord with accepted epistemological principles?" "Is the *via negativa,* or the apophatic way, a legitimate epistemological venue?" In a word, do the theological principles have adequate epistemological credentials?

For this reason, and others, I thought it best to entitle this work a commentary dealing with St. John's mystical *"philosophy"*, and not his "theology" as such, for a much broader range of issues, especially epistemological issues, are clearly necessary to the scope of this type of endeavor, issues which a purely theological analysis would otherwise, and legitimately, exclude. The reason I have done so will, I think, become apparent early on. I have essentially attempted to bring three related issues into focus within the present work:

8

the phenomenon that we have come to understand as the "mystical experience", the metaphysics ostensibly underlying it, and the consonance, if any, obtaining between the two when viewed under the objective lens of epistemology. The real question of the work, then, can be summarized simply as this: *"Is the mystical experience epistemologically coherent?"* There are, of course, inevitably a subset of questions latent within this: "Are the conclusions drawn from St. John's arguments consistent with the premises implied?" "Do the premises and conclusions themselves coherently accord with the metaphysics?" In short, is the mystical experience described by St. John of the Cross at the very least epistemologically credible?

But why St. John of the Cross? Why not Eckhardt, Gerson, or Tauler? Even the briefest historical survey of the great Western Christian Mystics offers, especially in the way of speculative mysticism, a wide variety of other and perhaps better known candidates. The reason that I have chosen St. John is simply this: the works of St. John of the Cross, particularly the *Ascent of Mount Carmel* and *The Dark Night of the Soul*, stand, I think, as the culmination of the Western tradition of mysticism. Every other representative of this tradition is either in some way defective or deficient in articulating what has come to be accepted as *orthodox doctrine* in mystical theology. It is, in retrospect, no small token to the depth and scope of his writings that St. John was declared the first "Doctor of Mystical Theology" within the Roman Catholic Church. Much of this remains to be discussed later.

As a final note in the way of explaining what this book *is*, or at least endeavors to be, I think it necessary to say something briefly about the term "mysticism" itself. It has always appeared to me somewhat regrettable that the term "mysticism" is used to define what would really be more accurately described as "contemplative theology". With the term "mystical" we are likely to conjure up a good deal that is either unrelated, or deeply inimical to the contemplative theology that comes to us in the writings of the great Christian mystics. Mystical theology, in one of its typical paradoxes, is essentially a *rational* enterprise despite the fact that the mystical experience itself is not. While basically a practical undertaking, in presuming to set forth reasons for this practical task, it is at least implicitly a rational justification as well. And it is precisely this rational aspect of the mystical experience that is the focus of this book.

On the other hand, it is equally important to the reader to understand what this book is *not*. This book is *not* a compendium. While it carefully attempts to chronologically accompany the text where possible, it does not blench from a departure where an examination of concurrent issues is warranted. Some will undoubtedly find this vexing. And while it adverts to the Mystical Tradition in general, a tradition out of which the thought of St. John very clearly emerges, it does not presume to exhaustively treat of the many notable figures who have contributed to this long-standing tradition. Deidre Carabine's "*The Unknown God: Negative*

Theology in the Platonic Tradition: Plato to Eriugena", I suggest, would be much more suitable to this purpose. The goal of this book is unabashedly epistemological. Neither do I presume the reader to be intimately acquainted with Thomism as such, from which many of the metaphysical doctrines articulated by St. John unquestionably derive. For the sake of clarity, and the convenience of the reader, I have endeavored to reiterate them when necessary, providing pertinent documentation should the reader wish to explore the issue further. As dearly as I wish this work to be all things to all people, I have settled for the more modest goal of providing epistemological perspective on the sometimes fluid, sometimes volatile, but always paradoxical issues that mysticism perpetually engenders.

* In the end, we know God as unknown (In Boetium de Trinitate, q. 1, a. 2, ad 1um)

Preface to the Philosophy of St. John of the Cross

The Search for Coherence

If there is one unifying feature that appears to bind the great diversity of philosophic thought as it has occurred throughout history, it may well be found in the search for *coherence*. While the passionate and resolute pursuit of truth is certainly more exalted, it has for some time suffered rather badly, and for good reason has been denigrated as the pure impulse behind every philosophical system. The dispassionate search for coherence, on the other hand, has been, and is likely to remain, fundamental to all good philosophy. It is no less the driving force behind the great *Platonic Dialogues*, or Aristotle's *Posterior Analytics*, than Kant's abstruse *Critique*

14

of Pure Reason or Hegel's involuted *Logic*. On every philosophical frontier we essentially encounter problematics that demand explanation because they confront us as *facts*. What is more, these intractable, often vexing elements of experience do not always readily lend themselves to understanding, or if they do, it is sometimes upon terms not entirely of our own making. Such occurrences invite inquiry, challenge us to coherently respond to them, and even in the face of indifference resolutely refuse to be turned aside. They defy us, and therefore challenge us. By their persistent recurrence, they effectively demand of us accountability; demand, in fact, to be *coherently* incorporated into that philosophic purview toward which all inquiry inexorably moves as toward a universal comprehending every fact.

However elusive this pursuit may be, the impulse which motivates us to exact from *experience* the epistemological tribute which coherence demands, remains the same always and everywhere: the pursuit of understanding. To leave unexplained – or worse yet – to *ignore* any recurrent element in experience simply because it proves either inconvenient or recalcitrant, is not merely bad philosophy; it is contradictory to the philosophic impulse itself, an impulse which not merely derives from, but thrives within, the fertile matrix of inquiry.

If this indeed is so, it is particularly apropos of a study of arguably the single greatest – certainly the most voluble and articulate – figure in the Western tradition of mysticism, St. John of the Cross (1542-1591). Mystical experience, despite its many cultural and often conflicting interpretations, remains undeniably a fact *of* experience. This alone is sufficient warrant for examination. Its credentials lie in the *repeated*, which is to say, the historical experiences of men and women, and philosophy essentially demands no more of the subject of its review.

It is, however, equally clear that such an investigation suffers a regrettably persistent, if popular handicap: the general consensus seems to be, prior to any real critical reflection on the matter, that in and of itself mysticism is something entirely and irredeemably *irrational*, and inasmuch as it is beyond reason it is beyond the legitimate scope of rational inquiry altogether. Indeed, apart from the possibility of what appear to be otherwise solipsistic utterances meaningful only among the mystics themselves, it really has nothing to recommend itself to the type of inquiry to which other and decidedly less refractory experiences legitimately lend themselves. This is to be much mistaken. It is precisely this fundamental and pervasive misconception about mysticism that remains, I think, the chief obstacle to a study of mystical philosophy in its own right, the credibility of which, as a consequence, has suffered unnecessarily.

But there is more to the problem we confront at the outset than simply this. Semantics has played no small part in contributing to the confusion that surrounds the very term itself. As William James astutely observed:

"The words "mysticism" and "mystical" are often used as terms of mere reproach, to throw at any opinion which we regard as vague and vast and sentimental, and without a base in either facts or logic. For some writers a "mystic" is any person who believes in thought-transference, or spirit return. Employed in this way the word has little value." [1]

As a consequence, the term "mysticism" has come to acquire a kind of pseudo-metaphysical connotation, or perhaps better yet, an *esoteric* pathos of the most reprehensible sort – evoking, as it does, a type of vague intellectual empathy to which nothing in any sense coherent and meaningful corresponds. This essential misunderstanding of mysticism, however, is quickly dispelled upon a close examination of the works of St. John of the Cross: immediately we confront facticity and discern logic; facticity and logic so compelling, in fact, that a *philosophy of mysticism* may well offer a unique contribution to epistemology itself. To wit, In Part II of our commentary we shall examine, among other things, the possibility of a type of experience in which the redoubtable *Problem of Induction* – first introduced by the 18th century Scottish philosopher David Hume – and a thorn in the side of philosophy ever since – fails to obtain. This of itself would be no small recompense for our efforts given the magnitude of this problem to which philosophy, in one form or another, has attempted to respond since the publication of Hume's *Enquiry Concerning Human Understanding* in 1740. In short, we find reason in the mystical philosophy of St. John of the Cross, coherence and logic. Indeed, we find that, externally considered, the mystical experience is a profoundly *rational* experience – and it is this discovery, sweeping aside many long-borne misconceptions about mysticism which, if justification at all is required, suffices to justify an epistemology of mysticism.

To be sure, there are central elements in the mystical experience essentially inaccessible to reason. St. Thomas Aquinas perhaps summed it up

19

best in the terse statement, *"In finem nostrae cognitionis Deum tamquam ignotum cognoscimus."* [2] It is this *unknowing,* this first and most fundamental principle of the metaphysics of mysticism which, in our examination, we shall find to assume profoundly rational dimensions in the mystical philosophy of St. John of the Cross.

Geoffrey K. Mondello

---

[1] *Varieties of Religious Experience,* Lect. 16

[2] *We know God as unknown*

Foreword

In this short commentary on the two principle works of St. John of the Cross – the *Ascent of Mount Carmel* and the *Dark Night of the Soul* – we will, as I stated earlier, be primarily concerned with examining the possibilities of developing a coherent mystical epistemology, that is to say, a *theory of knowledge* relative to the mystical experience in which the rational elements of this unique experience will become explicit to us, and so enable us to usher at least some very crucial aspects of this phenomenon into the arena of rational discourse. Certainly, this will not make mystics of us. Indeed, this understanding itself is by no means propadeutic to the mystical experience, as we shall later see; that is to say, an understanding of the metaphysical principles underlying the mystical experience is not requisite in the way that, say, an understanding of the relation between rational numbers is presupposed in the exercise of pure mathematics.

The mystic, unlike the mathematician, may in fact dispense with such an understanding altogether.

This type of understanding, however, *is* requisite to the inquiring mind, which is to say, to those of us standing, as it were, outside, peering in through the sometimes-obfuscated lens of rational inquiry. We can, however, only achieve this through carefully examining the various and sometimes involuted arguments which St. John articulates in the development of what must be understood as his mystical philosophy; a philosophy which only gradually, even reluctantly, emerges from the text. Our inquiry, then, essentially boils down to an examination of certain rational features of the mystical experience which lend themselves to the possibility of being so organized as to constitute something systematic enough to be incorporated into what we have come to understand as epistemology. And this, of course, presumes order, sense, meaning and logic. One surprising consequence of our analysis, in short, will be the disclosure of the mystical experience not as antipodal to reason (as some have supposed), but as profoundly consonant with it. However, this *reason* we seek in St. John's account is, we hasten to add, and for reasons that we shall later explain, *implicit only*; from the outset it often requires patient analysis, but the results will be no less, – in fact, all the more – compelling for the effort.

Given the broad and inevitable complexity of the issues involved, it appeared to me that the best way to proceed in this type of examination would be through an analysis of the central *moments* in the movement to mystical union as they logically occur in the two texts. Where there is logical or chronological order to begin with, it seemed to me best to construct an analysis parallel to the already existing continuum. Not only should this help us in a comparative analysis of the text, but it serves to constrain us to the text as well – while at the same time allowing us the necessary latitude to extrapolate from it in an attempt to construct an epistemological analysis of our own. In doing so we will find ourselves moving from an examination of those factors external to the mystical experience and generally spoken of in terms of *predisposition*, to those elements more or less explicitly involved in the actual mystical experience itself and in turn generally spoken of in terms of *union*. Our purpose, then, is to examine the normative, as well as the descriptive elements in St. John's account. To do this, it is vital for us to provide the often-isolated elements which occur in the text with a coherent epistemological framework. This in turn requires us to draw out the logical implications of his statements, examine their premises, however suppressed, elicit their conclusions, however latent, and in the end attempt to demonstrate the coherence, if any, which obtains between them.

A certain antagonism with the text is inevitable. These are fertile but not necessarily congenial grounds for purely philosophical inquiry. There are, for example, certain tacit assumptions, both theological and philosophical in nature, to which St. John often adverts; assumptions, more often than not, in the form of suppressed theses which, if we are at all to succeed in our examination, must be *lifted* from the text as so many copulas to the intelligibility or our account. We must endeavor, then, to show not merely *that* certain experiences or consequences follow any given moment in the account, but *why* they follow logically (that is to say, deductively, or necessarily) from the given moments. As we examine St. John's arguments in greater detail, we come to realize that it is not so much an antagonism that we contend with in the account as it is a recalcitrance encountered within the text itself: that certain later statements and arguments essentially derive from earlier statements and arguments is not always clear in the writings of St. John. It remains for us to attempt to render these connections explicit, to endeavor to demonstrate their logical coherence, and to organize them into something systematic if we hope to succeed in articulating an epistemology of mysticism – at least St. John's mysticism. The ultimate aim of this commentary, in the end, is to give philosophic form to St. John's arguments, in effect to develop a *coherent* philosophy of mysticism, especially in light of the epistemological dimensions suggested within it.

St. John's works can be divided into three logical moments: *Predisposition, Transition,* and *Union. Part I* of the Commentary, which I have entitled the *Presuppositions* is principally concerned with the moment of *predisposition*, that is to say, with the merely mechanical features of mysticism which the latter two moments presuppose. It forms the foundation upon which the mystical momentum builds and in virtue of which much of the subsequent mystical experience is explainable. Its principal feature, we will find, is the apophatic way, better known as the *Via Negativa* (the Way of Negation, or the Negative Way) in all its mechanical aspects upon which the entire metaphysical infrastructure of mysticism depends. Detailed discussion of this central feature in mystical philosophy is dealt with in *Part II* of this commentary where it will be examined in detail.

Working from the various principles elicited from St. John's foundational work, the *Ascent of Mount Carmel, Part II*, entitled the *Metaphysics*, is an attempt to relate the evolving mystical experiences *to* these principles (the *via negativa*, notions of participation, proximity, proportion, contrariety, etc.) in order to demonstrate the latter to be, in fact, the logical consequences of the former. It is an attempt to show that, given certain statements concerning the function of these principles, other statements about certain unique types of experience (essentially states-of-being) not just follow, but *necessarily*, that is to say, *deductively*, follow. But at the same time we must also come to terms with the limitations inherent in the *kind* of books St. John was writing; books addressing issues vital to a distinct group of readers (issues that we shall discuss later in *Part II*). As a result, deductive relations which do in fact obtain between the various elements in his philosophy are often obscure to the casual reader. Suffice it to say at this point that St. John did not understand himself to be writing an enchiridion on mystical theology replete with deductive schematics to be later analyzed by, and subsequently vex, systematic theologians. Deductive relations do in fact exist, but because of this literary limitation, they must be elicited through careful reading if we are to arrive at that philosophic coherence we strive for in the works of St. John; a coherence that, in fact, is *always* latent, even in his most abstruse writings.

In the way of explanation, I should like to point out that I have omitted treatment of St. John's last two works – the *Spiritual Canticle* and the *Living Flame of Love* – not as an oversight, but simply because, for our own purposes, the pertinent material found in these two treatises derives from, and are largely more elaborate iterations of, the first two principal works in which *all* the elements in his philosophy are contained in much greater detail. As a final note, an addendum in the form of a prolepsis follows the commentary proper. Within it, various objections posed by skepticism, psychology, and orthodoxy, are briefly considered and answered in light of our examination. This, in turn, is followed by a brief biographical sketch, and an overview of the mystical tradition culminating in the thought of St. John.

The abbreviations used in this commentary are as follows:

AMC : *Ascent of Mount Carmel*
DNS : *Dark Night of the Soul*
SC : *Spiritual Canticle*
LFL : *Living Flame of Love*
ST : *Summa Theologica* (St. Thomas Aquinas)

Documentary references are based upon the translation of St. John's works by E. Allison Peers: *Ascent of Mount Carmel, Dark Night of the Soul, Living Flame of Love*, and *Spiritual Canticle, Image Books, Doubleday & Co., Garden City, NY, 1958, 1959, 1961, and 1962.*

Scriptural references are from the ***Biblia Sacra, Juxta Vulgatam Clementinam*** *Baronius Press Ltd., London, United Kingdom, Copyright 2008*

An Introduction to the Philosophy of St. John of the Cross

The Epistemological Paradox: the Knower, Unknowing, and the Unknown

Any study of St. John's mystical philosophy must first come to terms with the nature of mystical theology itself; what its object is, what its limits are: in short, what particular universe of discourse we are addressing in our attempt to understand the mystical experience described by St. John of the Cross. A good definition, it appears to me, must be broad enough to subsume the many interpretations we encounter outside any specific tradition. The advantages of this are at once obvious, for such an approach, broadly chronological in its purview, provides us with a much needed sense of historical continuity inasmuch as many of the doctrines found in the writings of St. John have very clear historical antecedents that are not, in fact, rooted in Christianity at all. Some precede it. Indeed, some are deeply inimical to it. On the other hand, it is equally clear that our definition must be sufficiently specific to the tradition to which St. John so clearly belongs and in light of which alone his mystical doctrine becomes coherent. One extremely useful definition, a definition embracing what is both specific and general, would construe mystical theology as essentially the *consummate* theology. Why consummate? Because it is the *cognitive* apex of an otherwise largely speculative theological enterprise. Mystical theology, in short, is concerned with the *direct intuition* – experience, if you will – of God [1]; the immediate and unmodified apprehension of the Absolute through what has come to be understood as *'unio mystica'*, or mystical union.

Perhaps the clearest, certainly the most concise, definition offered is, I think, summarized in the

words of the great fourteenth century theologian
and mystic, Jean Gerson:

"Theologia mystica est experimentalis cognitio
habita de Deo per amoris unitivi complexum" [2]

Natural Theology, by contrast, concerns itself
exclusively with the knowledge of God arrived at
through natural, or discursive reason: that is to say,
in Natural Theology an understanding of God is
abstractly achieved through a rational process much
in the way that a logical argument is constructed
through a sorites. St. Anselm's famous 'Ontological
Argument' is a fine example of this type of
theological reasoning. The God it broaches upon,
however, remains as abstract as the syllogistic
reasoning that deduced him, and, practically
speaking, few people undergo conversion
experiences as a result of this line of reasoning,
however impeccable.

Dogmatic Theology, on the other hand, takes a
somewhat different tack: it is primarily concerned

with the knowledge of God obtained through divine revelation principally embodied in Sacred Scripture, and has come to assume a rather monolithic architectonic through a long-standing and erudite tradition of Patristic exegesis. The force of reason and the appeal to authority (Scriptural, patristic, and philosophical) which typically characterizes dogmatic theology is a powerful combination, a combination so effective, in fact, that it is arguably the single most vital element in any individual's – including the mystic's – orthodox religious formation. It is, in a sense, the springboard off which the mystic leaps into less certain waters. St. Thomas Aquinas is an eminent example of both disciplines, artfully incorporating elements of the Natural and the Dogmatic into that remarkable synthesis culminating in his *Summa Theologica,* considered by many to be the greatest theological treatise ever written.

Reason as Propadeutic: the *Ex Hypothesi*

Mystical theology approaches God quite differently. Its path lies neither through the narrow corridors of reason, nor through the rigid architectonics of dogmatic exegesis. It either leaps off at the point where the scholar is left stammering, or may prescind altogether from the cumbersome intellectual impedimenta that becomes effectively superfluous in the ecstatic momentum that impels the soul to union with God. This, of course, is to disparage neither reason nor dogma. Each in measure is an indispensable tributary to the depth of that inexorable movement toward God, as we shall later see. It remains, nevertheless, that even a scholar of the caliber of St. Thomas Aquinas had subsequently come to view all that he had written, and this was considerable to say the least, as "so much straw" in light of the *direct experience* of God which he briefly encountered in a moment of ecstatic union. So overwhelming, so all embracing, so utterly definitive was this experience that St. Thomas immediately ceased writing.

Shall we then toss aside the *Summa*? It is clear that St. John did not. Neither, in fact, did Tauler, Suso, or Eckhardt. And for good reason: Mystical Theology, properly understood, neither compromises nor invalidates its Rational and Dogmatic counterparts. Rather, it *surpasses* them in the way that the act of *seeing* surpasses the most definitive description of sight. The description itself remains true; it is entirely accurate inasmuch as words signify, and in signifying attempt to communicate, what is essentially an *experience*. But the disproportion between the *experience itself* and any description subsequent to it remains nearly irreconcilable. To one who is color-deficient (to carry the analogy a little further) and who has never seen the color purple, the most precise and detailed description of this absolutely unique chromatic phenomenon called purple, even when coupled with appeals to extrapolate from colors with which one *is*

35

familiar, yields at best only a vague conception, and in the end brings that person no closer to the *experience* of the color itself. In short, we must come to terms with limitations inherent in language, especially descriptive language; limitations that are radicated in *shared* experiences outside of which the power of language reaches a cognitive terminus. No more can meaningfully be said. And this is precisely the plight of the mystic, and, therefore, that of mystical theology itself.

But let us take this a little further. While each of the several branches of theology take God as their cognitive object, something of a sense of theological fragmentation inevitably occurs. Somehow a universal and unitary comprehension of God is not so much lost, as never quite achieved. If a synthesis is obtained, however comprehensive and integrated, it only leaves us in the vestibule of the Divine, and the antechamber is yet obscure and unoccupied. Each discipline within theology, in other words, is possessed of quite definite and intrinsic limitations in addressing the Absolute;

36

insuperable limitations, we shall find, that derive from a *metaphysical* finitude inextricably bound up with nature as subsuming under itself everything created in opposition to the Uncreated Absolute. Each approach to God is irremediably limited; hence the extent of the possibility of its cognition of God is determined *a priori*. In other words, the knowledge of God we acquire through Natural Theology is mediated, and therefore limited, by *reason*. It addresses the inexhaustible Absolute strictly as the object of rational inquiry. On the other hand, the knowledge acquired through Dogmatic Theology, while not prescinding from reason, is nevertheless itself equally mediated, and therefore limited, by *revelation*, pertaining to the infinite God only insofar as he has revealed some aspect of his infinite being in finite human history. Our acquaintance, our cognition of God through reason and revelation, then, is necessarily incomplete. The contributions of traditional theological disciplines are not, for that reason, understood to be irrelevant. To the contrary, St.

John was well schooled in scholasticism at the University of Salamanca and relies a great deal on Dogmatic Theology as a propadeutic to the mystical journey. As a journey of faith, it is Dogmatic Theology which enables us to the reach the vestibule safely; it is the compass whose unchanging ordinals, divinely illumined, give us bearing in the *dark night of the soul*. Constituting, as it does, an index of truth in the form of dogmatic certainties, it provides essential definition in the face of gathering obscurity, and so disabuses us of *error,* which St. John sees as constituting one of the principal impediments to the soul in its journey to union with God.

This is not to say, as we suggested earlier, that the mystic must first thoroughly acquaint himself with Dogmatic Theology if he hopes to arrive at union with God. God of his own predilection brings whom he wills to this exalted state, and makes no inquiries into the mystic's theological credentials. *However*, the likelihood of achieving this state, given the many obstacles likely to be encountered on the journey, will in some measure be commensurable with the mystic's certain grounding in fundamental dogmatic issues. One's prospect of attaining to ecstatic union with the One, Most Holy, and Uncreated Absolute is considerably diminished if ones conception of God is grossly and fundamentally divergent from the Divine reality toward which one aspires. It is not unlike one attempting to find the solution to some complex algorithm by sorting out the entrails of owls. Some measure of correspondence is presumed between the objective and the means, and it is Dogmatic Theology which ensures this, not by delimiting the inexhaustible Absolute, but in defining certain irrefragable aspects of it. Unfortunately, or fortunately, the egalitarianism so dear to the human heart is shattered as much on the frontiers of heaven as it is on the formulas of mathematics. However dearly we would that two and two equal five, we strive for it in vain, or hold to a fiction, but never quite achieve true mathematics. This would appear to be no less true of the quest for God. However dearly we would that God conform his being to our wishes, our sensitivities, our inclinations, even our mistaken beliefs, the invincible reality will continue to elude us until we are prepared to settle upon terms not entirely of our own making and more in accord with the reality we pursue. Dogmatic Theology simply makes some of these terms clear.

A good deal more, however, must be said about reason. To begin with, inasmuch as reason *mediates* our approach to God, in so doing, it simultaneously *modifies* our perception of the Absolute; our apprehension of God is not, without stringent qualification, entirely veridical. Certainly it is not a perception of God in the plenitude of his being. Rather, it is a perception modified by, in being accommodated to, reason and revelation. God is essentially construed as a being upon whom rational categories are imposed, and who in himself, defined as infinite, transcends these intrinsically limiting and modifying categories. The nature of God, in other words, infinitely exceeds the narrow architectonics of reason, and while it is clearly

40

arguable that the intelligibility of God requires at least a minimal availability to reason, it is no less clear that the divine essence is incapable of being exhausted by reason alone, for the rational availability of God is only, merely, one dimension of God's infinite being. And this is really to say that we understand by *God* something *more* than the merely rational.

Transcendence through Immanence?

What emerges from all this is perhaps the most interesting question of all: is there in fact, beside reason, perhaps even above reason, some alternative mode of cognition which must be admitted into our epistemological account? One which, while not abrogating reason, somehow *surpasses* reason, much in the way that, to advert to our earlier analogy, *seeing* infinitely exceeds the description of *sight* – while in no way invalidating the description itself?

At the same time it is important to recognize that the deliverances of reason, however limited, nevertheless remain authentic. What reason predicates of God is not abolished in mystical experiences; such experiences, rather, are found to corroborate them. It is vitally important for us to understand this, for it means that those of us who stand outside this unique experience nevertheless have an understanding of God that is not in the end merely one of so many superlative fictions. In some albeit limited way our conception of God actually corresponds to the reality of the Absolute. Were this not so, the Christian understanding of salvific history would otherwise be emptied of meaning and our relationship to God would not so much be a matter of *disproportion* as one of utter incommensurability. In other words, if God cannot be known, in some sense meaningfully understood, then, practically speaking, he simply does not exist for us; no more so than we may hold anything to exist in any meaningful way about which we know nothing.

Nevertheless, it is precisely this genuine perceptual capacity within the mystic which undergoes a profound transformation in ecstatic union; a transformation in which the encounter with God is more accurately described as an *intuition*, that is, an *immediate* experience, one unconditioned by reason and sensibility – and if unconditioned, then totally unmodified. It is, for the mystic, a supernatural apprehension of God as he is *in himself.*

This claim, perhaps the most controversial, certainly the most central aspect of mystical experience, inevitably invites contradiction, and for good reason. Since Immanuel Kant, the notion of a perception of anything *in itself* (*an sich*) – the noumenal insight into unmodified being – has become epistemologically problematic. According to this line of reasoning, the presumably pristine data presented us in any possible encounter is modified in the very act of perceiving it: our perception, in other words, invests data with logical and aesthetic qualities that do not inhere in the data themselves, but which are present as a *condition* to the very possibility of their being perceived at all. And these qualities themselves are present as a result of our own epistemological activity which first *conditions* data in order to accommodate it. We can, therefore, never know *anything* in and of itself. We are acquainted merely with the phenomenal appearance, but never the noumenal substance, the unmodified reality forever concealed beneath a phenomenal framework of our own epistemological making. [3]

Reason and sensibility, then, having largely defined the terms (and subsequently the limits) of any epistemological analysis since Kant, must in some way be cogently accounted for in mystical theology as well. At the same time, by its very nature mystical theology cannot be arbitrarily constrained to the scope limiting other types of epistemological pursuits since its objective is understood at the outset to transcend the phenomena legitimate to them. This, however, is latitude, not license; a latitude which must nevertheless hold to terms mutually recognized in any competent epistemological endeavor whatever. The problem is that the terms themselves become much more fluid precisely at the point where epistemology and mystical theology converge. Consequently, there is perpetual tension in this convergence, a tension fraught with misunderstanding. What is vitally needed from the outset, then, is a clarification of terms. And what I am suggesting is that much of the confusion surrounding mysticism itself results from the fact that mystical theology has, at this point, essentially *redefined* the terms.

It is equally important to understand that it has done so not by abolishing these terms, but by prescinding from them. Mystical theology does not contradict the terms which largely define other types of epistemological pursuits. It recognizes that they are, in fact, entirely valid within their own legitimate province. But while it does not *contradict* these terms, it is nevertheless ineluctably constrained to *negate* them. And this is quite another matter altogether. Recognizing that an epistemological analysis defined solely in terms of reason and sensibility is *inherently* inadequate to its own unique enterprise, mystical theology has not abrogated the terms – it has simply redefined them. And this is really the critical point of our departure. In redefining the terms it redefines the epistemological enterprise itself which is no longer understood so much as attaining to *knowledge* as attaining to *being*. Its objective is not the *acquisition* of an end, but a *participating* in it. *Participation*, in a word, becomes not simply an alternative to knowledge – it altogether supersedes it. At best, "knowing", to the mystic, is penultimate to "being". In a larger sense, within the concept of participation the implicit distinction between the "knower" and the "known", a distinction otherwise constituting one of the most fundamental epistemological premises [4], becomes effectively superfluous. In the state of ecstatic union, the "knower" and the "known" are ultimately understood, in a carefully qualified sense, to in fact be one.

So crucial is the concept of participation, in fact, that it is fundamental to understanding the very *possibility* itself of the type of absolutely unconditioned and therefore veridical perception which the mystics claim to possess in ecstatic union. The epistemological margin between subject and object, the knower and the known, which gradually evanesces until it is totally transcended in the moment of the mystic's apotheosis in God, only becomes coherent through an understanding of a metaphysics radicated in the notion of participation.

The Doctrine of Original Sin as an Epistemological Tangent

But we are getting ahead of ourselves. At this point it is probably best to address some of the other fundamental issues that inevitably influence our understanding of mysticism before venturing further into our account. One such issue concerns the doctrine of Original Sin. According to this doctrine, mankind in its first state of innocence (moral impeccability) enjoyed familiarity with God. This innocence, however, is held to have been lost, together with the intuitive apprehension of God which attended it, through an act of Original Sin. The consequences of this breach not only profoundly altered and vitiated our relationship with God, but our very cognition of the Divinity is held to have been subsequently impaired as well. From this perspective the task of mystical theology, at least implicitly, must be understood as restorative: somehow man must once again be reconciled to that state of innocence in which his relationship to God is once again consonant and, consequently, his apprehension of God immediate.

The return, so to speak, to this original state can only be achieved, or perhaps better yet, approximated by the mystic through what is essentially a purgative process in which the mystic strives to center consciousness entirely and exclusively upon God. This process, we will later see, basically consists in the categorical negation of all that is *not* God, both externally according to the senses, and internally according to the spirit. Mystical theology therefore employs a *negative epistemology*, proceeding through what is known as the *via negativa* (or the negative way) to arrive at a veridical cognition of God.

At the same time, we observe in the mystic an epistemological striving for centricity: as a result of our fallen state, our relationship to God has become, as it were, eccentric. That is to say, God is no longer central to ordinary consciousness, but rather exists on its periphery as only one of a multiplicity of notions competing to varying degrees for primacy in consciousness, and often entertained simultaneously – if indeed God occupies a place in consciousness at all. As long as a *plurality* of necessarily discrete, and often competing notions alternately occupy consciousness, just so long is man's relationship to God eccentric. And it is precisely this type of epistemological diffusion which, for St. John, engenders what he calls "contrariety" to God in the soul. It is essentially a diffusion among incommensurable categories. If the soul, then, is to reestablish itself in its original state of consonance with God, it must in some way succeed in negating this plurality.

Let us attempt to sort this out for a moment. Assuming the intentionality of consciousness, that is to say, that consciousness itself presupposes as a condition of consciousness, an object or notion *of which it is conscious* – the soul in having but *one* item of consciousness is exclusively united with this object as the sole *condition* of its epistemological activity. We do not "know" *in vacuo*: the act of knowing, however vigorously abstracted and reduced, presupposes *something* being concurrently known, even if only the knower himself. Indeed, we understand the state of not knowing anything at all as *unconsciousness*. Consciousness, then, is not some dogmatically independent noesis apart from the data through which it is actualized. In this

50

rigorously exclusive state of focused awareness, consciousness is *contingent upon* its solitary object – it is, in fact, united with this object as a *consciousness of* this object. And it is precisely this type of epistemological centricity toward which the *via negativa* moves. The *via negativa*, then, must be viewed not simply as inseparable from, but as intrinsic to the *epistemological predisposition* to mystical union, for it ultimately enables an epistemological union of the soul as the *possibility*, on the one hand, and the activity of God on the other, as the *condition* of any subsequent state of consciousness.

In the state of mystical union, however, we may be surprised to find that cognitive agency is *not* ascribable to the contemplative himself except insofar as he is engaged in the purely negative, if you will, the purgative process of eradicating within himself all that is not God preparatory to receiving the divine infusion. In the mystical experience of St. John, the notion of agency is directly ascribable to God only: the contemplative merely disposes himself to receive this infusion which God alone initiates and consummates, both according to his will, and that degree to which the soul has succeeded in eliminating within itself all the epistemological debris which effectively obstructs the clear and immediate vision of God. Mystical experience, then, is seen to consist in a dialectic between the passivity of the soul on the one hand, and the activity of God on the other. Given this dialectic, the soul appears to be --- despite the fall --- yet latently disposed to that authentic cognition of God which marked the ordinary awareness of man prior to his fall from the state of original justice. So we find that the very possibility of mystical experience presupposes the soul to be at least implicitly disposed to a veridical cognition of God. When actualized, when rendered explicit in the mystical experience, this cognition is, as it were, a dimension of the state of innocence re-achieved. This does not, however, mean that man is therefore rendered impeccable, as the Illuminist believed: while epistemological consonance may be re-established in mystical union, the contemplative is not for that reason abstracted from the penalty of original sin and therefore incapable of subsequently sinning. His nature, radicated in genealogy and inherited from Adam, remains intact – despite God's predilection – and the invitation to union is apt to be viewed by the mystic not as a violation of nature, but as extraordinary testimony to the ability of God to work *super*naturally in the soul.

The Problem with Language: the Limitations of the Intelligible

One of the most challenging issue to be addressed, and fundamental no less to the philosophy than the theology of mysticism, concerns the role of language in the mystical experience. It is a linguistic tradition – and problematic – the antecedents of which, at least for our purposes, go as far back as the Neoplatonists in the third century, and, arguably, earlier, to St. Paul himself. Within the tradition from which St. John writes, the works of Dionysius the Pseudo-Areopagite, particularly his treatise entitled *De Divinis Nominibus* (Concerning the Divine Names), are an eminent example of the difficulties language encounters in addressing the Absolute. This problem becomes critical in the often attenuated discourses of the mystic, so let us look at this issue a little more closely. For the contemplative, words characteristically fail to *adequately* express or convey his experience of the Absolute, and any linguistic description drawing its categories from *experience* is found to be inadequate to, and radically distinct from, that *unique* experience of God in mystical union. So entirely dissimilar is this experience to all others, that the mystic typically finds it difficult to establish any commensurability at all.

At best, God may only be spoken of analogically. But even this becomes problematic in St. John's exposition, for any analogy at all presupposes at least *some* common categories between the analogized. To wit, in the first book of the *Ascent of Mount Carmel*, St. John outlines a cosmological relationship characterized by *opposition* between the created order and God. Each is possessed of ontological categories radically dissimilar in nature. How then, we must ask, is the role of analogy, which figures as largely in St. John's poetry as in his philosophy, possible? For the answer, I think, we must look to the nature of St. John's two principal analogies: the relationship of the Lover to the beloved, and that of the Bridegroom to the bride. Quite obviously, it is the notion of *love* that is fundamental to and essentially characterizes each relationship. And it is precisely this notion that, for St. John, becomes the common denominator between the contemplative and the Absolute. The analogy, we will find, is adequate precisely because commensurability is possible through man's basic ontological status as the *image* of God. And this image of God in man is, for St. John, love, for God Himself is love.[5]

And yet the very nature of love itself is incapable of being adequately expressed. Words, however well chosen, and descriptions, however articulate and exhaustive, are found in the end to be profoundly impoverished. The essence remains ineffable, to be *experienced* immediately, intuitively. And so the analogy itself breaks down linguistically: our experience of God can only be analogized to our experience of love – and our experience of love is essentially recalcitrant to language. The experience of God in mystical union, like the experience of love between the bride and the bridegroom, remains intuitive and essentially unavailable to language. The experiences are comparable because they share common intuitions, and while certain subjective states attendant upon, and, as it were, accidental to, such experiences may in fact be vaguely described, the intuitive affinity itself evidently derives from some source in itself spontaneous, ever-immediate, and self-creating.

This serves to underscore yet another dimension of the persistent problem with language. Descriptive language purports to convey to us, or to signify, some aspect of reality typically not immediately available to us; it serves, then, to *mediate* or to approximate the reality. But it is only able to do so by *presupposing* an entire spectrum of *shared experience* necessary to intelligibility in any particular universe of discourse. In this sense, language may be viewed as an expedient in lieu of direct experience. And yet we have found that the nature of the mystical experience is essentially intuitive, immediate, direct. It is, in short, an *experience* – and any language endeavoring to describe this experience necessarily *presupposes* this experience as a condition to the intelligibility of the account it would render. Let us suppose an individual with a rare sensory dysfunction who has never experienced the sensation "hot". No matter what linguistic categories we invoke, from the cup of hot tea to the arcana of thermodynamics, our attempts to communicate this sensation to that individual will be in vain until he has *shared* that experience with us, and only in light of that experience will the word "hot", and all that attends our understanding of it, become intelligible, meaningful, to him. In other words, our admission into any *meaningful* universe of discourse presumes shared experiences upon which it is grounded. Apart from this essential condition, any description of mystical experience, however detailed and definitive, is necessarily emptied of intelligibility. Mystical union, then, or infused contemplation as it is often called, remains to be experienced, and when spoken of is only done so analogically. Coupled with the problem of *absolute incommensurability* deriving from any attempt to relate the finite to the Infinite, the created conditional to the Uncreated Absolute, the mystic who would attempt to relate his experience faces a redoubtable challenge indeed.

Perhaps in some small way we have already succeeded in understanding some of the very fundamental issues involved in the Western tradition of mysticism. It by now be reasonably clear, for example, that the relatively esoteric nature of mysticism, coupled with the mystic's insistence upon the ineffability of the experience itself, derives from two closely related factors: the relatively small number of shared experiences upon which this tradition rests, and, of course, the limitations inherent in language itself. Experience, we find, inevitably outstrips language – it is the antecedent which language presupposes as a condition to the intelligibility of language at all. An alternative, then, must be sought beyond purely descriptive language. And while language clearly cannot be abandoned in any attempt to at least approximate meaning in the mystic's account, it can, nevertheless be modified, articulated, inflected, to form a linguistic tangent on the Absolute – and this, I think, is what St. John strives to achieve in his poetry. It seems to me very significant that St. John treats of the mystical experience in poetic form, and then proceeds to comment on each line and stanza with an often involuted exposition on its theological or philosophic import. It appears to be of the very essence of poetry that the words of themselves are merely vehicles, often to non-verbalizable meanings. The meanings arise, hover as it were, enigmatically above the hard and fast signification of the words and often defy our most persistent efforts to impose some determinate form upon them. That one line of St. John's verse may be followed by ten paragraphs of closely reasoned, discursive analysis merely brings to relief the fact that poetic form contains within itself a near infinitude of meaning which transcends the finite words. In short, the enigmatically communicative form of poetry demonstrates itself to be the only *proximate* means of communicating the mystical experience – while at once underscoring the inadequacy of words to describe it.

Why indeed, we must ask, given these extraordinary obstacles, does St. John, or any mystic, for that matter, endeavor to write of these experiences at all? The answer, I think – at least for St. John – is that while this experience is extraordinary and seldom encountered, it is not for a lack of predilection on the part of God. Indeed, St. John insists that ecstatic union in this life is merely the prelude to that everlasting and ecstatic union with God that is inaugurated in heaven as the culmination of our life on earth – and that it is God who ceaselessly calls us to this union. And while many, called to perfection, turn aside like the rich young man of the Gospels, either through an arrogance as ancient as the angels, or simply through a lack of perspicacity, there will always be generous souls quick to answer, and it is to these that St. John addresses his works. What remains obscure in the text will become at once luminously clear in the experience.

---

[1] Although we shall eventually find that the notion of experience itself is inadequate to our understanding of the mystical experience.

[2] Mystical theology is knowledge of God by experience arrived at through the embrace of unifying love. (De Mystica Theologia Speculativa).

[3] cf. Critique of Pure Reason (Immanuel Kant), Transcendental

Doctrine of Elements, I, A20/B34 - A46/B73

[4] This, incidentally, is no less true of Solipsism, or the epistemological theory which holds that we know only ourselves and modifications of that self. Every modification eventually constitutes a known datum contributing to, but no longer concurrent with, the personal continuity (identity) that remains (as the present knower) throughout these modifications.

[5] 1. Jn. 4.

The Mystical Tradition and St. John of the Cross

Confluence, Divergence, and Coherence

From the outset, as it must be clear by now, it will not be our purpose, nor does it lie within the scope of this book to seek parallels between the doctrine of St. John of the Cross and the many mystics which preceded him within the tradition to which he very clearly belongs. It is, rather, my express wish to examine the philosophy of St. John upon its own terms, in and of itself, without cluttering the text or confusing an already difficult issue with a plethora of distracting references and historical asides that, while providing a broader overview, inevitably vex us by pulling us away from the focus required to grasp this profound work. Historical perspective is very valuable; indeed, indispensable to an understanding of mysticism at large, and while clear parallels do in fact exist between the doctrine of St. John and the doctrines of earlier mystics, the reader who would have both – the breadth of historical perspective and the rigorous focus of a clearly defined examination – must inevitably decide upon one or the other. I have opted for the latter. But I also recognize the necessity of some perspective from the former. As E. Allison Peers had correctly pointed out, in the works of St. John we find ourselves at the confluence of a great mystical tradition to which many prior writers had contributed – each uniquely, but only in part – to the culmination of that unified and disciplined whole systematically, and for the first time coherently, articulated in the thought of one writer: St. John of the Cross.

But St. John is no mere synthesizer. His unique and profound contribution, not merely to the literature, but to the theology of mysticism, is unparalleled, and unrivaled by any of his predecessors, many of whom unquestionably contributed to the development of his thought. But one would not, for that reason, hold the creative genius of, say, Heisenberg, to be diminished simply because prior physicists had made separate and distinct contributions which the creative genius of Heisenberg – grasping *in toto* what each had only succeeded in articulating in part – molded into a successful physics no less original for these prior contributions, than it was creative in articulating the whole. Our notion of creativity as such quite often and unconsciously appears to derive its paradigm from God understood as having literally created *ex nihilo*. But in man, in any man, creativity is not something that suddenly emerges quite spontaneously and in isolation. There are always antecedents from which creative genius springs, distilling something pure from the brackish tributaries upon which it draws. Within the Christian tradition this was certainly so of St.

Thomas Aquinas. It is no less true of St. John of the Cross.

Mystical theology, we might say, appropriately begins, as it ends – in a paradox. The most direct, and certainly the most widely accepted interpretation of the development of the tradition of Western Christian Mysticism traces its origins back to Plotinus in the third century [1] But where Plato had endeavored to preserve the fluid dialogical nature of what was essentially philosophic *inquiry*, the Neoplatonists in general, and particularly Proclus in his tremendously influential *Elements of Theology*, strove toward a rigorously architectonic form, a form through which they sought to elaborate not so much a synoptic philosophy, but a coherent and essentially reactionary *doctrine*. This doctrine, only casually derived from Platonism, emerged from what essentially began as dialogues between Plotinus and Ammonius Saccas – a long-standing oral tradition to which Plotinus himself adhered until he was fifty and had begun making notes of his lectures. It was these notes which his pupil

Porphyry subsequently edited and organized into the Enneads [2] – and the reason this was done at all is the whole point of the paradox to which we had adverted at the beginning.

The Bursting Chrysalis: Antagonism, Assimilation and Articulation

While Plotinus himself makes no reference whatever to Christianity, confining his criticisms specifically to Gnosticism, it nevertheless remains that the mystical doctrine of Plotinus that had been subsequently developed by Porphyry and Iamblichus [3] – and especially as it had been systematically articulated by Proclus – cannot be understood apart *from*, because in fact it was in large measure a calculated response *to*, the burgeoning threat of the still nascent Christianity. Not only was Christianity winning converts to the cause, but more importantly, it was simultaneously encroaching upon the state religion – and with it, making decided inroads against what the Neoplatonists saw as the last vestiges of classical culture. Neoplatonism was, in this very clear sense, a reactionary philosophy – it was articulated in response to, and essentially to compete with, the new religion of Christianity which was sweeping the Empire, and along with it, the Hellenic tradition that had become a part of the unraveling fabric of post-classical society. And this is to say that even the systematic origin of the phenomenon of mysticism has its historical roots in antithesis.

It is important to understand in this connection that early Christianity, imbued as it was with the anticipation of the imminent Parousia, or Second Coming of Christ, had more urgent, and certainly more practical objectives in light of its impending redemption, and, consequently, little interest in speculation. With the passage of time, this sense of imminence, of impendence, while not entirely lost, inevitably receded before the more immediate demands thrust upon it by an antagonistic culture. The early Christian community soon came to the realization that it had to cogently evaluate its own doctrines in the very terms of its antagonists; to coherently interpret their deepest convictions in light of the increasingly critical and hostile position of the Neoplatonists. While it is true that the Neoplatonists could claim an historical continuity with classical antiquity through the fusion of Platonic and Aristotelian philosophical concepts, it is also true that Neoplatonism had effectively exceeded the legitimate bounds of classical philosophy. In fact, Neoplatonism had radically *redefined* philosophy by no longer understanding its objective to lay simply in the attainment of truth, but by transforming truth into religious insight through a specifically epistemological enterprise in which philosophic knowledge culminated in the knowledge of God, or better yet, in God as the culmination of philosophical knowledge. Through this transformation it successfully, if superficially, combined the official gods of the Empire reinterpreted through Plotinus, with the prestige that classical philosophy enjoyed at large. It was, after all, a doctrine clearly more congenial to, because it more closely accorded with, the prevailing Hellenistic tradition through its unique interpretation of Plato, and had, moreover, the distinct advantage of preserving important and popular elements of pagan religion. The official polytheism of the state, now reinterpreted in pseudo-Platonic terms – however tentative – in turn lent philosophical legitimacy to Neoplatonism, a legitimacy it would not have otherwise enjoyed apart from the prevailing cultural affinity for Plato.

Neoplatonism, then, effectively forced Christianity out of the slumber of its own critical naiveté. In a larger sense, the conflict which had long existed between Rome and Galilee had now emerged from the narrow and patently futile gauntlet of the Roman arena, where even blood had failed to attenuate the conflict, into the decisive arena of the mind. Faith would wither under the light of unrelenting reason – and reason would succeed where duress not only

70

had miserably failed, but had served to fuel the fervor of this growing, unreasoned, and recalcitrant sect. Another approach was clearly necessary to preserve what was left of the respectability of Hellenism in a declining empire, and Plotinus found in Platonism the most effective instrument to this end. This is not to say that the essentially reactionary impulse of Plotinus was exercised, or even conceived, in the interests of the state, at least in a way that we would understand in contemporary terms; still less that he did not have a genuine philosophical commitment to, if coupled with a defective understanding of, the tradition of Platonism – but the fact remains that the doctrine itself unquestionably evolved as a response to both cultural and contemporary considerations.

Inevitably, however, even this perspective is too myopic. Very clearly, systematic mysticism cannot be discussed apart from Plotinus, Porphyry, and especially Proclus – who first made the distinction between the *via affirmativa* and the *via negativa* in the epistemological approach to God – and whose synthesis of Neoplatonic concepts through Aristotelian logic was to prove so influential in later Scholastic thought. But the mystical enterprise must be understood within a much larger historical context. The bankrupt philosophies of the classical era, Eclecticism, Epicureanism, Skepticism and Stoicism, all of which had promised – and failed – to deliver happiness, resulted in a general disillusion with philosophy as a viable means of rescuing post-classical society from its impending dissolution. And while it is true that Neoplatonism attempted to provide that alternative by vying with Christianity, it is no less true that the mystical impulse itself clearly predated the advent of Neoplatonism as the first systematic formulation of the basic mystical thesis; an impulse which cuts across all traditions and cultures and has been universal in every age. It is fundamentally a human response that is as ancient as the Divine invitation echoed in the cool of the evening in the garden of the first paradise: "*Vocavitque Dominus Deus Adam, et dixit ei: 'Ubi es?'* "[4] The Divine solicitation to union with God, then, is as ancient as the creation of the heart of man. The human susceptibility to God cannot be confined to a culture, a tradition, a doctrine, or even any one religion. This is no invitation to indifferentism; it is merely a realization, a recognition, that this susceptibility is rooted in the ontology of the soul itself, and is therefore universal to all men, in all ages, in every culture. It is obviously another case altogether how each culture has interpreted this invitation and responded to it. For the Christian mystic, however, this invitation takes the decisive and definitive form of God Incarnate in the Person of Jesus Christ, a point to which we alluded earlier, and for which reason we needn't reexamine now.

The concatenation of persons and ideas which had culminated in the lucid exposition of St. John is more or less clearly defined along an historical continuum that is nevertheless worth exploring, for the thought of St. John cannot be exscinded from the tradition out of which alone it coherently arises. We had already briefly adverted to Plotinus,

Porphyry, and Proclus as the systematic progenitors of the mystical doctrine that had come to be subsequently elaborated within Christian metaphysics. There are many intermediary figures, to be sure: Iamblichus, the Syrian pupil of Porphyry; Marinus, the disciple of Proclus; and commentators like John Philoponus who subsequently converted to Christianity, among a host of other less significant figures after whom Neoplatonism, as a viable philosophy in its own right, had effectively come to a conclusion, having been supplanted by the decidedly more cogent and closely reasoned Christian interpretation. Christian thought, in the end, did not abolish Neoplatonism, as Neoplatonism had been intended to abolish Christianity, but rather reinterpreted it, and in the process had not so much adopted, as assimilated significant features of Neoplatonism, and incorporated them, with some residual tension, within the philosophic body of Christian doctrine.

The Neoplatonic emphasis on the dialectic approach to God is a good illustration. For the Neoplatonist

74

there are essentially three dialectical moments culminating in the knowledge of God. These may broadly be summarized as the predicative, in which we affirm something about God; the dispredicative, in which, paradoxically, we deny what we have affirmed, at least in a *univocal* sense; and finally the superlative, in which we reaffirm what we had denied, but in an *equivocal* sense; this latter finally achieving the most adequate approximation not simply linguistically available, but epistemologically possible. An example will prove helpful. For the Neoplatonist, the *only* ascriptions proper to God are the One and the Good. The most fundamental concept of *being*, however, is not predicated of God except equivocally, or analogically: it is not predicated of the One or the Good – because it is absolutely transcendent – in the way that it is predicated of other things in the universe of experience. So much had at least been suggested by Plato in his *Republic* and *Symposium*, although with a good deal of vacillation and, we might add, with sufficient enough ambiguity, if not ambivalence, to provide stable enough a platform for Plotinus to make his leap to super-reality where Aristotle through that same ambiguity stepped down to the world of experience. The fact remains, however, that every instantiation of being in the world of ordinary events is, without exception, determinate, limited, and therefore finite. In other words, each is possessed of being in a way that is not just different from, but radically dissimilar to, the completely transcendent Being of God. We cannot, as a consequence, univocally ascribe being to God – who is without limitation, determination, and finitude – in the way that we ascribe being to a man or, for that matter, to a tree. In *this* sense, then, God is not being; at least not being ordinarily understood. To arrive at an adequate understanding of the nature of God, then, we must effectively dispredicate him of being in the way that being is understood of everything else apart from God. God, as a result, must essentially be understood neither as being, nor as not-being. His being is, in the terminology of the Neoplatonists, *above* being.

A good deal more, of course, is involved in this dialectic which is extrapolated to every other possible predicate of God with essentially the same result: the thesis, having been established, is at once abrogated through its antithesis, and the erstwhile contradiction is sublated into a synthesis reconciling this apparent opposition. The synthesis itself, however, is at best only tentative, resting as it does upon a precarious balance between the univocal and the equivocal use of language – and the problems this inevitably creates for language, together with the paradoxes it subsequently engenders, are by now obvious and have become intrinsic to mystical discourse ever since. In other words, what has become conceptually synthetized through *language* does not translate into an *ontological* opposition that in the end is understood as apparent only. The ontological opposition remains unmitigated and intact. What *has* been conceptually reconciled are merely the terms of opposition *applied* to the Absolute – an opposition which, in any event, is entirely extraneous to the One in virtue of its utter transcendence – a synthesis which the Neoplatonist tentatively achieves through the use of the superlative. And this, of course, is simply another way of saying that the Absolute is only susceptible of being addressed analogically.

As we may well anticipate, such an analysis – at least relative to the paramount concept of being – was fraught with problems upon its own terms, and, as it stood, was not entirely amenable to thinkers struggling to articulate a Christian philosophy within an otherwise useful Neoplatonic framework. Systematically sound, the metaphysical architecture around which Plotinus constructed his doctrine stood largely in need of rehabilitation only – specifically along the lines of its cosmological and ontological interpretations. And it is precisely on this point, in one of the first crucial breaks with unchristened Neoplatonism, that the 4th century Marius Victorinus, considered by some to be the first Christian Neoplatonist in the Western tradition, took exception. Significantly, Victorinus held *being* or *esse* to be, if not the most appropriate, at least the most accurate name for God in one of the earliest, if only inchoate, formulations of Christian philosophical thought. A tension, then – one never entirely resolved – ineluctably emerges from the Christianizing of Neoplatonism; a tension, we can see, essentially resulting from the incorporation of significant features of Neoplatonism, both metaphysically and cosmologically, together with the repudiation of one of its most basic tenets concerning the fundamental concept of being.

In other words, while much of the *metaphysical* infrastructure of Neoplatonism remained intact despite its adaptation to specifically Christian concepts; *ontologically*, the abstract, superessential *being* of, say, Proclus, is clearly not identical, nor can it be equated, with the personal *Being* of the Christian Neoplatonists. Although the One identified by Plotinus is indeed, and almost parenthetically described as "the paternal divinity," [5] the god of Plotinus, Porphyry, and Proclus is, in a manner of speaking, not the God of Abraham, Isaac, and Jacob. To begin with, it is not a personal being

79

to whom, for example, prayers are addressed; a being understood as intimately involved in the lives and the affairs of men. For the Neoplatonist, there is no predilection for man in the abstract being of the Absolute. The whole point, however, is that not just the Being, but the *personal* Being of God, *is* unquestionably the most fundamental tenet of Christianity; in fact, it is unquestionably the first principle of any specifically Christian metaphysics.

As a consequence, the categorical transcendence of the Absolute of Plotinus – a transcendence so complete that it does not so much as admit of the predication of "being" to a proper conception of the Absolute except by way of pure analogy – becomes an immediate point of contention in the adaptation of Neoplatonism to Christianity. This, paradoxically, but no less obviously, is not to say that the Christian philosopher does not attribute transcendence to God; he merely interprets this transcendence, not in less categorical, but in less stringently ontological terms; terms which, in the end, find their most coherent definition in a metaphysics involving the notion of participation.

The Areopagitica

Certainly in terms of the influence exercised by
any one Neoplatonist, the most central figure, and
unquestionably the most instrumental in this
transformative assimilation is Dionysius the
Pseudo-Areopagite, or as he is often simply called,
the Pseudo-Dionysius, the fifth century Christian
philosopher (probably a disciple of Proclus) whose
actual identity remains unknown, although largely
conjectured upon. He is generally believed to have
been an ecclesiastic of some sort whose
pseudonymous authorship of this body of writings
that has come to be known as the Areopagitica, is
ostensibly attributed to one of the judges of the
Areopagus, or the supreme tribunal in Athens,
before which St. Paul had stood to defend his
evangel, and subsequent to whose eloquent defense,
converted to Christianity [6]. We now know this not

to be the case, and the reasons put forth for this pseudonymity are many and varied, but few of them seriously suggest anything more than the type of pious literary imposture that appears to have been commonly practiced at the time. In any event, the authorship of these works is largely beside the point considering the systematic coherence achieved in which Neoplatonic concepts were successfully synthesized with accepted Christian doctrine. These treatises, which were to have an impact well into the middle ages and beyond, and which *in toto* constitute the Areopagitica, are four: *De Divinis Nominibus* (a paradigm of the *via affirmativa*), *Caelestis Hierarchia*, *Ecclesiastica Hierarchia*, and *Theologia Mystica* (an even more celebrated paradigm of the *via negativa*) [7] The latter, though extremely brief – having only five chapters – distills elements essentially derived from the other three treatises which then form the basic principles to mystical union with God. Anyone who has read anything of the medieval mystics will be immediately acquainted with much of the imagery and many of the analogies, to say nothing of the method, in this work. And while we do not intend to go into a detailed analysis of the Christianized Neoplatonism of the Pseudo-Dionysius, it is sufficient for this brief summary to note that the Areopagitica is the *locus classicus* not only of the linguistics of mysticism, together with the inchoate development of a distinctive mystical epistemology, but of the *via negativa*, or the negative way, the concept perhaps most central to the later metaphysical thought of the medieval mystics in particular, and Christian mysticism in general.

It is very clear from the outset that the author of the Areopagitica was profoundly influenced by Proclus, the last and arguably the most systematic thinker of the Neoplatonic school, who was deeply antagonistic to Christianity. Despite this marked influence, however, the synthesis which the Pseudo-Dionysius had effected between Neoplatonism and Christianity was so successful that the Areopagitica very early on were invoked as competent documents on both sides of the Monophysite controversies in the 6th century, and in the dispute over Monothelism in the 7th. Within the latter part of that same century we find St. John Damascene, the last of the Greek Fathers, appealing to the Pseudo-Areopagite in discussing the limitations of language in addressing the Absolute, particularly in his references to the essential incomprehensibility of God. [8] Widespread as his influence had been, however, it was St. Maximus Confessor, the 7th century theologian who, by successfully integrating dogmatics into the Pseudo-Dionysian schema through his lucid commentaries on all four treatises, had provided the necessary theological glosses to obvious ambiguities in the texts, bringing the works of the Pseudo-Dionysius into closer alignment with orthodox doctrine and thus effectively preparing them for, and greatly contributing toward, their general recognition in the later Middle Ages.

Ironically, the profound influence that the Pseudo-Dionysius was to exercise upon the later development of medieval mystical thought was nearly lost to the West together with the knowledge of classical Greek that had all but vanished in the four hundred years preceding the Carolingian reforms and the subsequent revival of letters, culture, and learning. Greek at this time, indeed, the pursuit of learning in general, appears to have been preserved exclusively in the monasteries of Ireland, which alone had been spared the barbarian incursions that had ravaged the Continent and extended as far as Britain. Fortunately, however, they had failed to press farther west, and at the behest of Charles the Bald, it was the Irish philosopher and theologian, Johannes Scotus Erigena, one of a handful of theologians in the West who had acquired facility in classical Greek, who was largely responsible for bringing the Areopagitica [9] (together with St. Maximus Confessor's *Ambigua*) into the mainstream of medieval theological thought through his translation in 858 of the works from their original Greek into Latin. At the same time, he incorporated significant features of these works into his own speculative theology that itself had become prominent in his most celebrated, if controversial work, *De Divisione Naturae* [10], otherwise known as the *Periphyseon*, which was widely read by mystical theologians in the 13th century and exerted considerable influence upon such later figures as Johann Eckhart. With the isolated exception of Johannes Scotus Erigena, however, a significant hiatus occurred in the development of mystical-theological thought between the 9th and the 11th centuries that coincided with the greater gap in continuity that had occurred within philosophy itself apart from a few notable exceptions such as Boethius in the early 6th century – considered by some the last of the Romans – whose *De Consolatione Philosophiae* (a philosophical and not an explicitly Christian work per se) bears the unmistakable stamp of Proclus, and possibly St. Isadore of Seville in the 7th century, more properly an encyclopedist in his attempt to compile a sort of summa of universal knowledge, parts of which, incidentally, preserved important fragments of classical learning that would otherwise have been lost altogether.

Revival, Reason and Revelation: the Middle Ages and the Mystical Tradition

Not until the revival of letters and learning in general under the auspices of Charlemagne (principally through Alcuin, the great architect of the Carolingian renaissance) will we find the literature of mysticism reintroduced through the reintroduction of classical learning itself. This, as we have seen, was the impetus that brought the Pseudo-Dionysius to Johannes Scotus Erigena in the first place. While the assimilative process, as we may expect, was gradual, so effective was the reform in education and learning that had been brought about largely through the efforts of Alcuin that the educational system it produced survived the collapse of the Carolingian Empire, which had effectively ended with the death of Charles the Fat in 888. However, the wealth of classical learning it had succeeded in acquiring was preserved in the

Cathedral schools and monasteries through which it subsequently became available to the mystics who would later flourish in the 12th century

It would seem to appear that these two distinct repositories of classical literature were largely responsible for the two equally distinct approaches to mysticism that we find emerging in the 12th century. While clearly not separate traditions, the divergent interpretations found their clearest expressions respectively in the Cistercian monasteries, most notably at Clairvaux and Signy, under the auspices of St. Bernard – widely regarded as the first medieval mystic – and at the Abbey School of St. Victor in Paris founded in 1108 by William of Champeaux, but which really came to renown under the leadership of Hugh of St. Victor, one of the foremost theologians of the 12th century and one of the principal architects of scholasticism. In many respects it was St. Bernard, however, who, in his "homilies on the Canticle", and elsewhere, put the indelible stamp of Christianity upon the Neoplatonic mysticism of the Pseudo-Areopagite by contending that *grace*, and not simply the abstracting process of contemplation, was essential, indeed, indispensable to the knowledge of God that culminates in mystical union; a union, moreover, achieved not through the intellect, but through the will; not through reason, but essentially through love, and for whom the very possibility of union at all presumed the *imago Dei* in the soul.

William of St. Thierry, a close friend and colleague of St. Bernard, provided perhaps the clearest expression of the Cistercian emphasis upon the role of the will in the realization of union:

"When the object of thought is God, and the will reaches the stage at which it becomes love, the Holy Spirit at once infuses Himself by way of love [such that] the understanding of the one thinking becomes the contemplation of the one loving" [11]

In this respect it would appear that St. John of the Cross is much closer to St. Bernard and William of St. Thierry than to Hugh of St. Victor to whom he is in other respects nevertheless indebted. While not prescinding from the necessity of revelation, and always within the bounds of orthodoxy, Hugh of St. Victor nevertheless strongly emphasizes the role of *reason* in attaining to the knowledge of God. His contribution to the literature of mysticism, principally in the form of his five mystical works, *De Arca Noe Morali et Mystica*; *De Vanitate Mundi*; *De Arrha Animae*; and *De Contemplatione et eius speciebus* was significant and the Neoplatonic influence upon his thought unquestionable as we see in his *Commentariorum in Hierarchiam Caelestem Sancte Dionysii Areopagitae secundum interpretationem Joannnis Scoti libri x*. The emphasis upon reason, which characterized the Victorines in general, is particularly evident in the mystical works *Beniamin maior* and *Beniamin minor* by Richard of St. Victor for whom contemplation formed the terminus of a progression of knowledge to the point of pure reason beyond which – and only with divine assistance – the soul attains to union. In an interesting aside nevertheless apropos of St. John, Richard invokes a particularly useful analogy in the way of underscoring the importance of dogma and Scripture to the mystical experience by seeing in the Mount of the Transfiguration a prototype of certain "visions" accompanying this experience, and claiming that such essentially peripheral phenomena, if they are in fact genuinely divine in origin, must be corroborated by Moses and Elijah, who for Richard symbolize the Church and Sacred Scripture. If they accord with neither, they are to be rejected. Certainly the tradition that culminates in the thought of St. John owes a considerable debt to the Victorine School in further elaborating the Christian synthesis that derived its impulse from the Pseudo-Areopagite. The extent to which St. John of the Cross was influenced by this important school of thought is, I think, most clearly evidenced in his use of the allegorical interpretation of Scripture, certainly not in the Victorine emphasis upon reason. It would also seem probable that St. John's metaphysics of participation through love owes at least an historical debt to Richard of St. Victor in whose *De Trinitate* God is emphasized as love itself, as the Evangelist John had beautifully summarized, and not merely as a perfectly loving being.

This tradition continues to be developed in the writings of the13th century Franciscan mystic Giovanni Fidanza, better known as St. Bonaventure, a contemporary and close friend of St. Thomas Aquinas, whose *Itinerarium mentis in Deum*, or Journey of the Mind to God, and *De Triplici Via*, or the Three-fold Way – essentially a compendium of the mystical theology of the Victorine School – were widely read by such diverse later 14th century mystics as Blessed Henry Suso and Jean Gerson. It is really in the 14th century, however, that we come the flowering of mysticism, and more specifically, to the apex of speculative mysticism. The various earlier systems, both rational and affective – that is to say, emphasizing either reason or the will respectively – converge at that academic crossroads where the increasingly abstract, dry, and often contentious schools encountered a popular yearning for depth and renewal in the most basic spiritual aspirations of which the academics had seemingly lost sight in the pursuit of matters abstruse and trivial by comparison. Here we find such familiar and notable figures as Eckhart, Ruysbroeck, Suso, Tauler, and Gerson, all of whom, directly or indirectly, to some extent influenced St. John of the Cross. Within the limited scope of this book we cannot possibly attempt to detail the individual contribution to the thought of St. John of each of these figures who were, at least chronologically, his most immediate predecessors; it is nevertheless clear, however, that the most direct sources to which St. John had access were in any event themselves indebted to the contributions of previous figures within the same tradition. And while we may safely advert to the earliest systematic formulations of this doctrine in the Neoplatonists in general and the Pseudo-Dionysius in particular, and see every subsequent development essentially in light of this basic metaphysical doctrine, we cannot, and quite obviously, for that reason prescind from those unique contributions that were instrumental in articulating this early and largely inchoate doctrine in a way that progressively succeeded in making it consistent with both Christianity and reason.

To a large degree, each figure in the mystical tradition owes a greater debt to the influence of another and preceding figure in a way that is more clearly recognized than his debt to the rest. But we must equally recognize that every mystic is essentially eclectic in drawing upon the distinct universe of ideas that constitute the tradition out of which his own thought emerges, sometimes subscribing to certain aspects of one doctrine while largely rejecting the rest, as in the case of Blessed Henri Suso's rehabilitation of some of the faulty doctrines of Johann Eckhart. In a sense, to say that St. John owes his most immediate debt to Ruysbroeck, as some maintain, even if true in a purely chronological or immediate sense, is to fail to see in Ruysbroeck the myriad other mystics, indeed, the entire mystical continuum to which the doctrine of Ruysbroeck or any other mystic is indebted. Every mystic, then, incorporates something of the thought of not merely one particular mystic preceding him, but of the entire tradition implicitly comprehended within the doctrine of that mystical figure to whom he himself is most immediately indebted. And distinct elements within this tradition extend back well beyond the Pseudo-Areopagite himself; in fact, at least as far back as the 3rd century AD, some two hundred years prior to the appearance of the Areopagitica. And the whole point is this: whether or not say, Maximus Confessor in the 9th century had read St. Athanasius's *Life of Antony* written around 357 AD or the Spiritual Homilies of the 5th century Pseudo-Macarius, and whether or not Maximus's *Ambigua* itself was the subject of study of say, Johann Tauler, may be impossible to ascertain. What is certain, however, is that an entire tradition consisting of a wide variety of writings by a great many different writers is brought to bear on the doctrines that later became articulated in the speculative systems of the great 14th and 15th century mystics.

Any brief survey, for example, must certainly include Origen, the 3rd century scholar and Church Father who stands not only as one of the most creative minds in the history of the Church, but as one of its earliest mystical teachers. Indeed, not only was Origen a contemporary of Plotinus, but he studied under the very same Ammonius Saccas from whom Plotinus derived his own mystical doctrine. In Origen, among other things, we find one of the earliest examples of the systematic use of allegory in the interpretation of Scripture [12], a literary device exercised no less by St. John of the Cross than it was by the Victorines some four centuries before him. Among the mystical doctrines to be found in his *Commentary on the Song of Songs* is a conception of union framed around the notion of the *imago Dei* and his writings clearly adumbrate the celebrated three-fold way of purgation, illumination, and union,[13] which had subsequently come to typify the mystical path to

God. But there are other aspects of mysticism to be considered as well. The 4th century St. Antony, for example, is widely acknowledged as having contributed indispensable elements to the development of the ascetic aspects of Western mysticism, which find their clearest expression in the form of what are basically the ascetical prescriptions mandated by the *via negativa*. The conception of a rehabilitation of man's nature to its original state of consonance with God, which had been forfeited as a result of the Fall, is equally addressed by St. Anthony, and in the context of a conception of union with God. His skeptical regard of supernatural phenomena and his admonitions concerning them (to be reiterated by Maximus later, and St. Bernard later still), his stress on the necessity of withdrawal from the world, together with his counsels concerning impediments likely to be encountered as a result of diabolical interference, are very familiar to us by now from a much later historical context.

More influential still upon the thought of the medieval mystics was the 4th century Desert Father St. Gregory of Nyssa to whom the mysticism of St. John is, directly or indirectly, indebted. In contradistinction to earlier (and some later) mystics, but very much like the Pseudo-Dionysius (whose writings were unquestionably influenced by St. Gregory of Nyssa) ecstatic union is to be attained through darkness, not light. Not surprisingly, in his *Life of Moses* (as St. John will much later describe it in his *Ascent of Mount Carmel*) we find that the journey to "… the knowledge of God … is a steep mountain difficult to ascend …", and in this ascent itself, moreover, the *imago Dei* figures largely in the mystical experience that follows. The Incarnation is, for St. Gregory, as it is for St. John, and for Maximus Confessor before either of them, absolutely essential to the very possibility itself of mystical union. The necessity of abstraction from sensibility, and the imperative of faith as the only proximate means to this union – this is no less the currency of the mysticism of St. Gregory than it is of St. John of the Cross.

In the writings of these early Fathers, particularly Origen and St. Gregory, we also find some of the earliest references to Divine love *inflicting a wound* whose pain is longing for union; a sentiment echoed only less eloquently but no less passionately by St. Bernard than by St. John of the Cross. Like St. Antony before him, and St. John after him, St. Gregory understood mystical union as essentially culminating in the restoration of the *imago Dei* obscured by sin. But our striving after parallels for their own sake, should we care to pursue them further, may well continue indefinitely, and in the end be quite pointless; the recognition of such antecedents itself suffices to our present purpose. For what I am suggesting in all this is merely what I had attempted to state with a good deal more brevity earlier: All the coherent, but fragmented elements of an entire historical tradition, dating at least as far back as the 3rd century, come into brilliant focus in the thought of St. John of the

Cross some thirteen hundred years later. Perhaps, in closing, an analogy of our own will be useful. This tradition comes to us more or less like the fragments of a mirror shattered at the dawn of time, each piece of which, in some diminished form, in and of itself reflects something authentic of the one same sun whose light is brought to bear upon it – but these scattered pieces are finally brought into proper orientation, aligned, reintegrated, and seamlessly conjoined only through a creative insight so flawless in perspective that the whole is for the first time reflected as unfragmented in all its parts, revealing a brilliance far greater in its unity than the sum of each distinct light reflecting in only the totality of its parts. Where each previous mystic, through the indomitable prompting of Unspeakable Love, had succeeded merely in hurling a star into the darkness, St. John, peering into that same night, grasped the divine dialectic of darkness and light – and with the finger of God traced the constellation that revealed, in the closing words of Dante's

Paradiso, "the love that moves the sun and every star."

---

[1] or literally, 'sets of nine' essays divided rather arbitrarily by Porphyry in his penchant for numerology into six groups.

[2] Apart from the Enneads, Porphyry himself had written several influential treatises, the most notable being his *Sentences*, essentially an exposition of the philosophy of Plotinus, and the *Isagoge* (or introduction to Aristotle's categories) which figured largely in later medieval thought especially in the controversy over universals in the 11th and 12th centuries.

[3] His principal works, broadly organized as the *Summary of Pythagorean Doctrines*, while less celebrated than those of Porphyry, were more speculative still, and contributed significantly to the modification of the basic metaphysical tenets of Neoplatonism, elements of which Proclus would subsequently take up in his final systematic synthesis.

[4] "… the Lord God called to the man, and said to him, "Where are you?" Gen. 3.9 (Vulgate)

[5] Ennead 5.1

[6] Acts 17.34

[7] Not including ten letters, apart from these treatises, attributed to the Pseudo-Dionysius as well. These were addressed severally to ecclesiastics of ranks ranging from the monk, Caius, to the Bishop of Titus, and one ostensibly to the Apostle John himself·

[8] *De Fide Orthodoxa* I.12

[9] The text of which, in the original Greek, had been archived by Pope Paul I in the Abbey of St. Denis just north of Paris in 757 where it had remained unread for the better part of a hundred years.

[10] A boldly speculative but unsuccessful attempt to synthesize the emanationisn, pantheism, and mysticism of the Neoplatonic schema with the empirical elements of Aristotle,

Christian theism, and the doctrine on creation.

[11] *Golden Epistle*, 249-250

[12] *Philocalia*, chapters 1-15

[13] intimated earlier still by St. Clement of Alexandria in his *Stromateis* in the 3rd century.

ASCENT of MOUNT CARMEL

The Presuppositions

Beyond Innocence

One of the fundamental principles of mystical theology, briefly touched upon in our introduction, is that the relation between the contemplative and God is marked by profound incommensurability in every category. Ontologically, this incommensurability derives from the relationship between two radically distinct natures: God, on the one hand, considered ontologically, is uncreated, infinite, eternal, immutable, autonomous, and self-sufficient. The ontological attributes of man, on the other hand, are diametrically opposite. While procreative, his nature itself remains created. He is finite in knowledge and power. His being exists, is enacted, radicated within, the distinct and limited physical locus circumscribed by his body. He is temporal, having historical antecedents in time: a beginning before which he was not, and an end toward which he ineluctably moves. He is mutable, inconstant, changing, evolving, maturing – not only physically, but intellectually and spiritually. He is altogether heteronymous. Subject to circumstances, forces, and occurrences quite often beyond his control – *despite* the most assiduous application of his will – he lacks complete self-determination. Finally, he is utterly contingent. His being, in every way, relies, depends, upon, requires, re sources beyond itself. Ultimately, the ontic reality of man is understood to be conditioned by the divine existence itself: his being, metaphysically considered, is ultimately dependent upon the being of God. The divine existence, however, is absolutely unconditioned, being completely sufficient unto itself.

Furthermore, this incommensurability between God and man in the realm of the ontological, is compounded by moral alienation in the universe of ethics. Prior to Adamic sin, or the fall, the gulf between God and man is held to have been mediated by grace which, according to Christian doctrine, is understood to be the created participation in the life of God – a life which, significantly, consisted in *familiar commune* with God. By some primordial act of sin, however, man fell from this state of grace; his communion with God was sundered and his nature, once consonant and harmonious with God, became corrupt, divided, disordered. He is yet possessed of an immortal soul in *essential* communication with God inasmuch as God continues to communicate *being* to the soul, but as a result of the fall and his subsequent alienation from God, his cognition of this fundamental source of his being – in a very real sense, his *vision* of God – has become inadequate and obscure. He is essentially communicated with, but noetically excommunicated from, God. In the state of innocence, the noetic apprehension of God is held to have been connatural to man – but this is no longer the case. In his fallen state, man is

105

deprived of this simple, *immediate* apprehension of God in which his original felicity consisted.

Thus divided, man, once empirically acquainted with the eternal – and now in isolation from it – is a being whose cognitive acquaintance is now limited to one dimension only, the temporal: and this really is the beginning of the mystical problematic, for it is precisely temporal categories that are incompatible with the eternal, and incommensurable with the infinite. It is the task of the contemplative, then, to somehow reintegrate these bifurcated dimensions, in fact, to pass beyond them by gathering the temporal *into* the eternal, and in so doing strive to attain that epistemological integrity which existed in the state of innocence – indeed, to go beyond innocence by achieving not simply communion with God, as Adam enjoyed prior to the fall – but *union* with God. To do so, the mystic must first abstract himself from that manifold of temporal categories which are metaphysically irreconcilable with the two basic ontological attributes of the Absolute: infinity and eternity. His quest for union with God must be *negatively* achieved through a series of *purgations* which will first attenuate, and then effectively abolish his metaphysical contrariety to God.

It is within this context that we first discern the first epistemological principle of the *via negativa*: in order to achieve that union with God which constitutes the soul's consummate perfection, it is necessary to undergo two distinct negative processes, or purgations, corresponding to what St. John calls the *sensuous* and *spiritual* parts of the soul.[1] The purgation of each part, moreover, is to proceed according to the three *faculties* of the soul – will, understanding, and memory – each in relation to *its* sensuous and spiritual parts. In a sense, St. John states his methodology early on and rather clearly in the *Ascent* and we are tempted to extrapolate prematurely if not hastily in light of it. This would be to err seriously. And perhaps we ourselves have begun too abruptly, for it is not only the method, but also the means with which we must first come to terms if we are to avoid confusion at the outset. It is extremely important for us to understand that the movement to mystical union is a *cooperative* enterprise throughout. The soul responds to, and passively cooperates with, that initiative which rests with God alone [2].

Perhaps we can render this in other terms nevertheless compatible with the thought of St. John; terms that may more clearly establish the dialectical relationship that exists between the soul of the contemplative and God. The *activity* of the soul of which St. John speaks in his opening discourse in the *Ascent*, while not of itself capable of inaugurating the union sought after, may nevertheless be regarded as *predispositional* to that union which God alone effects, and to which the soul is entirely passive. In an epistemological context, this state of negativity that the soul strives to achieve may be viewed as the *condition* of the possibility of a direct intuition of God. Understood in this sense, the dialectic between the soul and God becomes somewhat clearer. As the mere condition of the possibility of the direct apprehension of God, this negation at once presupposes passivity on the part of the soul, and activity on the part of God – an activity capable of actualizing this possibility through what St. John terms the *divine infusion.*

This, however, must be achieved systematically, or perhaps better yet, methodologically, and in keeping with the empirical foundations of knowledge articulated by his Scholastic predecessors, St. John begins this redoubtable task on the purely human level of sensibility. The first step, then, that we encounter in the *Ascent of Mount Carmel* (or the step toward the epistemological predisposition to mystical union) is the *negativity of sense.* And this, St. John maintains, consists in depriving the soul of distinct conceptions according to the *understanding,* alien desires and affections according to the *will,* and various images and representations according to the *memory.* [3] In other words, it calls for a centripetal movement toward the axis of the soul's being – a rigorous integrating and coordinating of the faculties in the intensely focused love of God alone, as the first prerequisite to infused

contemplation. And so we find St. John stating in
Book I of the *Ascent* that:

> "… the soul [in this state of negation] is, as it
> were, in the darkness of night, which is
> naught else than an emptiness within itself of all
> things."[4]

The emptiness of which he speaks in fact constitutes
the state of sheer passive receptivity; a receptivity
toward which the soul is constrained to move
preparatory to its union with God. In this *night of
sense* the pleasures and desires of the soul
preeminently involving the *will* are not so much
systematically abolished, as rigorously suspended,
so that the soul contains nothing appropriated
through the will, in the way of created nature that
would engender contrariety with the Uncreated
God. The precise metaphysical nature of this
opposition between the created order and God,
which figures so largely in the philosophy of St.
John, remains to be addressed in greater detail later;
for the moment, let us examine some of the more

salient implications involved in what we have considered so far.

The Problem of Union vs. Identity

We have already touched upon several notions that are indispensable to a clear understanding of mysticism, and our discussion up to this point has briefly focused upon predisposition, passivity, activity, and receptivity as central in the movement toward mystical union. But even at this early point in our account a closer examination of these central features brings us into an arena of considerably greater complexity than any clarity it has afforded us thus far. Ineluctably, even a preliminary analysis brings us, in fact, face to face with perhaps the single greatest problem confronted in mystical phenomenologies in general, and St. John's works in particular, and this is the problem of *union versus identity*. It is an unavoidable problem that becomes at times critical in some later passages that we will examine in which St. John appears to equate personal annihilation [5] with the virtual assimilation of the soul into the identity of God [6] To St. John's credit, however, it is equally important to note that in other passages he is quite careful in keeping the two natures distinct. [7]

What then is this problem? And no less importantly, what is the provenance of this confusion? In effect, the problem has always been latent in the account, for that attitude which is conducive, or better yet, predispositional, to union, consists precisely in the absolute *passivity* which follows the sensuous night of the soul. In every faculty, according to St. John, the soul is rendered empty, unoccupied. It is the *sheer possibility* of conscious actualization, but is not of itself in any epistemological sense actual – for its ordinary consciousness, we have seen, consisted in precisely those elements which had been systematically purged through the *via negativa*. In this state of epistemological suspension – completely void relative to nature broadly understood as the sum of all possible natural conditions of conscious actualization – the soul is then receptive only to God as *outside nature*, and who, as such, alone is capable of actualizing this mere possibility through the divine infusion. Consciousness is thus contingent *upon* God, is actualized *by* God, and is a consciousness *of* God. In other words, it is an *apotheosized* state of consciousness, a unitary and exclusive awareness of *God*. However, it is crucial for us to remember that prior to this infusion, the soul of itself possessed nothing but the *possibility* of conscious actualization, and that subsequent to union its sole epistemological datum – that in virtue of which alone it has been actualized – is God. And this is to say that only insofar as God communicates himself the soul – is the soul actual, in any consciously noetic sense. And this, rather succinctly, is the problem of identity. It appears to be not so much a union of distinct natures, as an identity resulting from the apotheosizing of the one through its noetic assimilation into the other.

But we also mentioned that St. John was careful in keeping the two natures distinct, for he quite clearly states that:

> "In thus allowing God to work in it, the soul is at
> once illumined and transformed
> in God, and God communicates to it His
> supernatural Being, in such wise that it
> , appears to be God Himself, and has all that God
> has. And this union comes to pass
> when God grants the soul this supernatural
> favor, that all the things of God and the
> soul are one in participant transformation; and
> the soul seems to be God rather than
> a soul, and is indeed God by participation;
> although it is true that its natural being,
> though thus transformed, is as distinct from the
> Being of God as it was before" [8]

What, then, in St. John's account may be invoked as the distinguishing feature between the notion of *union* on the one hand, and that of *identity* on the other – when the two quite often appear to be conflated? Until we arrive at a concept that will enable us to discriminate between the two, we can penetrate no further into St. John's mystical account, or, for that matter, effectively differentiate it from other competing accounts entirely outside the Christian tradition. This crucial concept – the *sine qua non* to the very intelligibility of Christian Mysticism – is to be found in the notion of *participation*; a notion that, while not prescinding entirely from a conception of *identity*, more clearly implies the idea of *union*. Perhaps it can better be explained this way: we understand by that which participates, something clearly distinct from that *in which* it participates. That is to say, while the notion of participation clearly implies unity between the participant and that in which it participates, we at once understand that it is a unity into which disparate elements enter. In a similar manner, we understand by the notion of *union*, a conjunction of two in which the individual natures entering into the union are preserved, rather than abolished; we should otherwise find it very difficult to understand the sense in which we speak of it as a union, rather than as a unity. Unlike identity which implies the reduction of a merely *apparent* plurality to an ultimate unity, the notion of participation is understood to involve the preservation of two authentically distinct elements entering into – while not simultaneously being abolished by – a union.

We should, moreover, find it largely problematic, and entirely incompatible with the doctrines that St. John later develops to view the type of infused contemplation that St. John describes as resulting in an identity, rather than a union. It is, I think, extremely important to the integrity of St. John's thought to emphasize this point, so let us take our previous discussion just a little further. The two elements entering into identity, we had said, are in fact seen to be one. We do not speak of one participating in the other, for there is no *other*, strictly speaking: the merely-apparent two are in fact identical, understood to be one and the same. We discover nothing of the sense of subordination or contingency implied in the idea of identity, for the very simple reason that the one *is* the other. The

116

distinction, in other words, is essentially spurious. Most often it is rendered in purely temporal, although sometimes spatial, terms: it is, in fact, the one thing understood at different points in time or space, or both.

Something quite different emerges, however in our understanding of union through participation; something which clearly suggests the contingent character of the participant relative to that in which it is understood to participate. The latter, it becomes clear, is presupposed as the *condition* of the possibility of a participant. Simply put, what participates already presupposes that in which it is participating. And *this*, needless to say, very clearly accords with St. John's understanding of the soul's relationship to God subsequent to the state of negation; a primarily noetic, but also an ontological relationship in which the soul is contingent upon, presupposes, that divine initiative in which alone it is actualized. While it is undeniably an apotheosized state of consciousness, it is nevertheless a consciousness contingent upon, subordinate to, and metaphysically distinct from, the divine agency through which alone it becomes actualized. So vital is an understanding of this crucial distinction to an understanding of St. John's works at large, that unless we now grasp it fully, any further attempt at understanding his sometimes involuted expositories will be either entirely remiss or completely in vain. The notion of participation is, as it were, the first premise in a mystico-logical sorites upon which the coherency of the epistemology of mysticism rests. Once we have succeeded in understanding this, we can begin to address the role that the *faculties* play in the movement toward mystical union.

---

[1] AMC 1.1.1-2
[2] AMC 1.1.5; 2.5.4
[3] AMC 1.4.1-5; 1.9.6; 2.6.1-6
[4] AMC 1.3.2
[5] AMC 2.7.1
[6] AMC 2.5.4
[7] AMC 2.5.6-7 + 2.21.1 Also cf. ST I 3 Q.2 art.1
[8] AMC 2.5.7 also cf. STQ.3 art.4

The Role of the WILL
in the Philosophy of St. John of
the Cross

We had briefly mentioned that in the state of
negation the soul is emptied of all desires and
pleasures according to the will [1] and that in such a
state the soul contains nothing in the way of created
nature which is contrary to God. But a good deal
more needs to be said about the metaphysical nature
of this contrariety before we can go further. Let us
take, for example, the contrariety which St. John
perceives to exist between the *finite* and the *infinite*.
First of all, it is important to understand that while
there appears to be logical polarity between the two,
they are not, in a metaphysical sense, *mutually*
contrary. It is not so much a matter of contrariety
that is eventually seen to exist, as of an insuperable
disproportion in magnitude; a disproportion which
so closely approximates categorical opposition that
it qualifies, in a practical sense, as contrariety. It is

magnitude, then, that is the essence of the finite and the infinite, as duration is the essence of the temporal and the eternal. So understood, the finite not only *can* be, but as a matter of course *is* accommodated to the infinite without engendering any contradiction whatever. The infinite divisibility of matter is one example that readily comes to mind in the way of illustrating something finite incorporating the infinite within itself while losing nothing of the nature of its own finitude. Everyone, I think, will agree that we can, at least conceptually, continue dividing matter ad infinitum. It is simply a matter of applied mathematics. However tedious we should find this to be, it serves to demonstrate that the infinite so incorporated really turns out to be pseudo-infinite after all. Starting with a discrete whole, we are at least conceptually capable of subjecting it to infinite reduction. However, we should find that at any given point in the reductive process (which may continue indefinitely, that is to say, infinitely), a reversal toward integration will eventually go no further than the discrete whole from which we started. In other words, it is only a disintegratively infinite process. It is only infinite, so to speak, from the top down. And this, obviously, is equally true of time *vis-a-vis* eternity. While of itself infinitely reductive, divisible into days, hours, minutes, seconds, etc., an abrupt reversal of this process will never bring us beyond the present.

What is the point of this aside? In each instance we find that the finite, while unable to comprehend the infinite, is at least metaphysically susceptible to it. We have seen, through two rather pedestrian examples, that the infinite may, in principle, be accommodated to the finite without contradiction. But it does so dis-unitively, by division, reduction, disintegration. It is, paradoxically, a unilateral infinity coextensive with the finite: it is infinitely retrogressive, but only finitely progressive. It will always have its terminus in the unity from which it began. But the fact nevertheless remains that the matrix of the infinite is at least *implicit* in the finite. A latent, if limited correspondence *does in fact* exist, and it is in virtue of this fact alone that any

121

correlation between the two becomes possible – and only on terms which abrogate the metaphysical nature of neither. It is only when we try to pass *beyond* the finite to the infinite that we encounter difficulties. Whereas the infinite is capable of *instantiating* itself within the finite by subsuming the finite under itself while yet remaining infinite, the finite on the other hand is incapable of extrapolating itself into the infinite, of passing beyond itself without at once ceasing to be finite. The bearing this has on our understanding of the metaphysics underlying mystical union should be fairly evident by now. It is simply this: In mystical union, it is not a matter of the finite being poured, as it were, into the infinite – the finite can never comprehend, fill, be coextensive with, the infinite; rather it is a matter of the infinite instantiating itself within, as it were, being poured into, the finite. And this is precisely why it is termed the *divine infusion*; an infusion that can only be effected through an *approximation* of the infinite through the negation of all that is finite in the soul. That is to say, the soul, created *in imago Dei*, is the approximation of the infinite in its fundamental ontological nature. The infinite, as we had said earlier, clearly cannot exhaust itself in the finite, but it *can* fill the finite – to the extent that the finite has abolished every limiting category possible to its being, leaving only the image, the ontic nucleus of its being – a being which, for St. John, together with a great many mystics within the Christian tradition – is *being* an image.

The *Via Negativa*: Notions of Contrariety and Co-existence

As we had begun to say in opening our discussion on the role of the will, in the state of negation occasioned by the *via negativa* the soul contains nothing in the way of created nature which is contrary to God. Inasmuch as God is ontologically *other* to created nature, he is essentially contrary to nature as Not-nature, and inasmuch as nature is ontologically *other* to God, it is essentially contrary to God as not-God–and this, fundamentally, is the basis for the categorical opposition found between the created order and God, a point upon which St. John is clear in a number of passages:

> "All the affections which [the soul] has for creatures are pure darkness in the eyes of God [2] [and] all the being of creation compared with the infinite being of God, is nothing [3] How great a distance there is between all that the creatures are in themselves and that which God is in Himself [4] for there is the greatest possible distance between these things and that which comes to pass in this estate which is naught else than transformation in God [5] Thus, he that will love some other thing together with God of a certainty makes little account of God, for he weighs in the balance

against God that which, as we
have said, is at the greatest possible distance
from God [6] the soul, then, must
be stripped of all things created [7]"

The soul, then, aspiring to transformation in God
through mystical union is only receptive to God
insofar as it has succeeded in negating within itself
all that is other to God in the way of created nature,
until at last only that divine *speculum* remains in the
form of the *image* of God which mirrors, reflects,
only God, and is so utterly consonant with God as
to effectively be in union with him. But even in
stating this, we've anticipated a good deal too
much, for our most elementary understanding is as
yet far from complete. What are we to say, for
example, of the following principle upon which the
argument rests that St. John has just articulated
above, and which is the *sine qua non* of every
instance of the *via negativa*:

"Two contraries cannot co-exit in one person." [8]

Indeed, if one principle is held to summarize the most basic metaphysical contention of the mystic, of any mystic, in any tradition, it is this. But a clear understanding of this principle is particularly critical – indeed, it is indispensable, to an understanding not simply of the thought of St. John as a mystic, but of the entire metaphysics underlying the phenomenon of mysticism itself. How are we to understand this principle? Is St. John simply, merely, invoking the law of the excluded middle? And more importantly, precisely how are we to construe this principle relative to the mystical experience? For the moment it must suffice to say that the *application* of this principle to the mystical experience presupposes the *entire* mystical thesis that consciousness is unified in God thorough the direct and intuitive participation in the divine existence.

As it is formulated by St. John, the principle itself, that two contraries cannot coexist in one person, certainly admits of some very pedestrian exceptions. In our ordinary states of consciousness, for example, we regularly entertain, indeed, cannot dispense with, a wide variety of opposites in the routine exercise of the dialectic of reason. St. John, however, is not concerned with *ordinary* states of consciousness except insofar as they stand in need of remediation through the *via negativa*. This having been achieved (and here St. John is really anticipating the full development of his doctrine), we must advert to the mystical thesis itself, which we briefly touched upon above, and which, we suggested, is concerned with the exclusive and singular occupation of consciousness with God. And this is quite another thing. Ordinary consciousness is always diffuse, always engaging a multiplicity. In the state of mystical awareness, on the other hand, consciousness is actualized by, and unified in, its *singular* object, God, – or lacking that object, exists in a terrible night in abstraction from everything else. Clearly, then, the principle, as it stands, is in need of some qualification. Perhaps we can restate it more consistently in the following way:

The coexistence of
two contraries within
unified consciousness
is impossible.

At first there appears to be something subreptive
about this. A consciousness, after all, *unified* in
being rigorously focused – either upon nothing (the
dark night of the soul) in anticipation of the divine
infusion, or upon God (in ecstatic union) – by
definition would seem to exclude the notion of any
coexistence whatever, contrary or otherwise.
Consciousness totally unified in a single
apprehension exclusive of all else, by *definition*
precludes the possibility of coexistence relative to
other apprehensions– but it does not, by definition,
necessarily entail contrariety. The notion of
contrariety, in other words, appears to be
superfluous and the principle could as well be
applied to any state of affairs. But a closer reading
of the mystical thesis reveals otherwise. Since it is
God who occupies (or would occupy)
consciousness, everything else that could possibly

128

coexist with God *would* be *other* to God – it would, in fact, be *nature*, and thus involve contrariety with God. In short, within the limitations of space and time, there is a mutual ontological tolerance, often a complementarity, in nature among things created. This rather congenial arrangement, however, does not extend to nature *vis-à-vis* God. As a *sui generis*, God is forever opaque to nature. Metaphysically, the being of God stands diametrically against nature, not in the way of opposition suggestive of antagonism but in the way of contrariety suggesting incompatibility. And it is this to which I think St. John alludes when he adverts to this *Principle of Non-Contrariety* – a principle which, in the logic of mysticism, is not simply equivalent to, but is identical with, the Principle of the Excluded Middle or the Law of Non-Contradiction within formal logic. But it is *applied* logic, a logic rigorously applied not to concepts but to existential categories through the agency of the *via negativa*. A clearly discernible connection, then, is seen to exist between the principle of non-contrariety (the coexistence of two contraries within unified consciousness is impossible), and the mystical thesis (that consciousness is unified in God thorough the direct and intuitive participation in the divine existence).

But something more must be said about this pervasive principle of non-contrariety which figures so largely in the thought of St. John; a principle which, in the logic of mysticism, effectively constitutes the antecedent to nearly every subsequent premise. So far, we have merely succeeded in establishing the relation of this principle to the mystical thesis, and while this is clearly indispensable to the task we have put before us, the more important question to be asked, I think, is simply this: precisely what role does this principle play in the opposition that we find between God and created nature – in both articulating the opposition occasioned by the encounter between God and nature – and at once bridging that ontological gulf; translating that opposition into union? Well, to begin with, the principle of non-contrariety may in fact be seen as the *nexus* between the *via negativa* and the mystical thesis. It is presupposed by both: by the *via negativa* as the principle upon which it functions in negating all contrariety to God – and by the *mystical thesis* in rigorously defining the parameters around which alone the possibility of ecstatic union may occur. Moreover, it relates the one to the other: the *via negativa* as the means, and the mystical thesis as the end. The role, then, of the principle of non-contrariety is twofold: it functions in the *via negativa* to mediate the opposition between God and nature, and it is the conditional upon which the realization of the mystical thesis rests. That is to say, it acts through the *via negativa* to actualize the mystical thesis.

In the *Ascent of Mount Carmel*, we first see this principle at work in the relationship that obtains between what St. John calls the created will, and God – a relationship that, in turn, can only be understood in light of the opposition existing between the created order and the Absolute. And while it is an opposition primarily radicated in ontology (finite versus infinite, etc.), it inevitably reflects itself epistemologically in man's inability to adequately comprehend God. And the mystic, of course, cannot hope to achieve union with that of which he knows nothing, or to perfect union with that of which his knowledge is defective. The mystic must first *know* God if he wishes to embrace him, and this knowledge must be relative to what is authentic, and not a mere fiction. The mystic who would aspire to union with God conceived of as golden calf would aspire toward a fiction, and all his misdirected efforts would bring him no closer to union with the calf than to the real God of whom he knows nothing. But in St. John's epistemology there is an antecedent to knowledge, an indispensable faculty presupposed by knowledge and constituted as the will:

> "Two contraries cannot coexist in one
> person and darkness, which is affection
> set upon the creatures, and light, which is
> God, are contrary to each other, and

have no likeness or accord between one
another" [9]

It is through the will (affection), then, that
contrariety is first acquired by the soul; the will as
the affective faculty for appropriating anything
within the created order.[10] But, we are inclined to
ask, is it not the case that we must first *know* what
we *will* to possess? For St. John, I think, the answer
must be, emphatically, no. *First* we must will to
know – and then will to possess what we have
willed to know. And this is to say that the Thomistic
apothegm, "*Deum tamquam ignotum
cognoscimus*"– "We know God as unknown"–
essentially constitutes the first epistemological
principle in mystical theology: that we know God
paradoxically – as unknown. To wit, every category
in human experience that we have appealed to in
our quest to know God has left us empty-handed.
Each category has either proven itself to be contrary
to, or incommensurable with, the inexhaustible
Absolute. Our epistemological approach to God has
been, at its best, merely analogical. It is not that the

mystic's plight is so abysmal that he has no inkling *whatever* of God. *Some* acquaintance, however inadequate, however primordial clearly must exist: we do not seek what we utterly do not know. Rather, we seek what we know in part, or as St. Paul had eloquently put it, what we see "through a glass darkly."[11] And it is this impoverished perception, this only dim acquaintance with the Absolute perceived, experienced, as the Good and the Holy – this only marginal acquaintance with what is invincibly loving – so loving, in fact, that it compels *our* love – that appears to be the germ of mysticism. At its most fundamental level, it is the experience of *love*, then, that is the impetus to *know*. And because we *desire* what we *will* to acquire, St. John quite appropriately speaks of the will in terms of "affection".

An understanding of the difference between *knowledge* and casual acquaintance – both empirical and rational – we must, regrettably, but of necessity, presume at this point in our account. It is a topic that simply cannot be adequately addressed without involving us in too lengthy an aside. Knowledge for St. John, we must simply say for now, constitutes a good deal more than casual acquaintance, and, relative to God, a good deal less than perfect understanding. The issue of interest to us here involves not so much the concept of knowledge as that of opposition. The *matrix* of contrariety – not a problematic of itself – we have said, is found in ontology. But it is the will which is the *locus* of contrariety: the will as the agency through which the soul then appropriates created things to itself – and in so doing engendering *actual*, if you will, existential, contrariety in its attempt to come to union with the Uncreated Absolute. The incompatibility is no longer merely conceptual – it becomes actual, concrete in terms of existential impediments to union. The soul, possessed of God's contrary in nature through the appropriation of the will, is incapable of realizing union with God, inasmuch as two contraries are incapable of being reconciled without abrogating one. So let us look a little further into the nature of this opposition itself.

135

The will, St. John is clear, must be rendered passive through its subjection to the *via negativa*, desiring nothing and finding pleasure in nothing.[12] It must remain empty and receptive to God alone, appropriating nothing to itself which may be antagonistic to union. The reason for this passivity on the part of the will should be relatively clear by now: any activity of the will entails that *preoccupation* of the will which precludes its being occupied by God. But, we are compelled to ask, does not the will, in willing nothing, still will? Yes. But willing nothing is quite different from willing anything – for literally *nothing* is appropriated through the will willing nothing. Nothing in the way of contrariety, and therefore nothing that constitutes an impediment to union.

Contrariety, then – while always metaphysically latent – is first introduced, acquired, through the will. How then, we ask, does the soul as the *image of God* in a fundamental metaphysical sense (as we shall later see) come to be characterized by that contrariety which we have found to be otherwise universal throughout nature. Before we can begin to answer this, however, I think it is extremely important for us to be clear about what St. John understands by the concept of *nature*. For St. John, nature quite simply constitutes all that exists outside of (and in this sense, *other to*) the Divine Simplicity – a universe created *ex nihilo* and characterized by multiplicity and finitude – that is to say, in a real metaphysical sense, entirely distinct from God. On the one hand, St. John seems to understand by nature simply the material universe, the universe of experience ordinarily understood, contributing, for example, data to the understanding, or things appropriable through the will, susceptible to the senses.[13] But in a broader sense, St. John clearly includes in this understanding of nature, the non-material universe as well, generally spoken of in terms of spirit [14] : angelic and demonic agencies, the human soul. However understood, the outstanding feature of nature is its categorical contrariety to God. It is the finite, the temporal, conceived not simply as distinct from the infinite and the eternal but as metaphysically diametric to them.

The *IMAGO DEI*:
The Concept of Participation
and the Notion of Mitigated
Contrariety

But while all created natures exhibit contrariety to God, we shall later find that some measure of commensurability does in fact exist and is seen to obtain between creatures and God through a metaphysics essentially constructed around the central notion of *participation*. And this is to say that the contrariety, the opposition if you will, found in nature somehow falls short of being absolute – that there is, despite real opposition, a latent commensurability to be elicited from nature in varying degrees according to its participative relation to God – some more, some less. And this, we will find, is why the soul, albeit a created nature, is capable of realizing union with God. Ultimately, through the soul's ontological status as the *imago Dei*, the categories of opposition are realized to be tentative, superficial aspects of a more fundamental participative being. But between this unique human nature, itself only intermediate between the highest hierarchies of being and the lowest [15] – a familiar medieval schema – that is to say, above human nature and below it on this ontological gradient, the entire spectrum of being ranges from that which exhibits the greatest contrariety to and the least commensurability with God, to the greatest commensurability and the least contrariety. All this, however, remains to be examined in greater detail later on.

Now that we have a clearer understanding of what St. John means whenever he invokes the concept of nature – broad as this articulation may be – we can return to our original question: how does the soul, as the *image of God*, come to acquire contrariety through nature? Perhaps we can put the question

139

another way. How can the soul, which is *essentially*, that is to say, metaphysically, constituted as the image or reflection of God [16], be contrary to that of which it is constituted an image? This is a central paradox among the many that abound in the literature of mysticism. The soul is held to have been created as the image of the Absolute – and nevertheless assumes real metaphysical polarity to God. How does St. John answer this? As we already have seen, the opposition between God and nature poses no special problematic in and of itself. The two quite simply are categorically distinct. It only becomes problematic when the soul aspires not simply to a vis-à-vis encounter with God, that is to say, toward apposition with God – but to *union* with God. Some connection, therefore, must exist between the soul as the *imago Dei*, and nature as instantiating within itself opposition to God, such that the direct relation of the soul to God becomes problematic by virtue of nature. A sort of inverse participation must somehow occur by which the soul comes to share in that character of opposition

140

to God which is fundamentally a hallmark of nature. We must then look to the *will* if we are to understand the provenance of this contrariety, for it is the will which had been found to be the faculty through which contrariety is first appropriated by the soul. But how, precisely, is this contrariety acquired? St. John's answer ultimately is formulated around what must be regarded as one of the most important metaphysical principles he invokes throughout his four treatises relative to union, and which, for our purposes we will simply call the *Principle of Similitude*. Quite simply, for St. John, the will in its love for anything is, by virtue of that love, somehow rendered similar and equal to its object. *This* is the reason that the soul is placed in an attitude of opposition to God through the exercise of the will upon created objects of nature. The relation of the soul to God at once becomes problematic because it is a relation essentially characterized by opposition:

> "... the affection and attachment which the soul has for creatures renders the

141

soul like to these creatures; and the greater is

its affection, the closer is the

equality and likeness between them; for love

creates likeness between that

which loves and that which is loved he that

loves a creature becomes as low

as that creature, and in some ways lower, for

love not only makes the lover

equal to the object of his love, but even

subjects him to it love makes equality

and similitude" [17]

This principle – in fact, this passage – adumbrates a significant feature about what, for St. John, constitutes *man's essentially reflective ontology*, a topic which shall be the subject of some rather detailed discussion in *Part II* of our commentary. Here it is only important to note that man's nature as such is closely connected with, and in an important sense, realized in, its relation to the universe of experience – even, as we have already seen, in the presuppositions of consciousness. Ultimately, we shall find that, for St. John, man is not a being-in-himself, or being autonomously considered, due precisely to his ontology as image of the Absolute.

The Principle of Similitude: Conformity and Contrariety

Much, unfortunately, is left unsaid by St. John about the Principle of Similitude that is so central to his thought and so crucial to our understanding of his discussion of mysticism. He does not, for example, extrapolate upon the mechanics of this principle, and while this is regrettable, it is also clearly understandable given the nature of the task he took to himself. We must bear in mind that virtually all his major works were, despite their exegetical format, written not as speculative treatises concerned with exploring theoretical principles in mystical theology, but rather, each of these works must be understood as eminently *practical* in both intention and scope; they were written more in the way of enchiridions for contemplatives in general – and the Reformed Discalced Carmelite Nuns in particular – not as a kind of *"Summa Mystica Theologica"* compiled for scholars, theologians, and philosophers. This in no way denigrates the meticulous, forceful and incisive reasoning that is evident in every page of his works – and for which, in large part, he would later be acclaimed Doctor of the Church Universal – rather, it serves only to delimit the scope of his work, which in turn enables us to understand why many speculative elements implicit within them are not subject to the otherwise rigorous examination that the more practical issues are.

Without an understanding of the metaphysics implied in the Principle of Similitude, however, we will be unable to arrive at an understanding of the epistemology involved. So what are we to make of this rather recondite principle? What basis has this principle in a coherent metaphysics? Indeed, is there one at all? It certainly *sounds* very mystical – in Lovejoy's pejorative sense – that "love makes likeness." But how? Since St. John does not elaborate upon this in any strictly analytical sense, we must look for the answer ourselves. And here, I think, our earlier discussion will prove helpful to us in avoiding an otherwise purely conjectural analysis, for the answer, I suggest, is at least implicit in metaphysics we have already briefly addressed. For St. John of the Cross, man's fundamental ontological nature, we had found, is essentially *reflective*, consisting as it does in the *imago Dei*. We had further suggested earlier that *consciousness* cannot be understood apart from the data essentially constituting it a *consciousness of*. Consciousness and data, empirical or rational, are always understood copulatively. To speak of someone who is conscious, but is conscious *of* nothing, is to utter a contradiction. Consciousness always implies a *consciousness of*. And this is another way of saying that consciousness not simply presupposes data of which it can subsequently become conscious, but that consciousness is *actualized by* data. Apart from data, it remains only, merely, the *possibility* of consciousness. It has, as it were, no autonomous being, no actuality apart from the data in virtue of which it becomes actualized. And this is further to say that consciousness is essentially a *reflective* faculty, a faculty that becomes actualized only upon its imaging data in becoming a consciousness *of* that data. A *union*, we might say, is seen to exist between consciousness and its data in its becoming a consciousness of that data. The data, St. John's argument would seem to suggest, become not merely the condition of our being conscious, but in fact an integral part of our being conscious. Man's reflective ontology, then, is clearly evidenced, at least implicitly for St. John, in the way in which he is constituted epistemologically – indeed, in the most fundamental presuppositions of consciousness itself.

How is this related to the problem at hand? How does this bring us any closer to understanding how love makes likeness as St. John asserts? Well, first of all we have established something fundamental

146

about man's epistemology in general: that not merely a nexus, but a union obtains in the actualization of consciousness by data. But if consciousness is a consciousness *of* data, our consciousness is *characterized* by that data of which it is conscious – and this is to say that a likeness occurs or results between the data and our consciousness of that data. But we had also said earlier that consciousness characteristically engages a multiplicity. The intentionality of consciousness is typically diffuse among a manifold, whether this manifold is yielded through sensory experience or engaged in the manipulation of rational concepts– wherein no particular aspect of that manifold assumes a preponderance exclusive of the rest.

The Preliminary Role of the Will

But here the role of the will enters. Seizing upon several aspects of that multiplicity it focuses consciousness on the few to the exclusion of the many. That is to say, the *scope* of consciousness is correspondingly diminished as the will exercises increasing discrimination in its selection of the data which it in turn submits to consciousness. As the data diminishes, the focus increases. Consciousness becomes less and less diffuse among fewer and fewer data; data which are, we will remember, appropriated to consciousness through the *will*. This increasingly discriminatory process *may* conceivably continue until the will eventually appropriates only one datum to the exclusion of the rest. This one datum, then, as the sole object of the will, becomes the sole focus of consciousness – which reflects the datum as a consciousness *of* that datum. It is not at all inappropriate, then, to say that

148

a *likeness* is engendered between the two, between data and consciousness of the data. Consciousness becomes, in effect, the *image* of the datum. So understood, St. John's thesis suddenly begins to seem a good deal more creditable than we were initially disposed to view it. But we must carry our explanation one step further in order to synthesize the whole.

What, we must ask, first disposes the will to seize upon one aspect of the manifold of experience to the exclusion of the rest? St. John is quite unequivocal about this, and the answer lies in his understanding of the nature of love. It is love, which St. John variously renders in terms of "affection", "attachment", and "desire", which first moves the will to appropriate the object desired.[18] But just a moment. Did we not say earlier that the soul must *first* will to know and then will to possess what we have willed to know? Yes, but we also said that *acquaintance* (which is quite different from *knowledge*) of necessity preceded the movement of the will. St. John is very clear upon this:

149

"... although it is true that the soul cannot help hearing and seeing and smelling and tasting and touching, this is of no great import ... for we are not here treating of the lack of things, since this implies no detachment on the part of the soul if it has a desire for them; but we are treating of the detachment from them of the taste and desire, for it is this that leaves the soul free and void of them, although it may have them; for it is not the things of this world that either occupy the soul or cause it harm, since they enter it not, but rather the will and desire for them, for it is these that dwell within it." [19]

St. John is no pure theorist. He does not deal with man as though abstracted from the world of common experience. The mystic does not prescind from his surroundings. From the phenomena that constitute man's environment – objects with which

man has either empirical or rational acquaintance –
the will, in virtue of this acquaintance, *and through
desire*, that is to say, motivated by desire,
appropriates the object to consciousness. We have
already seen that a kind of union is engendered by
the application of consciousness to data in general,
as a consciousness *of* that data. When, however, the
purely noetic apprehension of an object is
augmented by the catalyst of desire, (attachment,
affection), the will inaugurates a process of
discrimination in what it tenders to consciousness,
and the exclusionary process, the increased focus to
the exclusion of other data, is directly proportional
to the intensity of the desire. The result is
consciousness more or less unified in the object
appropriated by the will – according to the *degree*
of its desire. A relatively common experience may
suffice to illustrate the point: Our experience of
romantic love is typically one characterized by a
desire for, a preoccupation with, someone – in a real
sense an intensified consciousness of someone that
so completely occupies our awareness that we

effectively *become* the beloved in the sense that the beloved is comprehensively within us, filling our thoughts, our awareness, our consciousness – even to the *forgetfulness* of ourselves in our preoccupation with the beloved. We *identify* with the beloved, see ourselves in the beloved just as surely as we see them within us. We may, in a sense, be said to *participate* in the beloved – precisely to the measure or degree of our affection or love for them. St. John therefore argues that any degree of affection that thus unites us with what we love in the created order makes us, according to the degree of our desire, affection, or attachment, more or less contrary to God in our assuming the created character of what we love in nature and have appropriated to ourselves through the will. We can now see more clearly why a relation of opposition is held by St. John to exist prior to the soul's subjection to the rigors of the *via negativa*. The exercise of the will, motivated by desire, engenders contrariety through the Principle of Similitude: the soul is rendered equal and similar to the opposite of

God in nature. In light of this, the problematic of participation becomes increasingly clear:

> "... affection for God and affection for creatures are contraries, there cannot be contained within one will affection for creatures and affection for God. For what has the creature to do with the Creator? What has the sensual to do with the spiritual? Visible with invisible? Temporal with eternal? ... Wherefore ... no form can be introduced unless the preceding contrary form is first expelled from the subject, which form while present is an impediment to the other by reason of the contrariety which the two have between each other." [20]

Sensuous negation, or what St. John calls the "night of the senses", is therefore absolutely necessary to that union in which the soul becomes one with God – not, as we shall see, through identity, but rather, through created participation. [21] Certainly a good deal more is involved in a adequate understanding of this concept than we are prepared to set forth and discuss at this point, but unless we have at the very least a basic understanding of what is directly involved in the notion of participation we will be unable to understand much of what will follow in our account. In a noteworthy break from the scholastic tradition to which St. John is otherwise and fundamentally faithful, he departs from the prevailing theology which saw the *intellect* or *reason* as the image of God in man. [22] Although he never explicitly formulates it as such, it is extremely clear from his arguments, especially relative to the Principle of Similitude, that for St. John the image of God in man lies not in his intellect, but in his *love* – even as the Apostle John tells us that "God is love." [23] And since God created man in his image [24], *love, for St. John, is the created participation of man in God*.

This is not to say that reason, or the intellect, does not in some measure reflect, as the scholastics had maintained, the mind of God and so constitute an

154

aspect of that image in which man was created. As the image of God, it would seem that certain – by no means, all – aspects of the Absolute are reflected, however imperfectly, in the ontological composition of man. But only one, love, is capable of effecting a more than epistemological union of merely the knower to the Known – a union fundamentally ontological in the soul's not merely knowing, but *participating in* God. And love, for St. John, is the only principle capable of attaining to this type of union which, embracing the soul in its entirety is ecstatic.

A number of further implications remain to be drawn from St. John's treatment of the will as the seat of love and all the affections, especially in its relation to the Mystical Thesis and the Principle of Similitude. We find, for example, that while the will, as the seat of love, is an *active* principle of union relative to the created order (as we have seen), it is on the other hand a *passive* principle of union in its relation to God. And it is *rendered* passive by its subjection to the *via negativa*

155

according to the demands of the Mystical Thesis: that is to say, if consciousness is to be unified in God, the will must cease appropriating contrariety to itself through the exercise of the will – whose sole activity subsequent to its purgation through the *via negativa* is itself rendered entirely negative in willing not to will. The Principle of Similitude coupled with the Mystical Thesis, therefore, figures largely in the transition to union and serves to underscore the *cooperative* effort necessary to the realization of that union, for although it is ultimately God alone who both initiates and consummates this union, the soul nevertheless cooperates toward this "union of likeness" [25], as St. John sometimes calls it, by passing through the crucible of the *via negativa* and removing every impediment to union by eliminating every contrariety to God. Having done so, the soul remains passively disposed to the divine initiative and through the exclusive love which the it bears toward God alone – the love which is the image become explicit – the soul, St. John contends, will become equal and similar to God. This rather startling conclusion, however, remains to be properly explained later in our examination of the Night of the Spirit.

The Two-Edged WILL: Propadeutic or Impediment?

The contemplative, then, in his quest for union must first strive to empty his will relative to the created order. Exercised only in the love of God, and detached in the way of its love, desires, and affections from the order of nature, the created will is thus prepared to become transformed into the will of God [26] both through the absence of contrariety to God in the form of nature – that is, through transformation *negatively* considered – and through that similitude and equality generated through its singular love of God, or transformation positively considered. The created will, assimilated into the will of God in the state of infused contemplation, is then indistinguishable from God's own will, for in and of itself it is totally passive, having become, as it were, a created expression of the uncreated will of the Absolute:

> " [the soul] must cast away all strange gods
> – namely, all strange affections
> and attachments it must purify itself of the
> remnants which the desires
> aforementioned have left in the soul in order
> to reach the summit of this high
> mount, it must have changed its garments
> which God will change for it, from
> old to new, by giving it a new love of God in
> God, the will being now
> stripped of all its old desires and human
> pleasures ... So that its operation,
> which before was human, has become
> divine, which is that is attained in the
> state of union ... " [27]

Possessing nothing of itself in the way of desires and affections, the will remains passive and totally receptive to the will of God which, as other to the negated in nature – a nature no longer appropriated through the will – is that alone in which it is possible for the created will to be subsequently exercised.

But does this mean, then, that the soul in ecstasy is incapable of sin? This would appear to be the logical conclusion if the will is rendered completely passive. Are we to understand, in other words, that, given no act directly attributable to the created will, the soul is therefore no longer liable to sin? Is any subsequent act, then, deserving of approbation? Indeed, is it still *free,* with all the moral and deontological considerations that the notion of a free will entails? In regard to the second question, – concerning the soul's liability to sin – a careful reading of the text would reveal that St. John's answer would most emphatically be, no. And for this reason: the soul in the state of infused contemplation becomes, as we have said, a created expression of the uncreated will of God. In its total passivity, every movement of the will is directly ascribable to God. And since God is incapable of peccancy, the soul so moved by God – and, it is important to emphasize, *only in the state of ecstatic union–* is, likewise, incapable of sin. This obviously does not mean that the mystic who has attained to sporadic union can no longer sin, for it is also the case that the state of ecstasy in this life is characteristically brief, and upon his return from ecstasy the contemplative, despite the obvious predilection of God, nevertheless remains in his created humanity liable to sin through the penalty that inescapably accrues to mankind at large through the sin of Adam; a penalty from which none, even the most holy, are held to be exempt. Only when that state of ecstasy – which the mystic now only intermittently realizes – becomes indefectible before the beatific vision acquired after death, will the soul no longer be susceptible to sin. Mystical union is, after all, as St. John repeatedly states, a foretaste of heaven, and not an indefectible state on earth.

Bi-Dimensionality, Free Will
and Impeccancy:
The Mystic as Man

In reply to the remaining questions – to wit, is the soul yet free in the state of ecstasy, and are its acts within that state deserving of approbation – St. John's answer must be yes, and for the following reasons. In acceding to the will of God, which the soul recognizes as the sovereign good , and that in which the good universally consists, the soul freely consents to the exercise not only of *that* will but of every *good* in which that will consists. Among these are the good of the soul, which preeminently lies in its conformity to the will of God. But the notion of the good as it relates to the created will specifically, cannot prescind from the notion of freedom, both as a good in itself, and as a necessary condition of the moral soul. In choosing perfect conformity to the will of God, then, the soul simultaneously chooses that freedom apart from which the soul is neither

161

good nor moral. The created will, then, being subsumed into the divine will, nevertheless remains distinct and free. Furthermore, it is not so much that the passive will ceases to will, as that it ceases to will what is *contrary* to God – its will is, *in its created nature, both parallel to* and *identical with,* the will of God. That is to say, it wills not merely that God should move it, but that its will should freely coincide with the will of God. The volition of the soul, then, remains intact – for the created will so exercised in choosing to coincide with the will of God is in itself a free act of ratification, appropriating as its own the will of God to which it perfectly corresponds through an act of free will. And this is simply another way of saying that the created will *participates* in the uncreated will of God. And since the appropriation of the divine will is a free act of the created will, it may indeed be recognized as meritorious, as is every act ascribable to the free will which wills the good.

The precise mechanics involved in this transition are, regrettably, left obscure by St. John – but not so obscure that some very clear inferences are not available to us. It is a basic Christian premise that man as essentially *bi-dimensional*. He is possessed of a body and a soul. He is composed of matter and spirit. By and large rational, he is also sensuous. As intrinsic a component to his being as natural, is the supernatural. His existence is enacted in time but consummated in eternity. Nature, in short, subsuming under itself body, matter, and time, constitutes only one dimension of bi-dimensional man. An inverse metaphysical relation exists between the natural and the supernatural such that the more attenuated the natural dimension of his being, the more amplified the supernatural dimension; as the one recedes the other becomes increasingly manifest. Any *categorical negation* of this nature, then, would effectively result in a unilateral suspension of the corresponding natural dimension of man. And this means that the soul in having been negated to the *natural* dimension of its being relative to the will, becomes, with respect to this particular faculty, necessarily *supra-natural*;

that is to say, it is reduced exclusively to the remaining supernatural dimension of this bi-dimensional faculty in having passed beyond nature.

But to pass beyond nature is also to pass into the *other* of nature – which, on the one hand is spirit. Thus we find that the will, as described by St. John, is transformed from what he calls the sensuous into the spiritual; this erstwhile suppressed dimension of man's spiritual being now gradually emerging into existential relief. On the other hand, however, the other to nature, considered absolutely, was seen to be God. Thus in passing beyond nature the will, while yet remaining distinct from, is equally and simultaneously transformed into, the will of God. This admittedly requires some sorting out. The first level of negation we had seen to consist in *the negation of nature according to the will* in which the soul ceases to appropriate anything in the created order according to its desires and affections. We had already briefly touched upon this. The *second* level of negation, however, implicitly follows from the first, and this is *the negation of the will according to nature* in which the will in the state of negativity is effectively suspended relative to its natural function, thus becoming the functional expression of another in its subsequent activity – and that agency, St. John is clear, of which the will becomes the functional expression is God:

> "... this Divine union consists in the soul's total transformation, according to the will, in the will of God, so that there may be naught in the soul that is contrary to the will of God, but that in all and through all, its movement may be that of the will of God alone." [28]

We can now more clearly see that in negating the contrary to God in nature, the will becomes preeminently, if only passively, predisposed to the divine infusion. In being transformed from the sensuous into the spiritual, the will is rendered more proximate *to* God – and in the state of passivity (presuming, of course, that divine election that results in the actuality of union) subsequent movement of the will proceeds *from* God. As we shall later see, this entire process ultimately presupposes the transformation of the will into its corresponding theological virtue in the unified and integrated love of God. [29] In this state of transformation, the created will consummately participates in the uncreated will of God. This transition, however, is not accomplished without penalty. Very clearly, a transformation of this sort entails a privation of man's being – which, in its divinely constituted nature, is a being bi-dimensional – and every privation of being, of that perfection connatural to any being, will, despite its divine provenance, and its movement to greater perfection still, be experienced as an evil, as surely the pain of this transition, often described at length by St. John, is experienced by the mystic. It is, however, a redemptive suffering in a darkness about to broach upon light. But this is only realized in the very last stages of mystical union and already presumes the complete integration of the faculties in the love of God, which we shall examine at length in subsequent chapters.

---

[1] AMC 1.5.2
[2] AMC 1.4.1
[3] AMC 1.4.4
[4] AMC 1.5.1
[5] AMC 1.5.2
[6] AMC 1.5.4
[7] AMC 2.5.4
[8] AMC 1.4.2
[9] AMC 1.4.2; cf. ST Ques. 48 Art.3, also St. Augustine, *Enchiridion*, 14 (*Patrologiae Latinae*, 32, 1347)
[10] AMC 1.5.2
[11] 1 Cor. 13.12
[12] AMC 1.5.2
[13] cf. AMC 2.8.4-5; 1.4.1-4 etc.
[14] cf. AMC 3.4.1-2; 2.12.3-4
[15] AMC 2.12.3-4
[16] AMC 1.9.1
[17] AMC 1.4.3-4; also cf. 2.18.5; SC 15.4, 21.5, + 23.5. Emphasis added. This, of course, is essentially a reformulation of the doctrine articulated much earlier by the Pseudo-Dionysius that "it is of the nature of love to change a man into that which he loves."
[18] cf. ST Q.20 art.1
[19] AMC 1.3.4
[20] AMC 1.6.1-2
[21] AMC 2.5.4+7; 2.20.5; SC 11.6+7; LFL 2.30
[22] cf. ST Q.93 art.2 In this respect, St. John of the Cross is much more in line with St. Bernard than, say, the great mystical writers of the School of St. Victor.
[23] 1 Jn 4.8
[24] Gen. 1.27
[25] AMC 2.5.3

[26] AMC 1.11.2+3; 2.5.3+4
[27] AMC 1.5.7
[28] AMC 1.11.2+3, also cf. 2.5.3+4
[29] cf.

The Role of UNDERSTANDING in the Philosophy of St. John of the Cross

The *Via Negativa*

Book The Second of the *Ascent of Mount Carmel* is of particular importance to us in our exploring the possibilities of developing a coherent mystical epistemology. While, until now, we have tried to avoid some of the tedium inevitably involved in a commentary of this sort, the demand for accountability – within the greater demand for coherence – will sometimes require a somewhat detailed analysis of certain features of mystical doctrine. But this type of patient analysis will, in the long run, serve to illuminate a sometimes obscure and often abstruse metaphysics, enabling us to answer some very fundamental objections which we are likely to encounter further on. It is the fundamentals of St. John's metaphysics which we seek after here. And these in turn will lead us on to examine some of the more explicit epistemological features of St. John's account.

The profound disparity between created nature and God which was seen to characterize the relation between the unnegated will – the will prior to its subjection to the *via negativa* – and God, is brought to critical relief in St. John's extensive treatment of the second faculty of the soul, *understanding*. This is not to say that the same imperatives do not apply equally to each faculty, for the *via negativa* is a universal feature throughout the various movements toward mystical union. In St. John's analysis of the understanding, however, we have much clearer insight into some of the metaphysical difficulties to be overcome in a coherent account of mysticism. As the extraordinary object of ordinary understanding, God is essentially opaque to the natural intellect for reasons which by now may already be anticipated: God and the created intellect inform radically different and incommensurable categories – the nature, if you will, of the one is antipodal to the other. All, then, which the understanding can think, all that it is capable of conceiving in its natural capacity, is categorically, diametrically, opposed to the reality of God as He is in himself apart from the mediating and modifying categories of understanding:

> "... all that the imagination can imagine and
> the understanding can receive
> and understand in this life is not, nor can it
> be, a proximate means of union
> with God. For if we speak of natural things,
> since understanding can
> understand naught save that which is
> contained within, and comes under
> the category of, forms and imaginings of
> things that are received through
> the senses, the which things, we have said,
> cannot serve as means, it can
> make no use of natural intelligence [1] ... all
> that can be understood by the

171

understanding, that can be tasted by the will,

and that can be invented

by the imagination is most unlike to God

and bears no proportion to Him ... [2]

And thus a soul is greatly impeded from

reaching this high estate of union

with God, when it clings to any

understanding or feeling or imagination or

appearance or will or manner of its own ...

For as we say, the goal which it

seeks lies beyond all this, yea, even beyond

the highest thing that can be known

or experienced, and thus a soul must pass

beyond everything to unknowing." [3]

Since all that the faculty of understanding can conceivably think, or through its purely synthetic activity possibly imagine, is, *eo ipso*, *not* God, the soul aspiring to knowledge of the Absolute must proceed *paradoxically* – through a process of *unknowing* – a process, we shall find, that will ultimately translate the natural faculty of understanding into its corresponding theological virtue of *faith*. The epistemological doctrine of unknowing is, of course, but one of the many iridescent aspects of the *via negativa* which finds its clearest expression in Book One of the *Ascent*:

> "In order to arrive at pleasure in everything
> Desire to have pleasure in nothing.
> In order to arrive at possessing everything,
> Desire to possess nothing.
> In order to arrive at being everything
> Desire to be nothing.
> In order to arrive at knowing everything,
> Desire to know nothing.
> In order to arrive at that wherein thou hast no pleasure,
> Thou must go by a way wherein thou hast no pleasure.
> In order to arrive at that which thou knowest not
> Thou must go by a way thou knowest not.
> In order to arrive at that which thou possest not,

173

Thou must go by a way that thou possesst
not.
In order to arrive at that which thou art not,
Thou must go through that which thou art
not.
When thy mind dwells upon anything,
Thou art ceasing to cast thyself upon the All.
For in order to pass from the all to the All,
Thou hast to deny thyself wholly in all.
And when thou comest to possess it wholly,
Thou must possess it without desiring
anything.
For, if thou wilt have anything in having all,
Thou hast not thy treasure purely in God." [4]

Despite its largely negative format, clearly
illustrated above, the *via negativa* nevertheless
remains not only a viable, but indeed the *only*,
"way" of arriving at the Absolute. And if it is a
difficult way for the contemplative to travel, it is no
less a difficult route for the epistemologist to map,
for all its signs, every cue, each marker, is negative.

It is not unlike a series of signs that might say, not "Paris this way", but rather, "Paris *not* this way." That is well and good, but the traveler will most assuredly at once ask, "Well, then, if not *this* way, which way?" To which every sign he subsequently encounters simply answers, "not this way". The *via negativa* is much like this. It may be seen as a kind of epistemological compass that indicates not *where* to go, but where *not* to go; it is the negative of a map outlining the mystical terrain that tells you not so much *how* to get to the Absolute azimuth, but, rather, how *not* to get there. In essence, it is a cartographical paradox. It is clear, then, and most expedient that some other principle of direction must be invoked. Some principle that will provide us with a measure of certitude, not necessarily apart from the negative prescripts we have acquired thus far – which of themselves are extremely useful to us in disabusing us of error in finding our way – but which, while according with them, is more precise, or perhaps better yet, affirmative in direction.

A brief glance in retrospect may prove helpful. In the opening sequences of Book One of the *Ascent*, St. John discussed the night of the senses relative to the will. There we found that the disparity between God and created nature emphasized the lack of proportion, of commensurability, between God and the soul in its relation to God through created nature, and in so doing demonstrated the inherent impossibility of a sensuous apprehension of God. And the conclusion, of course, was that if God is to be apprehended at all, he must be apprehended *extra*-naturally; not through a sensuous manifold accessible to the will – nor, as St. John will *now* argue, through any conceptualization available through ordinary understanding. And much as we had found in the case of the will, a transition is required which will inevitably result in the positing of a theological correlate in which the function of understanding is explicitly suppressed through what St. John sees as the epistemological negativity of *faith*. Negativity, as we had seen, implies the absence of contrariety; so in stating that the three

theological virtues – faith, hope, and love – render
the soul "proximate" to God, St. John is actually
saying that each of these virtues are essentially
characterized by negativity – a negativity essentially
signifying the absence of contrariety to God.
Proximity and *non-contrariety*, then, are
interchangeable terms in the mystical vocabulary of
St. John.

For St. John, faith explicitly transcends the
limitations of sense and understanding, and in so
doing simultaneously transcends the inherent
limitations of nature and reason. [5] The limitations
implicit in *nature* are, by now, quite obvious: in
every respect it is finite. As such, not only is nature
ontologically distinct from God, but in its very
finitude and limitation it can never yield veridical
knowledge of God who is infinite and unlimited.
But the limitations of reason are less clear. In our
introduction we suggested that God, and indeed the
universe of experience itself, is not exhaustively
considered in its intelligible dimensions alone; that
any given item in experience affords something

more in the amplitude of its being than the merely rational dimensions to be elicited from it. Within reason itself, however, we discern even more fundamental limitations, and it is these that are of particular interest to us. For the most part, the mechanics involved in the limitations of reason are left unaddressed by St. John. Certainly is not the case that he was unable to articulate these limitations in greater detail, for St. John was, we had noted earlier, extremely well versed in scholastic philosophy. Still less warrant do we have to believe that he presumed them known in the mind of his readers who were, by and large, professed religious, and not necessarily scholars. In reading St. John, and I shall emphasize this point time and again, it is essential to bear in mind that he did not understand himself to be writing a philosophic treatise, still less a systematic organon in speculative mysticism, but rather an enchiridion for contemplatives, a fact we had pointed out earlier and will, no doubt, find it necessary to point out again. One goal, and one goal only, lay incessantly before St. John and everything else palled in significance before it: union with God. His own, and that of others. His readers did not need to know the law of the excluded middle in order to make a practical choice between mutually exclusive moral or spiritual ends. Less abstruse and far more effective means were available to them. These mechanics are, however, of interest to us – indeed, vital to us if we are to understand the epistemological dimensions of the mystical experience.

So what can we infer from St. John's discussion of the faculty of understanding, especially as it pertains to reason? It is, first of all, I think, fairly clear from his own exposition, that reason essentially functions upon, is limited to, and therefore requires a *manifold* – a manifold which is ontologically possible only in the universe of created nature, [6] for God of himself is one and simple. In requiring a manifold, reason is limited in three ways: first, and most obviously, by its limitation to a manifold itself – that is to say, by its

179

inability to function apart from a matrix of sheer multiplicity. The second limitation discernible in reason, concerns its scope. The manifold which reason addresses is comprised of the universe of finite entities broadly called nature, and both objects and concepts (the mind no less than matter) finite in nature, can never yield infinite, that is to say, unlimited information. Simply put, the synthetic and analytic activities of reason are incapable of eliciting more than is ontologically available in the finite data of experience. Reason, then, unable to transcend, is therefore limited to, an inherently exhaustible (finite) dimension of being. The last, but not the least, limitation of reason lies in the fact that it is ineluctably temporal – the discursions of reason are thoroughly conditioned by time which is presupposed and implicit in all its functions and activities. Time is the underlying medium through which the *successive* movements of discursive reason are enabled, enacted; and it is time which constrains reason from apprehending the simple simultaneity of existence. However comprehensive

180

its purview, reason is limited by time to discrete and successive moments in all its analytic and synthetic activity.

We have established, then, that reason requires a manifold which by definition consists of a plurality – plurality of necessarily finite entities, each limited and distinguishable one from another. Without plurality and differentiation, then, reason could not be discursive, that is, passing from one aspect under rational consideration to another in the dialectic we understand to be reason – it would, in fact, altogether and at once cease to be discursive. Which is to say that reason in its discursive capabilities would effectively be not so much abolished, as suspended. And this, in St. John's account, is precisely what occurs to reason in relation to God in the mystical experience. It remains inoperative, suspended, as it were, blindly staring into the Absolute, simply for the fact that God is One and simple, unchanging and eternal. Not reason, but the utility of reason, then, is, for St. John, forever abolished in the transcendence of plurality.

The Notion of "Proximate" Union

In transcending the limitations of nature and reason, St. John further argues, the soul then enters the state of what he calls *proximate* union with God [7] through having negated within itself the other to God in nature and reason. Considered carefully, this state of proximate union may be seen to follow for two reasons, although St. John only adverts to one. First of all, in passing beyond the *finite*, the soul quite logically – that is to say, *necessarily* – passes into the not-finite, or the infinite, and, according to the same logic, in passing beyond limitation, the soul passes into the unlimited. And in so doing – in passing into the infinite and the unlimited – the soul enters a state that is *proximate* to God inasmuch as God in himself is infinite and unlimited. This is not to say that the soul *itself* becomes infinite and unlimited in this transition – in a Christian metaphysics it can never become so: its created nature remains unviolated and unchanged despite the transition. What *has* changed, however, is the nature of the *experience* encountered by the mystic, one now characterized not by the familiar plurality, finitude, limitation and differentiation that are typical components in the experience of the created order. The mystic now, for the first time, encounters, *experiences* the infinite and the unlimited. Let us look at this more closely, and for the sake of clarity segregate the following line of reasoning for a more detailed examination:

We had said that in passing beyond the finite, the soul necessarily passes into the not-finite. Now that which is not-finite is either nothing or infinite. It is *nothing* if it is not-finite and not-infinite. It is infinite if it is not-finite and not-nothing. But the soul is not-infinite and not-nothing–which is to say that the soul is finite. Moreover, that which is not-limited is either nothing or unlimited. It is nothing if it is not-limited and not-unlimited. It is unlimited if it is not-limited and not-nothing. But the soul is not-

183

unlimited and not-nothing – which is to say the soul is limited. We have, then, the created soul which is finite and limited. In passing beyond the finite and the limited in created nature, the soul must encounter either nothing or the infinite. In either event, it will be the not-finite.

Further elaboration will, I think, make this rather concise formulation more readily understood. Whatever is, is either finite or infinite. If it is neither, it is nothing, for everything that is, or can conceivably be, is either finite or infinite. There is no conceivable third alternative. Obviously, then, the concept "nothing" pertains neither to the finite or the infinite. Were *nothing* infinite then there would be absolutely nothing, either finite or infinite – for the term infinite would be predicated of nothing. Conversely, were we to say that the infinite is nothing, we would involve ourselves in a hopeless tautology. We cannot, therefore, coherently speak of nothing as infinite. Our difficulty in apprehending this stems, I suggest, from our inclination to render the concept *nothing* spatially: we tend to conceptualize it not as nothing, but as empty *space*, a kind of amorphous negative configuration coterminous with and indefinitely configured by *something*, relative to which it is nothing; we are inclined to see it as the possible *place* of something else; in effect, *something* devoid of something else, when in fact it remains the absence of everything – which is another way of saying nothing. If, on the other hand, what we are considering is infinite, it clearly is not finite, for we *mean* by the infinite that which is not finite; nor can it be nothing, as we have just seen. The soul, on the other hand, is something, and not nothing, and it very clearly is finite in every aspect, and not infinite.

Now, if what we have argued in fact is the case, then a good deal more about the nature of the contemplative's experience prior to union becomes somewhat clearer. The *natural* or created soul is, as we have seen, finite and limited; and as we had further seen, no commensurability obtains between the finite and the infinite, the limited and the unlimited. The natural or created soul, then, has no epistemological capacity for the infinite as the *not-finite that is not-nothing*; it is incapable – *qua* created – of *experiencing* the infinite, (except under the species of the pseudo-infinite in number, etc., which we addressed earlier). But the created soul *does* have a capacity for experiencing the infinite as the *not-finite that is not-infinite*, that is to say, of experiencing the infinite as nothing – and it is *this* experience which, for the mystic, constitutes the *dark night of the soul*: not only is the soul in utterly unfamiliar metaphysical terrain, but the topography itself has metamorphosed into utter nothingness. Moreover, even *were* the *natural* soul capable of experiencing or epistemologically addressing the infinite, the experience of the oneness of the infinite, the unlimited, the undifferentiated – is no less effectively the experience of nothingness. The senses coupled with reason would falter and ultimately fail in their inability to grasp what cannot, by virtue of infinite magnitude, be grasped, apprehended, understood. The very mechanisms of reason and sense, relying upon limitation, finitude, and differentiation as the very tangents to comprehension – individuating characteristics now no longer available – would default into suspension. Natural faculties no longer suffice, for nature finds itself at the bourne between created and Uncreated being, at the outermost margin, the ontological periphery of creation where the gulf between man and God is sheer infinity, and as such, an ontic chasm, the primeval nothingness out of which man and the cosmos was created *ex nihilo*. St. John speaks of this experience as a terrible one, unparalleled by any other. We might say that in some small measure it may be likened to the experience of a man who, awaking from a dream filled with familiar images, finds himself not only in total darkness, but amidst incomprehensible emptiness, possessing no frame of reference whatever, nothing to see, nothing to touch, no sound, no smell, no sense of direction, no orientation. His experience is essentially one of complete sensory abstraction and total noetic suspension, of absolute undifferentiation. The extreme consternation, even terror, that such an experience is likely to provoke may, to some degree, resemble the plight of the mystic who has entered the antechamber of the Absolute. In this sense, darkness is a metaphor for infinity; and the awakening, the inauguration of the *dark night of the soul*.

Proximity versus Union

Up to this point we had seen that the soul, as a consequence of having transcended the limitations of nature and reason, occupies a state proximate to God inasmuch as God in himself is infinite and unlimited. While the soul in this state of proximity possesses no contrariety to God, this state of itself, St. John is clear, does not suffice to bring it to union. Rather, it makes the soul merely *receptive* to the divine infusion; metaphysically disposed to the *possibility* of infused contemplation. At this stage, the soul is brought to the extremity of its being, to

188

the irreducible, the most fundamental dimension of its ontology – beyond which lies only extinction. While it is indefectibly the image of God, at this point it neither reflects God whom it only anticipates, nor created nature which it has transcended. It is the possibility of both and the actuality of neither. In its sheer reflective ontology, it is like the image in a mirror possessing no actuality in itself apart from being the possibility of the reflection of something else; a mirror before which no image passes except the infinite toward which it is poised and which it apprehends as nothing. In this state, in reflecting nothing, it has no contrariety whatever to God, and inasmuch as it possesses nothing in the way of contrariety, it is understood as being proximate to God. So much is clear from our previous discussion.

The ontological implications of this argument, however, are two-fold and reciprocal: on the purely *metaphysical* level, the soul, St. John has argued, upon transcending the finite and the limited becomes proximate to God. So much is clear. In this

189

moment of transcendence, however, it appears that something *doxastic* emerges, not simply concomitantly, but logically, which is to say, necessarily, from this metaphysical transition.

St. John, we have seen, very clearly maintains that the soul achieves *proximate union* with God following the negation of nature and reason. He does not state *why* it follows, merely that it does in fact follow. A closer examination, however, suggests that the utility of reason and sense – relative to objects of created nature apprehensible through the will and understanding – have already been *abolished* through transcendence, or negation, and appear to be, *as a consequence* of this transition, now supplanted by the theological virtue of *faith* – which St. John argues, is *also* the state of proximate union with God.

The problem we now confront, however, is that if we hold faith to be *contingent* upon this essentially *metaphysical* transition – as the argument might appear to suggest – we divest faith of its supernatural character: it loses its provenance in God and becomes immediately subsumed under nature. It is a logical, and therefore *necessary* moment in a concatenation of events occurring within a clearly defined and purely metaphysical matrix. Faith, so understood, is not *concomitant* with transition, but is the *terminus* of the transition itself. It is not concurrent with the negation of nature and reason, it is *indistinguishable from* it; it is, in fact, synonymous with it. It becomes, in a word, metaphysically *legislated* – apart from any divine and free dispensation. As an erstwhile theological virtue, it immediately ceases as both theological and a virtue.

How can this be? The line of reasoning strikes us as sound, but is nevertheless deeply disconsonant with the most profound theological principles from which the impetus to ecstatic union emerges. Compelling as this argument may appear, it is nonetheless subreptive as we will soon see. It is, however, also extremely instructive, for it serves to underscore the complexities, as well as the tensions, that have often subverted many efforts to articulate a coherent mystical doctrine that is both consistent with the canons of reason and consonant with accepted theological tenets. The question, no less, still stands. Let us examine it more closely.

Transition or Translation?

We had stated earlier that we have observed something of the nature of *reciprocity* in this moment of transition, two distinct levels of proximity that, I will now suggest, *converge* – rather than *conflate*. The distinction is critical, for it is precisely at this juncture that much of the confusion and misconception surrounding so many attempts at explicating the notion of mystical union occurs. The metaphysical momentum that has culminated at this crucial ontological point subreptively lends itself to a spurious interpretation of what is a _transition in_ being as a _translation of being_; as a continuum of something metaphysically legislated, and not as a breach in that continuum through an autonomous leap of faith. Even while concurrent with it, faith entirely prescinds from this metaphysical momentum as a leap from the natural to the supernatural, from what is inherent in nature to what is inherent in faith.

At this point we stand, as it were, before the ontological chasm to which metaphysics has brought us and past which it can offer us nothing more legitimate, and we instinctively blench before what metaphysics legislates as the terminus of being. Metaphysics, we recognize, cannot make the transition to nothing, it has reached a point *in extremis* from which alone the soul cannot leap off to extinction. But in offering us translation, the translation of being, instead of its transition, it is offering us something counterfeit: it is offering us the nothing from which it shrinks, the nothing in which the *translation* of being is no more than the *termination* of being, the very point beyond which it cannot pass without abandoning the ontological infrastructure upon which it stands. Only faith can make that leap. And the supreme irony is that each essentially ratifies the other and both equally culminate in what appears to be the terminus of being: The Dark Night.

So what, precisely is occurring here? On the one hand, the state of proximity to God is achieved through transcendence (of the finite) on a purely metaphysical level. On the other hand, it is, as we have said, equally attained through the theological virtue of faith. Something more than mere congruity, or even concomitance, appears to occur; something deeply implicative of both mutuality and complementarity. It would appear that either faith corroborates the metaphysics, or that the metaphysics corroborates faith. The answer, I suggest, is both, inasmuch as faith implicitly accords with what metaphysics explicitly states.

It is not merely of the nature of faith, but of the essence of faith to assent to the very same propositions we find emerging from the metaphysics, not, however, as demanded by metaphysics, but as demanded by faith. In other words, this is not to understand faith as *proceeding* from metaphysics, any more than it is to understand the metaphysics proceeding from faith. At the point of convergence, however, it is imperative to understand that the deliverances of each are indistinguishable, for both arrive at the same impenetrable epicenter that is infinite, unlimited, and absolute. Nor is it simply coincidental that at precisely this point of convergence we arrive at the opacity of reason.

We are now, I think, in a position to understand that this reciprocity which we observe does not in any way abrogate or violate the unique integrity of what is either ontological or doxastic – a superficial bifurcation to the mystic at this point– but rather, is axiomatic of the traditional concept of nature cooperating with grace. What we find, in the end, is not the one through the abrogation of the other, but instead, a mutual corroboration of each at that critical point of convergence that St. John understands as the state of proximity to the

Absolute, To God.

The Role of Faith and Reason in the Transition to Proximity and Union

But how do we understand *faith* to be an implicit consequence of this transition? To answer this, let us look for a moment more carefully at the nature of faith. By faith we generally understand that theological virtue, divinely infused, which is *cognitive* in nature, and which expresses itself in the terms of clearly defined articles of *belief* – not knowledge – independent of any empirical acquaintance with the object in which belief is invested – specifically, God. The cognitive dimension of faith, in other words, is doxastic rather than noetic. Faith makes no appeal to reason. The object, or articles of faith *may* be entirely consonant with reason. On the other hand, they may completely *transcend*, not simply the canons, but the very capabilities of reason – and yet do so without abrogating them, since grace either perfects or exceeds, but never violates nature. While faith is essentially cognitive in nature relative to these articles of belief, the articles themselves are *supernatural* in character. And the legitimate province of reason, we had argued earlier, lies not in the supernatural, but in the matrix of nature, specifically created nature experienced in terms of plurality and finitude. The faculty of reason, then, has only limited access to the articles of faith, and only inasmuch as these articles, *among themselves* – prescinding entirely from the question of their authenticity, that is to say, considered formally, and not materially– demonstrate a coherence that accords with the canons of logic, of reason. Insofar as logical coherence is discernible among the relation of ideas that constitute the articles of belief around which the notion of faith revolves, reason *formally* ratifies faith, finds the relation of the ideas of faith to be consistent with reason, although it makes no pronouncement on the authenticity of the articles themselves. And to this limited extent, faith is found to be consonant with reason, or perhaps better yet, reason is found to be consonant with faith.

But faith also *transcends* reason, as we had said. In passing from that realm of finitude and plurality in which alone reason is capable of being discursively exercised, the only cognitive capacity remaining to the soul – with no data available to sense or reason – pertains to these articles of belief – in other words, faith – which the soul maintains despite empirical evidence to the contrary: the nothingness which the soul encounters on the brink of infinity. That some *form* of cognition remains is indisputable, otherwise we should hold the soul to be incognitive, which is to say unconscious, and this very clearly is not the case with the mystic. If anything, what we find is an intensified state of consciousness. It is, moreover, equally clear from our previous discussion that this form of cognition cannot be reason. So what alternative remains?

Confronted with that before which reason defaults into suspension, *faith* – independent of reason and uninformed by the senses – remains cognitive in the form of articles of belief which, themselves supernatural in character, were never dependent upon reason or sense to begin with – and thus remains fully as cognitive as it was prior to the transcendence of nature and reason. In this sense, then, faith is seen to follow the negation of nature and reason. But that faith transcends *nature*, as St. John further implies, seems at first a rather odd notion, and yet it nevertheless follows from and is consistent with the overall logic of St. John's account. Faith, we might say, transcends nature *through* reason as that plurality of finite entities which the exercise of discursive reason requires and therefore presumes. In transcending reason, then, faith has already transcended nature as implicit within reason.

As we may anticipate, the imperative of faith will continue to be not only a significant, but a multifaceted feature of the mystical doctrine which meticulously unfolds before us in the opening chapters of the *Ascent*. Nor can we prescind entirely from all the concomitant issues which faith touches upon if our epistemological account is to be complete. For example, St. John argues that the soul not only transcends time, finitude, and reason through its subjection to the *via negativa* and the subsequent positing of faith; but through this same faith the soul equally circumvents diabolical impediments to union as well.[8] While this issue may at first appear to be only incidental to any strictly epistemological analysis, a closer examination reveals otherwise, for we find that St. John's treatment of diabolical deception effectively serves to underscore a very fundamental epistemological issue concerning the notion of *error* – which is by no means incidental to any examination of the notion of understanding.

Let us pursue the point. Through faith, St. John has argued, the soul has passed beyond understanding. So much at least is immediately clear from St. John's account. However, as a consequence of this transition, that is to say, in passing *beyond* understanding, the soul has simultaneously, and for two reasons, passed beyond – is no longer subject to – the possibility of error. And for the following reasons: first of all, the notion of error exclusively, if obviously, pertains to the faculty of understanding: it is, fundamentally, a consequence of *mis*understanding, consisting in the intellectual assent to defective propositions delivered by, or illegitimate conclusions drawn from, discursive reasoning. But reason has been transcended – and along with it, the errors to which defective reasoning is liable. That is to say, the possibility of error as a consequence of *mis*understanding has been abolished as implicit within the utility of understanding itself which has already been negated.

Inerrancy and Impedimence

It is important to further understand that the second reason that faith, for St. John, is not held to be liable to error rests upon the *source* itself of the infused theological virtue of faith, which is God. The articles of belief constituting the virtue of faith have, for the mystic, no less a guarantor than God who, as both object and author of the articles of faith, is understood to be not simply the source of truth, but Truth itself. [9] So much, I think, is immediately clear from a cursory rendering of St. John's understanding of faith. But the question nevertheless remains, why in fact is it so pressing, so vitally important for the mystic to be free of error? Or more precisely, how is error to be understood as constituting an impediment to union? The answer for St. John, of course, is already implicit in an adequate understanding of the Divine nature itself. Aside from the simple misdirection – which is of no small consequence to the mystic – which liability to error affords, error is, quite simply, a form of contrariety to God who is Truth. While the mystic clearly has, in the form of the infused virtues, the assistance of God who invites the soul to the ecstatic state of union as a foretaste of the eternal felicity awaiting the faithful in heaven – it is also the case that the contemplative confronts an ancient antagonist who wishes to frustrate, confuse, and deceive the soul in its efforts to achieve union with God. And this, of course, is the devil who, within the Christian tradition, is preeminently understood as a liar and the father of lies.[10] St. John argues, however – and this is the critical issue – that diabolical artifice can only be exercised over the soul through its attachment to created things.[11] In transcending created nature, in having extinguished all attachment to the created order, the soul is then effectively brought beyond the pale of diabolical influence – and is therefore no longer subject to error instigated by the devil.

If this concern strikes the contemporary mind as quaint, it is, I suggest, only symptomatic of a more prevailing contemporary defection from the supernatural at large, and apart from which not only mysticism, but Christianity itself remains, in its most fundamental essence, incomprehensible. The two components of every error, then, either defective reasoning or diabolical malice, cease to be impediments to union in the soul's having transcended created nature and reason. Quite practically, moreover, any journey – especially the journey of the soul to God – whose course and direction, compass and map, are not free of error, will not, cannot, bring the traveler home. However he would that his bearings were correct, without truth as the declination to compass and map, the mystical terrain remains unrecognizable, and the wayfarer remains lost and without hope of achieving his end.

Truth, Faith, and Dogma: Triad or Trilogy?

Truth for the mystic, however, is inseparable from, and inextricably bound up with, faith – and faith, in turn, is ultimately informed by Dogmatics. The point is worth pursuing. Despite the negation of sense and understanding, the soul nevertheless remains cognitive through the infused theological virtue of faith which, at least from an epistemological point of view, constitutes a cognitive function, albeit an obscure one. [12] Faith, in other words, is at least implicitly cognitive of its object – and it is here that the doctrinal and mystical elements in St. John's philosophy converge. As we had noted earlier, the mystic of necessity adverts to certain clearly defined dogmatic tenets as propadeutic to his quest for union with God. Reason alone, as we had seen, defaults into suspension in the face of the Absolute. To a certain limited extent, reason may retrospectively ratify the dictates of faith – but never inform them. When we speak of faith as an infused theological virtue, however, we certainly do not mean that the articles of faith are supernaturally articulated in the soul independent of the avenues of nature. On the contrary, no less an authority than St. Paul tells us that faith originates in the hearing. [13] But hearing alone, quite obviously, does not necessarily translate into faith; it does not involve that consent implicit in faith which not

205

simply understands these articles, but understands them to be true; holds these articles to communicate factual information about certain aspects of reality, supernatural in character, which are unavailable to, and therefore cannot be authenticated by, sense and reason. This ability to posit what reason cannot corroborate, what sense cannot confirm, comes from God. In this sense it is understood as being divinely infused.

This a rather roundabout way of saying that the mystic's faith, if it is to be inerrant, must coincide precisely with the articles of faith tendered him by dogmatic theology which affirms certain things about God through the indefeasible guarantee of God's self-revelation in Sacred Scripture in general, and in the person of Jesus Christ in particular. These, together with that deposit of faith which the Church understands as Sacred Tradition, form for the mystic the repository of, while by no means exhaustive, nevertheless inviolable truth; they effectively define his objective, provide him with the compass, the map, and the lay of the metaphysical terrain, and detail the perils to which he will be exposed in the *dark night of the soul* – all indispensable elements to the soul's journey to that Absolute which is Truth and admits of no error. These dogmatic canons, in fact, logically precede faith in determining the object of faith. And while faith as such is ultimately abolished in the moment of ecstatic union when what has only been implicit in faith yields to the actuality of the Absolute, it nevertheless is indispensable not merely toward proximating, but in fact identifying the Absolute. Hence, St. John argues that faith induces our assent to divinely revealed truths which, though not necessarily in conflict with understanding and reason, nevertheless inexorably transcend them:

"... faith ... makes us believe truths revealed by God Himself, which transcend

all natural light, and exceed all human understanding, beyond all proportion ... Hence it follows that, for the soul, this excessive light of faith blinds it and deprives it of the sight that has been given to

207

it, inasmuch as its light is great
beyond all proportion and transcends the
faculty of vision ... The light of faith,
by its excessive greatness oppresses and
disables that of the understanding,
for the latter of its own power, extends only
to natural knowledge ... " [14]

The disproportion between faith and knowledge, St. John argues, becomes somewhat clearer by way of analogy. The analogy, I think, is particularly interesting, for it is frequently surprising to contemporary but ill-informed critics of medieval thought that the natural epistemology articulated in scholasticism – an epistemology by and large derived from Aristotle – is thoroughly empirical in nature as the following excerpt demonstrates relative to the inquiry at hand:

"... the soul, as soon as God infuses it into
the body, is like a smooth, blank
board upon which nothing is painted; and,
save for that which it experiences

through the senses, nothing is communicated
to it, in the course of nature,
 from any other source ... [15] Wherefore, if
one should speak to a man of things
which he has never been able to understand,
and whose likeness he has
never seen, he would have no more
illumination from them whatever than
if aught had been said of them to him ... If
one should describe to a man
that was born blind, and has never seen any
color, what is meant by a
white color or by a yellow, he would
understand it but indifferently,
 however fully one might describe it to him,
as he has never seen such colors
or anything like them by which he may
judge of them, only their names would
remain to him ... Even so is this faith with
respect to the soul; it tells us of
things which we have never seen or
understood, nor have we seen or

understood aught that resembles them at all.

And thus we have no light

of natural knowledge concerning them, since

that which we are told of

them bears no relation to any sense of ours;

we know it by ear alone,

believing that which we are taught" [16]

Common categories, St. John argues, are essential to the transmission, the communication, of knowledge – and any description, however exhaustive, however carefully nuanced, that cannot appeal to categories commonly shared, will avail nothing to understanding. And this, of course, is precisely the difficulty the mystic encounters in any effort to convey his experience of the Absolute. Since knowledge necessarily appeals to experience to meaningfully inform understanding, and the experience of the Absolute in the person of God is unavailable outside of ecstatic union, the cognitive faculty of understanding is not merely inadequate to, but is altogether incapable of addressing the Absolute. Understanding, then, must be not merely suppressed, but entirely superseded by a cognitive faculty that does not rely upon, derive its information from, the reports of the senses gathered through the medium of experience. And this cognitive faculty, of course, is the infused theological virtue of faith. The author of the Letter to the Hebrews summarizes it this way: "... faith is the assurance of things hoped for, the conviction of things not seen." [17] It is faith, then, that informs us, albeit obscurely, of things of which we have had no experience whatever; things so radically dissimilar to all other experiences that no adequate parallels, no analogies, will descriptively suffice. It is, in fact, very much along the lines of what St. Paul attempted to describe to the Corinthians:

> "... no eye has seen, nor ear heard, nor the
> heart of man conceived, what
> God has prepared for those who love him".[18]

Faith, then, is quite different from understanding. Each addresses entirely different spheres, and each are informed by radically different categories.

Understanding is determinate, clearly articulating and comprehending its object and verifying the data submitted to it by reports of the senses. Faith has far less specificity. While apodictically certain, it is indeterminate. It verges upon but does not clearly comprehend its object; it requires no corroboration, no authentication by sense, deferring instead to the veracity of the Author from whom it holds its articles to have been delivered. And it is only implicitly cognitive of these revealed articles as inarticulate expressions of the Absolute which itself is incapable of being exhausted by any and every expression of its being. Indispensable as they are, these articles of faith are only impoverished media of a true understanding which abolishes itself in the experience of, the immediate confrontation with, the Absolute. And this means that for St. John, faith, in transcending the canons of ordinary understanding, remains necessarily and eternally unavailable to it. The elements of dogma, the articles of faith – these self-expressions of the Absolute – ultimately involve, for St. John, the post-rational assent to the very doctrines held to be infallibly taught through the Magisterium of the Church concerning the revelation of God through Scripture and sacred tradition.[19] Unlike understanding which is proactive in acquiring knowledge, the object of faith, St. John insists, is passively received – either through revelation preceding union, or through the divine infusion in the state of ecstasy.

The Three Theological Virtues and the Impetus to Union

Our understanding of faith relative to the mystical experience now becomes somewhat clearer. Faith, to recapitulate, is the ill-defined and tenuous apprehension of something only implicitly understood. In transcending what is explicitly, determinately cognitive, faith passes from all the limiting frames of ordinary reference into that state of unknowing which is the explicit negation of all the contradictions to, and the contrarieties of, God

213

in the created and finite spheres of understanding and sensibility. The soul, St. John argues, is then rendered more proximate to God in having been negated to the other – the contraries – of God in nature and reason. Although in this state of simple proximity the soul is not yet what God is, it is not what God is not. And for this reason it is preeminently disposed to receiving God in mystical union.

By now it is probably clear, although somewhat prematurely, that the union of the soul with God is not, cannot be, achieved through the three natural faculties of the soul: will, understanding, and memory.[20] While much remains to be addressed especially in regard to the faculty of understanding, it is perhaps best that we pause at this point to better gain perspective of the whole. Mystical union, as we may already anticipate, is rather to be achieved through the three theological virtues corresponding to these three faculties:

"... the soul is not united with God in this
life through the understanding,
 nor through enjoyment, nor through
imagination, nor through any sense
whatsoever; but only through faith,
according to the understanding; and
through hope according to the memory; and
through love according to the
will. These three virtues ... all cause
emptiness in the faculties: faith in
the understanding, causes emptiness and
darkness with respect to the
understanding; hope, in the memory, causes
emptiness of all possessions;
and charity causes emptiness in the will and
detachment from all affection
and from rejoicing in all that is not God." [21]

Each infused theological virtue, we can see, is the
negation of its corresponding natural faculty, and
insofar as these virtues succeed in their negative
functions, just so is the soul disposed, or receptive,
to the state of infused contemplation. These virtues,

like many elements of the mystical experience that are steeped in polarity, are in fact double-sided. On the one hand they are seen to be negative, disabling the faculties which they supersede even as they are enacted within them. On the other hand, they are seen to be positive, informing the soul even as they displace the natural faculties they have negated. At this point, however, St. John considers them largely in their negative aspect. Faith is the explicit negation of understanding: it abolishes the mediatory function of reason in apprehending its object intuitively. The object of faith is transcendent, and therefore inaccessible, to the rigorously defined and therefore limited architectonics of the categories of understanding. While these are sufficient to addressing finite objects in the created order, they do not, cannot, suffice in addressing the Absolute. Consequently, they are abolished in the enactment of faith.

Hope, on the other hand, is equally the negation of its own corresponding faculty in the memory which, for St. John, is really a kind of residual faculty of understanding. Unlike understanding itself which is actively engaged in acquiring, coordinating, and, through the dialectic of reason, synthesizing the data delivered it by the senses, memory – strictly speaking – is a passive repository of either the synthetic fabrications of reason or of impressions acquired through the senses. And I say strictly speaking for this reason: memory of itself essentially consists in mere recollection; the recollection of things and concepts no longer contemporaneous with that exercise of reason or the immediate sense experience by which they were initially acquired. Once acquired, of course, these initial acquaintances – until repeated, in the case of sense experience – immediately devolve to memory. There they passively form the repository of acquired knowledge to which reason or understanding subsequently appeals, and consequently amplifies, when synthesizing or analyzing new data submitted by the senses or acquired through the activity of reason. Imagination, however, which for St. John is a subfaculty of memory – that in turn is subsumed beneath understanding – acts to creatively synthesize and manipulate the data deposited in memory in much the same way that understanding does – with two important exceptions. The exercise of the imagination, while not antithetical to, or even necessarily exclusive of, reason, is nevertheless unconstrained by the canons of syllogistic reasoning that apply to understanding. It quite freely, and quite often prescinds entirely from the protocols of logic.

Both analytic and synthetic, imagination systematically analyzes the part from the coherent whole and is quite capable of synthesizing incongruent and illogical fictions from essentially unrelated data. No laws, in other words, are discoverable in the exercise of the imagination apart from the route the data take to inform it. But more importantly, imagination is remote from immediacy: while initially informed by the senses, it subsequently acts independently of them. It may take its clues from the senses, but the products of the imagination have no correlate in reality. In short, they are not factual reports, but elaborate fictions. Fictions which, in the end, are composites of created things initially derived from the senses and ultimately sharing, with all other things in memory whose provenance lays in sense, in that contrariety to God which is preclusive of union. As faith was seen to abolish understanding, so now hope in supplanting memory abolishes it, for the theological virtue of hope, St. John tells us, is by definition, directed to that which is not yet possessed. [22]

But, we are likely to object, are not faith, hope, and love resident in memory as well? In that state of negativity preparatory to union, may not the contemplative be said to recollect, to remember the articles of faith, which in turn inform hope and articulate the object loved? After all, these were, St. John had argued earlier – and prior to being assented to – first learned, acquired through the hearing, and, we presume, deposited into memory. Is not the mystic, then, appealing to elements within the very deposit of data (memory) which we had understood to have been abolished by hope? St. John, unfortunately, is not at all clear on this point. But there is, I think, a semantic issue involved here concerning the notion of recollection which does not readily lend itself to the categorical opposition St. John seems to place between memory as a natural faculty and hope as an implicitly mnemonic virtue. We are, however, clear on one point, and that is that the memory as a natural faculty is in fact negated – effectively abolished – relative to things created. In being supplanted by hope, it is expropriated of every datum corresponding to the created order.[23] But the soul does not then possess no at least implicitly mnemonic faculty whatever. Hope, which has replaced memory, materially possesses nothing, but rather, formally anticipates the possession of something. Of what? It anticipates the possession of the object which the articles of faith address, the object of which faith is cognizant, God – which the soul does not yet possess, but only hopes to possess. That is to say, hope anticipates,

220

since it does not possess, what faith recognizes but does not clearly know. Faith is the reservoir of hope which appeals to things uncreated, and unlike memory, unpossessed. Hope then is seen as the antithesis of memory in possessing nothing, and as the supernatural counterpart to memory in anticipating what it does not possess, but what it nevertheless latently recognizes through faith.

There are, moreover, distinct differences discernible between the way in which data are preserved in memory, and the way that the articles of faith are preserved in the latently mnemonic theological virtue of hope. To begin with, we do not possess the articles of faith in the way we possess the impressions of the senses, or, say, the theorems of Euclidean geometry. Geometric theorems, for example, are rationally, and even empirically demonstrable; they are characterized by a deductive certainty deriving from analytical principles so clearly defined, so self-evident as to be unequivocal and incontrovertible. The inherent specificity of geometry as the paradigm of purely deductive reasoning, and therefore the paradigm of deductive certainty– of incontestable knowledge for philosophers from Plato onward – stands in stark contrast to the obscure and indeterminate articles of faith which very clearly are not the conclusions of syllogistic reasoning, possess nothing in the way of deductive certainty, and are by nature not susceptible to being demonstrated either rationally or empirically – although, as we have said, they may not of themselves necessarily be in conflict with reason. In short, the articles of faith do not qualify as knowledge – certainly not along the lines that would fit a purely rational paradigm. And knowledge, either derived analytically from the exercise of reason, or acquired through the reports of the senses, or indeed as the synthesis of both, is, after all, what we understand to be passively archived in memory.

But we might further object that this deposit of data in which memory consists typically comprehends a vast number of concepts which do not share, are not characterized by, the rigorous deductive certainty of the geometric model we have invoked. In fact, much of that deposit of knowledge that we call memory is really inchoate, and quite nearly as vague as the articles of faith themselves. However this may be, it nevertheless remains that they are also susceptible of being fully articulated by subsequent reasoning; or, more apropos of our argument, since we understand these incompletely articulated concepts to be merely deficient in formation, it is entirely possible for them to be fully informed by subsequent experience. Such concepts deriving from, and constructed around, empirical acquaintance, or the impressions of the senses, are, therefore, verifiable through, and capable of being augmented by, further experience. And this is to say that the object of faith implicit in hope does not constitute data in precisely the same way that rational concepts or sense impressions do.

To summarize, then, our understanding of the differences that obtain between hope and memory, we may say that memory, unlike hope, is characterized by specificity, and the data resident in

223

memory are susceptible of further elaboration subsequent to further investigation. The corresponding faculty of hope, on the other hand, is radicated in faith – not reason or sense – and its object, unlike memory, only vaguely, indeterminately, imprecisely, corresponds to a reality that was not empirically acquired, is not empirically available, and is, therefore, not verifiable. Memory and hope, then, while yet sharing parallel mnemonic functions, effectively qualify as contrarieties in the epistemological account of St. John.

This regrettably involuted account, necessary to distinguishing memory from hope, finally puts us in a position to understand why St. John will later argue that the soul is unified through the three theological virtues [24], why this unity results in the soul's singular intentionality in God (its being exclusively, absolutely centered upon God), and how this facilitates the soul in its movement toward God in the soul's possessing within itself no contrary to God. Let us look at this more closely.

Since the soul's faculties are no longer diffused among a multiplicity of objects, but are, rather, in a common state of negativity (or proximity) – each characterized by its respective theological virtue – the soul is unified both in this negativity, or night of the soul, common to each faculty, and by intentionality, in that each of these virtues are theological in nature, or exclusively directed to the one, singular object in God. Simply put, all the faculties have entered the one same night: negation. And all the theological virtues address the one same object: God. This translation of the natural faculties into their corresponding theological virtues constitutes what St. John will henceforth refer to as spiritual negation, or the spiritual night of the soul [25] which is a pivotal point in the movement to mystical union as we shall later find in Part 2.

Whereas we had found the night of the senses to consist in the detachment from the created external order in nature according to each faculty, so now the night of the spirit will be found to consist in a similar detachment from the created internal order of spirit. And once spiritual negation has been achieved, the soul will have entered into a state of absolute negativity, for it is the bilateral, absolute, and unqualified negation of the two created aspects of bi-dimensional man: the natural dimension relative to nature, and the spiritual dimension relative to spirit. This state of absolute negativity, in fact, corresponds to what St. John otherwise calls "annihilation" [26], for it is, as it were, the annihilation of the soul's natural existence:

> "... the soul must not only be disencumbered
> from that which belongs to
> creatures, but likewise, as it travels, must be
> annihilated and detached from
> all that belongs to its spirit ... This ... is death
> to the natural self, a death
> attained through the detachment and
> annihilation of that self, in order
> that the soul may travel by this narrow path,
> with respect to all its
> connections with sense, as we have said, and

according to the spirit as we
shall now say ..." [27]

Epistemology or Heterodoxy?
The Annihilation of the Soul

This is the inauguration of that "terrible night" of
which St. John so often speaks, the night which
must be traversed in faith alone. [28] Here every other
standard of reference to the world of experience
ordinarily understood, fails, evanesces, before the
negativity of night. And here it becomes absolutely
critical to the purpose of our commentary that we
correctly understand what St. John refers to in
speaking of the concept of "annihilation". The
various phenomenologies that have historically
evolved around the concept of mysticism are almost
universal in incorporating this mercurial and
extremely fragile term, and there is far from
unanimity among them concerning its significance.

This is particularly true for the Christian mystic. First of all, it is not, we must hasten to add, a type of nirvanic annihilation of the self much as we understand in certain Vedantic phenomenologies broadly construed as mystical, for in St. John's account the self, however attenuated through the process of negation, is nevertheless understood to be preserved in super-natural existence. Not, to be sure, in the exercise of its natural faculties ordinarily understood – but rather through the theological virtues which at once annihilate (negate) the self relative to the natural faculties, and preserve the self as the presupposition of that personal and residual consciousness within which the theological virtues are enacted, exercised.

Annihilation, because it is so easily misconstrued, is one of those volatile concepts within Christian mysticism that readily lends itself to charges of heterodoxy, the sanctions against which, at the height of the Counter-Reformation (1560-1648), were stringently applied. Despite this fact, it is not the case that St. John, as a contemporary figure in this tumultuous period, simply deferred to orthodoxy out of expedience as some may suppose, or worse yet, deliberately couched his terms in equivocal language to conceal a covert agendum antagonistic to accepted doctrine or ecclesiastical authority. There is not a shred of evidence to support this contention. St. John was unwavering in orthodoxy, and would undoubtedly have answered that, if his mystical doctrine was entirely consonant with the deposit of faith articulated by the Magisterium of the Church, it was not, for that reason, a procrustean accomplishment; a matter of merely accommodating his doctrine to the formal requirements of faith – but rather that the articles of faith must be seen as having informed his doctrine – as indeed they had – which in turn was a vindication of that dogma whose elements were subsequently authenticated in the mystical experience itself.

Identity and Individuation:
Noesis or Nuance?

But to return to our point, the annihilation of which
St. John speaks appears to be essentially the radical
reduction of the self to an irreducible state of
consciousness. This consciousness, we have already
said, necessarily presupposes something of which it
is conscious. To restate our point succinctly, our
consciousness is always a consciousness of. Of
what? Well, certainly of something. And this
something, of course, can no longer be the
deliverance of sense and reason already
transcended. It is, rather, an anticipatory
consciousness informed by the articles of faith
alone, and exclusively directed toward God apart
from any other object of intention. In essence, it is a
state of pure intentionality. The self has completely
receded from all relativity to everything outside
itself: it is perfectly receded from, and therefore
utterly without reference to, the non-self, both in

nature, as negated, and in God, as yet revealed. In this state of absolute recession, the soul has only the dim, merely formal cognition of God – unaccompanied as yet by any empirical acquaintance – provided it through the three theological virtues which are at once, paradoxically, the very principles behind this annihilation, and simultaneously the means of the preservation of the self subsequent to it. While much of this remains to be discussed in greater depth in Part II, it is nevertheless important to an understanding of St. John's thought at this point to recognize that the self – that is to say, personal consciousness – in fact survives the annihilation of which St. John speaks in his account. And it is precisely this residual self-consciousness, this implicit but nevertheless distinguishable apperception in the face of the Absolute which preserves a distinction in identity even as this union abolishes contrariety in nature.

The implications that evolve from this are worth considering further. We had, for example, spoken of the self earlier as having been brought to an irreducible state of consciousness epistemologically poised in an act of pure intentionality. But what, we must now ask, is the self so understood? Our very notion of identity, of our self, would seem to be bound up with a great many material and historical antecedents which must then necessarily be borne along with our identity beyond negativity. Our individual identity – who we are – defined, by and large, by our unique historical antecedents would appear to be a necessary component of a coherent conception of the self. But let us look at this anew from the phenomenological perspective of the mystic. We are accustomed to being individuated by precisely those elements which, through the *via negativa*, have been negated and transcended: namely finitude and temporality. We perceive ourselves to be such and such an individual apart from other individuals by virtue of certain clearly defined material limits – our bodies, for example, describe a finite area that is discrete from the bodies of others; our minds, while similar to others in their cognitive faculties, are unlike others in that our

232

thoughts are not identical to the thoughts of others; my experiences in all their subtleties, and the arrangement and chronological order of these experiences, are not identical with those of others, having been acquired, enacted, if not in different frames of time then in different locations in space; still yet, my parents are not your parents, or if they are, my birth was not precisely coincidental with yours, and I never had myself as my brother. In short, there are a thousand ways in which we individuate ourselves from others and acquire a sense of identity that is essentially composed differentially.

And so our question is: Can we in fact possess an identity apart from these individuating elements or circumstances? And if so, in what does that identity consist? Indeed, does one lose one's individual identity altogether in mystical experience, and does this consequently entail some absurd and essentially meaningless form of cosmic consciousness? These, and other questions like them, some rather frivolous, others quite serious, enable us to see why mysticism is often the breeding ground of redoubtable epistemological difficulties – as well as a good deal of nonsense. Within each of these instances or circumstances we find time or finitude or both as the individuating principle behind the conception of identity. But it is equally clear that the radically reduced notion of the self consequent to the mystic's subjection to the *via negativa* entirely prescinds from the self as historically articulated. The mystic in essence acquires a new identity, not that of the self reflexively identified – that is to say the self historically identified with the utterly personal existential enactment of its own being chronologically considered at a different, elapsed, point in time – rather, the mystic's identity now refers, not back to himself, reflexively – but to God. And this new identity, in fact, is merely the re-appropriation of the soul's primal identity as the imago Dei, the image of God. This notion of identity, which is always and essentially reciprocal in nature with an other relative to which it is the same, remains to be discussed more fully later on.

We only touch upon it here to further illustrate the point that the annihilation of the soul in no way compromises, but rather attenuates the identity of the soul which nevertheless remains intact beyond absolute negation.

Faith as Negativity: The Knower and the Unknown God

Returning once again to our discussion of the relation that obtains between faith and understanding, we had found that no proportion, or as St. John puts it, similitude, exists between the understanding and God for reasons already discussed and principally involving the notion of incommensurability:

> "... all that the imagination can imagine and the understanding can receive and

understand in this life is not, nor can it be, a

proximate means of union with God

... [for] all that can be understood by the

understanding, that can be tasted by

the will, and that can be invented by the

imagination is most unlike God and

bears no proportion to Him ..." [29]

 In the face of this incommensurability, a requisite
to union must consist in a transformation that will
bridge this gap which is infinite; that will, in effect,
restore a measure of commensurability between the
means and the end, cognition and God. This
transformation, however, cannot be effected by,
since it is clearly beyond the natural ability of, the
created and finite soul. It can only, therefore, be
divinely initiated. And this, we have seen, occurs
when God leads the soul, through faith, into the
state of negation. But how are we to understand
faith – which up to this point has largely been a
negative factor in St. John's account in the way of
abolishing understanding – as now capable of
restoring this commensurability? Well, to begin

236

with we had already seen that, for all its obscurity, faith nevertheless entails certain positive elements in the form of implicitly understood articles ultimately derived from the self-revelation of God to man; articles which, for St. John, are to be received in that simplicity which is consonant with faith:

> " ... the understanding, profoundly hushed
> and put to silence ... leans upon
> faith which alone is the proximate means
> whereby the soul is united with God;
> for such is the likeness between itself and
> God that there is no other difference,
> save that which exists between seeing God
> and believing in Him. For even as
> God is infinite, so faith sets Him before us
> as infinite; and as he is Three and
> One, it sets Him before us as Three and One;
> and as God is darkness to our understanding,
> even so does faith likewise blind and dazzle
> our understanding.
> And thus, by this means alone, God

237

manifests Himself to the soul in Divine
light, which passes all understanding." [30]

Faith, in other words, transcends the limitations of
understanding in affirming of God those attributes
which the understanding in its limitations, and
without involving itself in contradiction, could not
possibly affirm. And so in transcending
understanding, faith simultaneously transcends
limitation implicit within understanding – and in
doing so simultaneously establishes
commensurability with the infinite and the
unlimited. Such a transcendence will inevitably
entail a cognitive transformation as well.
Determinate understanding with all its limitations is
no longer sufficient. In fact, it has already been
abolished in the negativity of faith. Abolished – but
also superseded, as we had already seen, by a
faculty quite different, a faculty which, as the
negative of understanding with its distinct concepts
and determinate categories, will necessarily be
indistinct and indeterminate.[31] And this type of
cognition, not radicated in an acquaintance with its

object either empirically acquired through sense or rationally acquired through the analytic or synthetic activity of reason – that is to say, which does not acquire its object mediatively – is essentially intuitive in nature.

"Natural" and "Supernatural" Modes of Understanding

So we find that, despite the negativity of faith, it is, after all, not the case that all understanding categorically ceases, but merely a particular kind of understanding, for within the comprehensive faculty of understanding itself, St. John distinguishes two quite different modes: the natural and the supernatural. The former refers to the distinct and determinate mode of ordinary cognition both appropriate and sufficient to addressing the world of ordinary experience, and consisting in finite concepts actively applied to finite data. The latter corresponds to that intuitive mode of cognition subsequent to the state of negation in which faith has superseded natural understanding. The former we have already examined. It is the latter with which we are now concerned. This supernatural knowledge, as St. John calls it, is, to additionally complicate matters, then further subdivided into corporeal and spiritual modes through which knowledge is communicated to, and passively received by, the soul. [32] Understanding at this point becomes, as it were, rarefied in that epistemological margin between nature and spirit. It is at the outermost extremity of both, while completely sharing in the unique character of neither. Let us, then, look at each mode as it informs understanding and see what further conclusions remain to be drawn.

The "Corporeal" Mode of Understanding

The corporeal mode of supernatural understanding, St. John tells us, consists in those communications to the soul which proceed either through the external sensuous by way of the bodily senses, or through the internal sensuous according to the imagination. At this point we can safely say that St. John has already demonstrated [33] that the imagination is dependent upon empirical data acquired through experience, and that, therefore, no proportion whatever can possibly exist between God and the synthetic constructs of imagination. Incapable of proximating God, imagination is summarily disqualified as a proximate means to union with God. The very specific and determinate nature common to every product of the imagination is profoundly incommensurable with the infinite reality of God. Consequently, the internal sensuous according to the imagination must be negated of all the various forms and images which are either the products of its own synthetic activity, or which derive from a supernatural agency communicating these forms and images to it, [34] for without exception they entail contrariety to God. That this applies with equal and greater force to those supernatural phenomena sensuously embodied in the external order is already clear. Our treatment, then, of imagination, in an effort to leave no element unaddressed in our account, is really parenthetical to our articulating an epistemology of mysticism. By and large the constituent elements of imagination may be subsumed under the broader category of sense, and stand merely to be abolished in the movement toward contemplation.

The "Supernatural" Mode of Understanding

On the other hand, St. John's discussion of the supernatural mode of understanding is a good deal more illuminating. Even a casual reading of St. John reveals that, in an effort to be as precise as possible, his systematic treatment, especially in regard to the faculty understanding, becomes increasingly schematized. The category of understanding, for example, is further divided into sub-categories of natural and supernatural modes of understanding. The supernatural mode, to take just one element in this bifurcation, is then further analyzed into corporeal and spiritual modes, and the spiritual mode, in turn, further subdivided into distinct and special and confused and general modes. [35] This is no gratuitous exercise in speculative analysis. St. John's objective, we must remember, is always practical. In taking such a rigorous and systematic inventory of understanding, St. John effectively attempts to address an issue involving the single greatest liability to which not only the mystic, but the entire mystical enterprise itself, is exposed: the problem of error. Although we had briefly examined this problem earlier, let us look at it once again in light of the present context. Supernatural understanding, as St. John calls it, is either communicated distinctly and specially through visions, revelations, locutions, and the like – or generally and obscurely, that is to say, in a manner

243

lacking both in specificity and clarity. In essence, however, St. John's entire discussion of knowledge supernaturally communicated to – not actively acquired by – the soul, is at least implicitly his treatment of the impediment of error, both here and elsewhere.

Consequently it is, at one and the same time, an ad hoc critique of human understanding confronted with the supernatural – to the end of establishing a canon of authenticity to which the mystic may ultimately appeal with unquestionable certainty. And it is precisely this type of critical analysis – to which the Christian tradition of mysticism owes a great debt to St. John – that is central to our accreditation of the mystical experience as in fact veridical. For unless quite definite criteria are established concerning the authenticity of the contemplatives mystical experience – that it is a unique experience corresponding to, not simply a solipsistic or reflexively interpreted reality , but to a reality independent of the mind of the mystic – Christian mysticism will fail to exempt itself from the most remarkable and bizarre array of pseudo-mystical states, including delusional psychoses, which are often otherwise broadly, and erroneously, characterized as "mystical" .This problem, worthy of a chapter in itself, will be examined more extensively later on. For the moment it is sufficient to note that St. John is acutely aware of some of the problems created by this type of confusion. For example, he insists that,

> "... he that esteems such things errs greatly
> and exposes himself to the peril
> of being deceived [36] ... [for] a readiness to
> accept them opens the door to the
> devil that he may deceive the soul by other
> things like to them, which he very
> well knows how to dissimulate and disguise,
> so that they may appear to be good;
> for, as the Apostle says, he can transform
> himself into an angel of light." [37]

This premature and clearly parenthetical treatment of the problem of error equally serves to underscore

245

the imperative of faith in the soul's journey to union with God, for it is faith, as we will come to understand, which constitutes the one epistemological constant to which the several modes of understanding are subordinated throughout.

Dealing first with the distinct and special mode of supernatural understanding, St. John tells us that these very specialized apprehensions are, to begin with, sensuously communicated to the soul – understanding does not play an active, or intentional role in acquiring them much in the way that it does in its interpretive interaction with data delivered by the senses subsequent to being actively addressed by understanding. The notion of intentionality relative to the understanding is entirely absent in the case of these apprehensions as they come to the soul – which at this point, we will remember, is passive – through the five bodily senses. It is most urgent, St. John argues, that the soul maintain an attitude completely skeptical to these apprehensions; in fact, if at all possible, to entirely disregard them.[38]

A Dark Impedimence:
Diabolical Deception

Given the disproportion and contrariety which we have seen to exist between God and the created order (all that is not God), St. John further argues that the greater the apparent corporeity and exteriority of the apprehension, the less warrant we have to presume its origin to be in God. The possibility, if not the likelihood, both of human error and diabolical deception relative to these sensuously embodied communications is, for St. John, far greater than in communications to the spirit; and for this principal reason: our judgment, accustomed as it is to defer to the superficial reports of the senses – not just as an ordinarily reliable index of a reality, but characteristically of a reality presumed to in fact correspond to its appearance – is accurate only to the extent to which appearances actually coincide with the reality they ostensibly signify. And this is simply another way of saying that we characteristically, even necessarily, judge only on the basis of appearances. And while, on the one hand, real correspondence often exists – our interaction with the world around us would be impossible or chaotic otherwise – on the other hand disqualifying instances clearly abound: most often as a matter of mistaking appearances to authentically represent realities to which they actually do not conform, or less often but equally real, by subreption through diabolical malice – in either case the resulting misjudgment is what we call error. And what this effectively means is that sense experience does not necessarily constitute a confirmation of reality. And this is St. John's whole point. This is why the contemplative must not defer to the senses, however credible their reports may appear.

Moreover, St. John argues, in their tangible dimensions, these sensuous communications cannot in reality bear any proportion to, and are in fact the ontological opposite of, the spiritual reality which they purport to convey. [39] Even were such communications divine in origin, these supernatural reports would serve merely as the vehicle, the character of which invariably, ineluctably, colors our interpretation of the actual significance. Invested as they are with clarity and distinctness, the forms of these apprehensions further tend to overshadow the implicit spiritual significance they are intended to communicate independent of their sensuous expedient. It is, then, crucial for the mystic to act in utter disregard of any such communications, and in so doing avoiding the occasion of the two principle possibilities of error. However, it now becomes problematic as to how one thing (the sensuous) contrary to another (the spiritual) – as clearly they have been throughout our account so far – can be the vehicle of its antithesis, that is to say, how the spiritual can be sensuously embodied at all. St. John provides us with no clear answer to the problem. In a sense it stands clearly aside from his practical intent. But not from ours. I think, however, that one solution is suggested by the logic of the argument itself.

Any supernatural manifestation of necessity introduces itself within the natural order. This having occurred, a radical duality is subsequently generated, the two distinct components of which are nature and spirit On the one hand we have what we might call unqualified nature in the simple material sense, and for lack of a better term, qualified spirit. What we have called qualified spirit, we might say, is super-existent in nature. Although subsisting independently of the material order, it is nevertheless capable of assuming additional, if fundamentally extraneous, ontological characteristics essential to its introduction to, or appearance within, the material order. But it does so only under some clearly defined conditions ontologically dictated by the nature it assumes. Being in nature and assuming quasi-natural dimensions, it must conform to the two ultimate constituents of nature as the very ontological frames – the very matrices of finitude – presupposed in every conception of nature as such, namely, time and space. Simply put, any supernatural manifestations must occur somewhere and sometime. However these manifestations may be able to contravene every other protocol of nature through their yet undiminished supernatural character, as manifestations in nature, they are necessarily subject to these two laws governing all appearances in nature whatever. In other words, they must share definite characteristics common to, if in fact they are to occur as appearances within, the material order.

Despite this incorporation, however, this spirit-in-nature–which every supernatural manifestation essentially is – yet remains other to nature as spirit. That is to say, it nevertheless remains unqualified spirit, spirit unmodified or unconditioned by nature; spirit merely introduced within and only physically – not essentially – constrained by the laws of appearance, the two laws alone which it cannot contravene, but to which, as we have said, it must submit as a condition of any appearance whatever.

Assuming physical specificity as a condition of its appearance – not as essential to its nature – it becomes qualified, subject to laws from which it is characteristically, essentially immune, and to which it submits itself merely as an expedient to its appearance in nature. But if this, in fact, is how spirit is capable of being sensuously embodied, it does not answer why they are embodied at all. This question is answered by St. John.

‑

More on "Spiritual Communications"

Before going further we must point out that at this stage in the Ascent, St. John is treating of the mystical experience as it pertains to the beginner who is just being brought into the first stages of mystical union and who is not yet completely withdrawn from the senses.[40] As a result, these spiritual communications are given sensuous form in order to be rendered proximate to ordinary, sensuous understanding. In fact, as we have already seen, they are merely an expedient – addressed as it were to the determinate mode of ordinary understanding in order to lead it the further on in its desire for union with God.[41] The form which this communication takes is, to sensuous understanding, merely the necessary vehicle of the spiritual reality behind it which transcends the sensuous form, even as this reality is eclipsed by it in the immediacy of sense. But the nature of this super-existent reality concealed beneath the superficies of form is nevertheless such that it succeeds withal in producing its effect independently of the form. The noetic realization is obscured by, because the soul at this point is merely attentive to, the form of the communication. In the words of St. John, it is "secretly" communicated to the soul.

Now we must admit that this strikes us as rather odd. If these communications are capable of producing their effects independently of the sensuous form in which they are embodied; and if, furthermore, the phenomenal features which such

253

communications assume by way of mere expediency are to be ignored altogether as a likely source of error – then why are these communications not effected in the soul without the appearance of the sensuous form that is both unnecessary to their producing their effects and, at the very least, the likely occasion of misjudgment and error? I think that this is a serious question that requires an answer. And the answer, I suggest, is offered within the context out of which the problem arises. It is unquestionably within the power of God to produce effects within the soul of which the soul is not cognizant. Or even to produce effects within the soul which the soul acknowledges but does not apprehend in either an experiential or noetic sense. A few instances which immediately come to mind concern the sacraments of Baptism, Confirmation, and Holy Orders, each of which are held to impress certain indelible characters upon the soul – as well as supernatural capabilities – only the external significance of which is recognized and acknowledged. The actual character, seal, or impress of God upon the soul is neither cognitively accessible nor subject to empirical verification. In the case of Baptism, it is entirely possible for a child to be baptized and subsequently mature in complete ignorance of his faith and his own baptism – all the while possessing the baptismal seal, and all that it signifies, without recognizing it.

The power conferred in these instances, as well as the effect itself – not, of course, the ritual signifying the effect – may be said to have been secretly communicated to the soul. Now this analogy that we have chosen is not at all inappropriate to our purpose. We must recall, once again, that the present discussion revolves around the contemplative who is not yet totally withdrawn from the senses. While the effect of the communication is in fact wrought independently of the form, the sensuous form serves to signify the reality being enacted completely supernaturally, secretly, invisibly, within the soul. It is a sign to the soul – which is still sensuously oriented – of something being enacted supernaturally. And as a sign, it points to, signifies, something beyond itself of which the sign constitutes no material element. Moreover, as a sign, it is an indication of the proximity and presence of something else of which it is merely a sign. And this is precisely the manner in which God first moves the soul to greater desire for union with Himself. So in answer to our question, can God produce effects within the soul without adverting to sensuous phenomena, we must unequivocally state, yes. But his doing so with a soul still primarily oriented to the senses would effectively move the soul no closer to God, and so be apart from his purpose.

... And More on the Notion of the Impedimence of Error

Let us look a little closer now at the nature of the error to which the soul is liable in adverting to the sensuous form of these supernatural communications. First of all, St. John argues, the soul errs in judging these apprehensions to be as they sensuously appear. In pronouncing judgments that appeal to the sheer phenomenal features of such occurrences, the soul illegitimately insinuates a spurious commensurability between nature and spirit which does not, and cannot, metaphysically obtain. And it is precisely because of the disproportion that exists between spirit and nature that any such embodiments of spirit are pure contingencies, exigencies in which no necessary connection is discernible between the appearances and the realties ostensibly signified by them. The soul, in order to avoid error then, must not only prescind from the sheer phenomenal dimensions of such appearances, but suspend its judgment concerning them altogether [42]

There is, moreover, a second and potentially greater danger involved in giving credence to these communications and what they purport to convey, and this, for St. John, lies in the very real possibility of diabolical deception. The dysteleological presence of personified evil on the ontological fringe of spirit toward which the contemplative moves is of genuine concern to St. John. It is the perfectly disvaluable presence whom, as we had seen earlier, Jesus describes in no unclear terms as "... a liar and the father of lies." [43] and whom St. Peter calls "[the] adversary, the devil, [who] as a roaring lion, walks about seeking whom he may devour." [44] The mystic, then, in addition to the liability to error connatural with judgment, confronts the possibility of supernatural error foisted upon the soul by no less than an agency metaphysically diabolical in nature and historically inimical to the ultimate interests of man – which, not simply for the mystic but for every Christian as well, preeminently lies in union with God. Confronted with so redoubtable a foe, far more powerful, tremendously more resourceful, vastly more intelligent, and invincibly evil, the soul, for St. John, has but one recourse – and that is to advert once again to the methodological suspension of judgment. St. John maintains that since God is more disposed to communicate with the soul through the spirit, rather than through sense, all such sensuous communications should be least methodologically – to proceed, not from God, but rather, from the devil. St. John is clear on this point: the realm of matter and sense is particularly susceptible to the artifice of the devil who, through exercising his influence over the sensuous and material, actively endeavors to deceive the soul and to frustrate it in its efforts to achieve union with God.[45] All judgment, then, must be categorically suspended and the ordinary canons of interpretation which the mystic invokes before the world of appearances must be entirely relinquished as inadequate before such extraordinary occurrences if the soul is at all to succeed in avoiding the impediment constituted by error, and so achieve union with God.

For St. John the chief danger, however, in submitting to such communications – and ultimately, the diabolical stratagem is directed to this end – lies in the soul's subsequently abandoning the principal means of union with God which we have found to be faith. In failing to disregard these communications, the soul consequently abandons that faith which takes for its object the unrevealed – and in so doing proceeds, not according to the only proximate means of union with God – which is faith – but according to the understanding in relation to its proper object which is revealed, and which St. John has already demonstrated at length to have no proportion whatever to God. But what if this supernatural communication does in fact proceed from God – as very well it may? Does the soul not err in withholding its assent? This would appear to be a very cogent objection, for it would seem that by withholding its consent, the soul would then be subjecting itself to the very liability it is expressly committed to avoiding: error.

But this is not the case, St. John answers. If a given communication does in fact proceed from God, then it produces its effect on the soul independently of the soul's judgment and assent:

"... if [any communication] be of God, [it] produces its effect upon the soul at the very moment when it appears or is felt, without giving the soul time or opportunity to deliberate whether it will accept or reject it. For, even as God gives these things supernaturally, without effort on the part of the soul, and independently of its capacity, even so, likewise, without respect to its effort or capacity, God produces within it the effect that He desires by means of such things, for this is a thing that is wrought and brought to pass in the spirit passively ..." [46]

But why, we must now ask, would God continue in such supernatural communications if they are likely to be the occasion of error, or worse yet, a defection from faith? Considered more carefully, however, there is something subreptive in this objection that makes it spurious, for if we look closely we find that it is really anachronistic. We must answer that, essentially, God does not so continue. Through these communications, we have seen, God is leading the beginner into the state of contemplation, and in so doing, God initially cooperates with the limited nature of the soul by introducing sensuous forms and images to the understanding – principally, St. John tells us, in the act of meditation. Gradually, however, God leads the soul from the active state of meditation together with its various forms and images, into the passive state of contemplation in which the limited nature of sense in transcended through, and in fact supplanted by, the simple assent of faith.

To further emphasize the point, St. John uses an interesting analogy to demonstrate the necessity of the soul's remaining passive and exercising no judgment whatever relative to such apprehensions. We have, St. John argues, no less a paradigm than Scripture itself:

> "... although sayings and revelations may be
> of God, we cannot always be sure
> of their meaning; for we can very easily be

greatly deceived by them because

of our manner of understanding them. For

they are an abyss and a depth of the

spirit, and to try to limit them to what we

can understand [would be in vain] [47]

... let it be realized, therefore, that there is

no complete understanding of the

 sayings and things of God ... [48] [whereas in

themselves they] are always certain,

they are not always so with respect to

ourselves ... One reason is the defective

way in which we understand them ... To

many of the ancients many of the

prophesies and locutions from God came not

to pass as they expected because

they understood them after their own

manner ... " [49]

These communications, he continues, are equally

capable of being apprehended by the understanding

without the active mediation of either inner or outer

sense, without corresponding phenomena in the

external order, and, moreover, without the active engagement of the imagination:

"[These] four apprehensions of the understanding ... we call purely spiritual, for they do not (as do those that are corporeal and imaginary) communicate themselves to the understanding by way of the corporeal sense; but, without the intervention of any inward or outward corporeal sense, they present themselves to the understanding, clearly and distinctly, by supernatural means, passively – that is to say, without the performance of any act or operation on the part of the soul itself ... " [50]

Those apprehensions, then, that were previously invested with qualities distinctly accessible to the senses, are now received by the understanding with an intelligible clarity and distinctness which parallels in the intellect the definition with which these apprehensions were invested in order to be first accommodated to the senses. It is, however, an intelligible definition, a definition no longer concealed, as it were inchoate, within distinctly sensuous perimeters. In a word, it is completely unconditioned by corporeity and exteriority. But how can visions, locutions and the like can be rendered non-sensuous at all? Not only non-sensuous, but purely intelligible? It would seem, at first glance, as though St. John had inadvertently overstepped every criteria of meaning in his pursuit of ultimate realities – but a closer look reveals otherwise. The solution to this enigma, we find, is suggested in certain terminological transitions that occur within the text. To wit, at one point St. John describes these four apprehensions – including locutions and spiritual feelings – as "visions of the soul", and "intellectual visions" respectively. [51] It would appear, then, that the terms "revelations, "locutions", etc., as we find them variously applied to these supernatural apprehensions, are essentially employed analogically. [52] While some correlation, however attenuated, undeniably obtains between the terms in the analogy – otherwise it would be altogether useless –the complete amplitude of what is signified characteristically, even essentially, exceeds an inflexible criterion of meaning. And this, after all, is the whole purpose of adopting an analogy – to verge upon an amplitude of meaning accessible through no other means; by approximating – not by achieving – a satisfactory meaning. And, to enunciate the obvious, a totally satisfactory meaning would not require the use of analogy. So understood, the terms "visions", "locutions", etc., to which St. John adverts, are intended to approximate by way of analogy an aspect of reality that only remotely corresponds to the meanings imbedded in a language that is not, and cannot be, sufficient to the descriptive task. Language, predicated as it is upon shared experiences, is simply too impoverished to accommodate the amplitude, the infinite amplitude of the Absolute. Even the peripheral, the most marginal and obscure experience of the Absolute, in some sense, for St. John, analogically approximates a vision, or a locution, in its intelligible clarity:

> "... all these four apprehensions may be called visions of the soul; for we

266

term the understanding of the soul also its
sight. And since all these apprehensions
are intelligible to the understanding, they
are described, in a spiritual sense, as
'visible'. And thus the kinds of intelligence
that are formed in the understanding
may be called intellectual visions. [53] From
all these the soul derives spiritual
vision or intelligence without any kind of
apprehension concerning form, image,
or figure." [54]

But something more remains to be said about the
nature of these four apprehensions that figure so
largely and are treated so extensively in *Book II* of
the *Ascent*. All of them, we have found, are equally
subsumed under the comprehensive term "vision",
and this would seem to effectively attenuate any
radical distinction between them. There must, then,
be a single characteristic universally shared among
them such that either the mode of reception or the
mode of communication is the same in all relative
cases. And since a distinction, however tenuous,

nevertheless remains between these several communications – in that they are clearly and consistently differentiated within the schema St. John has developed – this unitary characteristic cannot be in the mode of communication; it must therefore be found in a certain mode of reception. And this receptive mode, we have seen, is described as a "vision" by St. John; a vision which may more properly be designated an intuition since it is explicitly unmediated in nature. As an intuition, then, this communication is non-sensuous; it is merely intuited without mediation of any type, rational or sensory. Moreover, the clarity and distinctness with which it is invested must not be mistaken as referring to the content of the communication – this still remains concealed from the understanding – rather, it is to be understood as referring to the experience itself which is clearly and distinctly perceived, not clearly and distinctly understood. This interpretation, I think, is clearly borne out in the following passages:

"... although these visions ... cannot be
unveiled and be clearly seen in this
life by the understanding, they can
nevertheless be felt in the substance of
the soul ... [55] And although at times, when
such knowledge is given to the
soul, words are used, the soul is well aware
that it has expressed no part of
what it has felt; for it knows that there is no
fit name by which it can name it ..." [56]

This very complex notion of intelligible
apprehensions or visions, then, is more readily
understood as, in clearly evidencing the
characteristics of, an intuition: they are immediately
apprehended, perceived as pure experiences
communicated to the soul spiritually, and without
any mediation whatever.

The Spurious and the Counterfeit:
The Imperative of Faith

But it is no less clear, as St. John once again points out, that these four apprehensions are equally susceptible to being contrived, or perhaps better yet, counterfeited, diabolically. It is of the first order of importance, then, that some very clear criteria be established to distinguish between the diabolical and the divine relative to these apprehensions. Although St. John fails to provide us with a clear answer on this subject, our most immediate question, I think, will inevitably be – why? Why indeed go to the trouble of establishing criteria to distinguish between what is authentically divine, and what is spuriously diabolical in origin? After all, St. John has forcefully argued that when confronted with such supernatural apprehensions, the contemplative must disregard them totally, both as inimical to faith which alone is the proximate means to union, and as the possible occasion of error. If in fact, then, the disregard is to be total, the source, or origin of such communications would seem to be entirely irrelevant. One and all they are to be dismissed. The mystic, in any event, is to act in disregard of them; however, St. John proceeds to argue, the subjective effects of these apprehensions – independent of the resolute disregard of the mystic – are to the soul who is not yet totally withdrawn from the senses, that is to say, to the soul who is just being brought into the preliminary stages of mystical union, indications of the predilection of God who, through the accidental qualities of these subjective effects, stirs the soul to a greater desire for union. In a sense, then, God is understood as permitting these accidental qualities, *ex mero motu*, to attend the effects being secretly wrought in the soul. They are essentially signs to which invisible realities, in the way of actual effects occurring in the soul, correspond. On the other hand, those apprehensions effected diabolically, St. John contends, are in every sense entirely fraudulent. That is to say, there is no authentic correspondence between the sign and the reality it spuriously signifies: no effect whatever is wrought in the soul – no effect, that is, apart from the soul's subjective response to the sign. And this is worth examining further.

For St. John, the only criteria to which the contemplative can appeal in attempting to discern the authenticity of what is perceived to be the divine invitation to mystical union consists, at this early stage – a stage, we will remember, in which the mystic is yet susceptible to the senses – largely in the subjective effects produced in the soul by the respective apprehensions. Diabolical communications, St. John argues, typically render the soul apathetic toward God; they characteristically foster inordinate pride, a pride in which the soul sees these communications as signal tokens of God's unique predilection for it, and consequently dispose the soul to be inclined toward precisely these types of phenomena which, in effect, are so many inducements to abandon pure faith. The soul must, then, and for this crucial reason, proceed in absolute detachment from them, irrespective of its judgment concerning their source, and continue in the darkness of faith alone. [57]

But does this really answer our question? In other words, if the soul is to prescind entirely from, not only the apprehension, but its accidental and subjective effects as well, how are we to reconcile this with the soul's acceptance of God's invitation through the very effects he is committed to disregarding? The answer, I suggest, is to be found in the very detachment that the soul is consistently exhorted to exercise. Perhaps we can put it another way. The mystic, through the accidental qualities that attend these phenomena, is, despite his intentional disregard, nevertheless perceptibly influenced by them – because they actually and simultaneously produce a real effect in his soul. They are, after all, and as we had said, authentic signs of invisible realities. On the other hand, there are no realities whatsoever effected in the soul by the merely fraudulent signs contrived by a diabolical agency. Both signs, then, may in fact be safely ignored – but only one produces an autonomous effect independent of the of the assent of the will.

But what of the criterion itself? Just how reliable can criteria be that appeal to what are fundamentally subjective impressions? Indeed, it is a commonplace in ordinary discourse there is hardly a less stringent or less qualified standard of discrimination to which we can appeal than the simplicity of feeling, nothing more naive than the subjectivity of sense. But the problem at hand is really quite an extraordinary one, and while this objection may indeed hold true in ordinary states of affairs, I think we are compelled to look at it more closely, certainly more critically, relative to the mystic's own unique predicament, for upon further consideration, it turns out that what appears to be, on St. John's part, an unsophisticated model of judgment, inevitably emerges as the only possible criterion available through the logic of the account. Our difficulty in accepting this criterion, I suggest, vanishes when, by simple substitution, we understand by the ambiguous term "feeling", the more accurate term "intuition".

We must bear in mind, even as we had argued earlier, that what we are in fact dealing with in this type of supernatural apprehension is ultimately a pure, unmediated experience. Not, of course, relative to the actual effects being produced in the soul – since these are accomplished "secretly"– but rather, relative to the accidental qualities attending these undisclosed effects. These accidents, concurrent with, but unessential to, the effects being actually achieved, are a matter of experience – and experience remains the only criteria available to judgment. All the canons of rational discrimination, we will remember, including every judgment inflected by reason, have been sublated according to the uncompromising demands of the *via negativa*. Reason, then, antecedently abolished, can pronounce no judgment, for it can apply no logic to elements of experience to which it has no access.

For the soul reduced to the passive simplicity of experience-only, there remains merely the intuition, or in the words of St. John, the feeling, in which this experience consists – and it is this simple subjective perception which alone can possibly constitute a criterion by which the soul is capable of evaluating the several types of experiences or apprehensions to which it is subject in this obscure night of the spirit. The distinct and special mode of supernatural understanding which we have discussed above is, as we had suggested earlier, really a parenthetical treatment of error which St. John addresses to emphasize the imperative of pure faith in the soul's journey to union. In a sense it is propadeutic to better understanding the general and obscure mode of supernatural understanding which is really the aspect that is of particular interest to us in developing a mystical epistemology, for here we are dealing with the direct, if confused, intuition of God. Unlike its distinct and special counterpart, this general and obscure mode begins, surprisingly enough, in the soul's active practice of meditation prior to its being brought into the advanced state of contemplation. And it is here that the relation between meditation and contemplation first becomes clear.

The "General" and the "Obscure" Modes of Understanding

Where the distinct and special mode of supernatural communication had its origin solely in the divine or diabolical initiative independent of the dispositional attitude of the soul – which was, in fact, exhorted to be entirely passive to these communications – the general and obscure mode, on the other hand, begins in the discursive act of meditation. Here the mystic endeavors to achieve, through increasingly articulated acts of reflection, a greater knowledge, and therefore a greater love of God (the two are clearly equated by St. John throughout the text). This knowledge and concomitant love of God, increasingly attending each particular discursive act, and amplified in the totality of these acts, through repetition ultimately generates what St. John calls a continuous and habitual knowledge and love of God as its familiar object:

> "... the end of reasoning and meditation on
> the things of God is the gaining
> of some knowledge and love of God, and
> each time that the soul gains this
> through meditation, it is an act; and just as
> many acts, of whatever kind, end
> by forming a habit in the soul, just so, many
> of these acts of loving knowledge
> which the soul has been making one after
> another from time to time come
> through repetition to be so continuous in it
> that they become habitual ...
> And thus that which aforetime the soul was
> gaining gradually through its
> labor of meditation upon particular facts has

now through practice ...

become converted and changed into a habit

and substance of loving

knowledge, of a general kind, and not

distinct and particular as before." [58]

What St. John appears to be saying is that the various discrete acts of meditation, by virtue of repetition, coalesce into a general sense of the numinous. Although generated collectively by these individual and discrete repetitive acts, this comprehensive sense of the numinous appears to transcend each of them in their particularity. The soul thus comes, through practice and habit, to what St. John calls a confused and general knowledge of God which may better be described as an intensely focused attentiveness to – and consequently a receptivity towards – that of which it has yet only obscure knowledge. [59]

Once again, and typically, the precise mechanics involved in this psychological transition remain unaddressed by – because in a real sense they are unnecessary to – St. John, and remain merely to speculated upon. By now, however, St. John has provided us with the necessary heuristic concepts to assist us in understanding this transition more completely. Having transcended the discrete and particular acts characteristic of meditation, the soul must be understood as having effectively transcended meditation itself, together with the specific and determinate forms apprehended within it. In transcending these distinct forms, then, the soul has transcended the activity itself by which they were acquired – and as a result has simultaneously entered into the passive state of contemplation. In other words, the general and numinous sense that resulted from a continuous and habitual knowledge and love of God has itself resulted in an epistemological transformation in which not only is the particularity of form transcended, but the activity that produced that form as well. The result, whatever it may be, cannot be an epistemological state characterized by a type of activity that has already been transcended. It must, then, as a result of this transition, be passive. And not simply passive, but as a consequence of the transcendence of distinct and clear form, it must of necessity be general and confused relative to God. In other words, in transcending this clearly discursive function which passes from one particular to another, the soul at once and necessarily undergoes a cognitive transformation resulting in, and characterized by, indeterminate generality – a generality in which the penumbra of hitherto distinct particulars merge into, effectively become continuous with, others in a way that a discursive faculty is no longer able to accommodate. And it is precisely this indeterminate type of cognition, this indistinct epistemological state precursive to contemplation, which St. John understands as the general and obscure mode.

But that this mode of understanding is supernaturally communicated to the soul – and St. John maintains that it is – is not entirely clear in the text, for we have seen it to essentially result from a process of repetition, practice, and habit, in all of which the soul itself appears to be the principal agent. But by the same token it is no less clear that in having transcended meditation the soul has simultaneously transcended what is fundamentally a formal manifold – a matrix of distinct forms – the features of which, however embellished by the imagination with supernatural qualities, remain natural objects addressed in the discursive activity of meditation. That is to say, the object taken in meditation, however meticulously constructed to represent our conception of a supernatural reality, is always invested with distinct formal features deriving from, and only occurring within, nature. They are, one and all, distinct, finite, temporal, and invariably represented as material. And necessarily so, otherwise they would be incapable of being apprehended by sensuous imagination as the synthetic faculty operant in every meditation.

Consequently, in transcending, in going beyond, natural objects properly addressed in the discursive act of meditation – regardless of the manner in which this is accomplished – the cognitive soul has

282

already, and necessarily, passed on to supernatural objects of contemplation. Nor can the soul be the author of these supernatural objects, still less the agent behind this transition, for as a natural agent it cannot produce supernatural effects, that is to say, effects which are categorically disproportionate to its nature. This kind of transition simply does not lie within the natural province of the soul. It must, therefore, be divinely initiated. And this is precisely the point argued by St. John who maintains that it is God alone who, from beginning to end, moves the soul – which, through the prompting of grace, cooperates with God – to union with him through infused contemplation. [60]

This is not to say, paradoxically, that the epistemological transition from meditation to contemplation is immediately recognized by, even as it is enacted within, the mystic. It is not, as we may suppose, a sudden quantum leap between utterly incommensurable categories, but rather a gradual transition from distinct and clear, to confused and general knowledge:

"... when this condition first begins, the soul
is hardly aware of this knowledge
 and that for two reasons. First, this loving
knowledge is apt at the beginning to
be very subtle and delicate, and almost
imperceptible to the senses. Secondly,
when the soul has been accustomed to that
other exercise of meditation, which
is wholly perceptible, it is unaware, and
hardly conscious, of this other new and
imperceptible condition, which is purely
spiritual ... [61] This general knowledge
is at times so subtle and delicate, particularly
when it is most pure and simple
and perfect, most spiritual and most interior,
that although the soul is occupied
therein, it can neither realize it nor perceive
it ... [in fact] when this knowledge
is purest and simplest and most perfect, the
understanding is least conscious
of it and thinks of it as most obscure." [62]

Apparently, then, in the transition from mediation to contemplation, this general and obscure knowledge is so subtly introduced, so insusceptible to determinate understanding, that it often escapes not so much a conscious realization, as understanding altogether. The soul only implicitly, tentatively, experiences God, understanding neither that which it only perceptibly experiences, nor how it experiences this obscure intuition of the Absolute. When this "knowledge", as St. John calls this intuitive apprehension, is "purest", or entirely imperceptible to sense, the transition from meditation to contemplation is effectively complete. Cognition transcends the perimeters that circumscribe – and in so defining, limit – the forms, figures and conceptions of natural understanding to which the experiences in contemplation remain forever and necessarily opaque. It is the "fleeting touch of union" of which St. John speaks, the pre-noetic confrontation with the Absolute before which understanding is abolished to nature.

---

[1] AMC 2.8.4
[2] AMC 2.8.5 cf. 1.4.4-7
[3] AMC 2.4.4 also cf. 2.26.18
[4] AMC 1.13.11+12 also cf. 1 Cor. 2.9 & 2 Cor. 6.10
[5] AMC 2.1.1
[6] Understood as encompassing the world of men and matter, as well as the celestial hierarchy of created spirits (cf. AMC 2.12.3+4).
[7] see page ___ of this commentary
[8] AMC 2.1.1 , DNS 2.23.2
[9] Jn. 14.6
[10] Jn. 8.44, Gen 3.1-15
[11] AMC 2.11.3
[12] AMC 2.10.4
[13] Rom. 10.14-17
[14] AMC 2.3.1 also cf. 2.9.1
[15] This surprisingly modern epistemological analysis, by the way, precedes the great 17th century empiricists by more than a century, and is treated in much greater detail by Saint Thomas Aquinas (1225-1274 AD) some four hundred years prior to Locke and Hume. Cf. S.T. I Q.84 Art. 1-8, Q.85 Art. 1-3 and *in passim*. Also, *De Potent. Dei* Q.3 Art. 5.
[16] AMC 2.3.2+3
[17] Heb.11.1
[18] 1 Cor. 2.9
[19] cf. AMC 2.22.11, 2.27.1+4, 2.29.12
[20] Books I, II, & III of AMC respectively
[21] AMC 2.6.1+2; cf. DNS 2.21.11
[22] AMC 2.6.1-4
[23] AMC 3.2.4
[24] AMC 3.16.2
[25] AMC 2.6.6
[26] AMC 2.7.4,7,+11; cf. DNS 2.4.2 & SC 17.11+12
[27] AMC 2.7.4+7
[28] AMC 2.2.1
[29] AMC 2.8.4-5
[30] AMC 2.9.1
[31] AMC 2.10.2-4
[32] AMC 2.10.2
[33] e.g. AMC 2.8.4-5, 1.3.3, & 2.3.2+3

[34] AMC 2.12.2-3
[35] AMC 2.10.4
[36] AMC 2.11.3 emphasis added
[37] AMC 2.11.7 cf. 2 Cor. 11.14
[38] AMC 2.11.2,5,7 & ff.
[39] AMC 2.11.2 & 2.19.5+11
[40] AMC 2.12.5 & 2.17.3
[41] AMC 2.11.9
[42] AMC 2.11.2 & 2.26.18
[43] Jn. 8.44
[44] 1 Pet. 5.8
[45] AMC 2.11.3
[46] AMC 2.11.6
[47] AMC 2.19.10
[48] AMC 2.20.6
[49] AMC 2.19.1
[50] AMC 2.23.1
[51] AMC 2.23.2&3
[52] AMC 2.23.3
[53] AMC 2.23.2
[54] AMC 2.23.3
[55] AMC 2.24.4
[56] AMC 2.26.4 emphases added
[57] AMC 2.24.8
[58] AMC 2.14.2
[59] AMC 2.15.2-5
[60] AMC 1.1.5 etc.
[61] AMC 2.14.7
[62] AMC 2.14.8

The Role of the Memory

The last faculty remaining to be discussed is memory. It is the subject of the third and final book of the Ascent and with it we will effectively conclude our examination of the fundamental principles presupposed in our analysis of St. John's metaphysics in Part II of our commentary. Our approach, to be sure, in dealing with memory, will be much the same as in our treatment of the will and understanding, and for this reason we shall be spared much unnecessary detail. But first, let us be clear about what St. John understands by memory, and in answering this, we shall at once discover the reason for the brevity of our account. For St. John, memory is simply the repository of forms received through the five senses [1] and in its subordinate capacity as imagination, it is capable of variously synthesizing these forms and producing still other forms with which the soul had hitherto been unacquainted, at least in their synthetic unity. In effect, then, memory is the subsumption of nature under the synthetic activity of imagination. All the imperatives, then, that apply to nature, and all the principles involved in its negation prior to union, equally apply to nature as internalized in memory and synthesized in imagination. Very briefly, then, since the memory is principally occupied with retaining and synthesizing various sensuous forms ultimately deriving from nature, we can succinctly state that, as Spirit, God is contrary to nature, and conversely, as subsumed under nature, form – delimited and finite – is contrary to God.[2] The soul, then, is once again constrained to subject itself – this time relative to the faculty of memory – to the rigors of the *via negativa*. just as it had done relative to the will and understanding, in order to eliminate within itself that contrariety to God which is preclusive of union. It must become transformed, together with the will and the understanding, into that otherness of God to nature, and as a consequence, rendered other to its own natural economy.

Once more we find that two levels of negation are discernible in this transformation: the negation of nature according to memory, in which the soul ceases to appropriate and synthesize forms variously derived from the senses, thus negating nature. And, implicitly following from this first order of negation, the negation of memory according to nature in which the memory, having ceased from appropriating and synthesizing these sensuously derived forms, has effectively ceased in its natural function qua mnemonic. This resulting state of absolute negativity – the categorical negation of nature and memory – is, for St. John, simultaneously the transformation of the memory into the negativity of hope, its corresponding theological virtue which is understood by St. John to essentially constitute a state of radical dispossession. [3]

There is, interestingly enough, one notable exception – and this only occurs in the Alcalà edition of 1618 – to the rule which requires the memory to be completely emptied of all forms and images: and this is the Sacred Humanity of Christ who, as both True God and True Man, remains, for St. John, the most proper object of both meditation and contemplation.[4] However true this may be, to leave our answer simply at this is to gloss over some very real difficulties that arise as a result of this exception, for a good deal more than the simple humanity of Christ is insinuated into our account through it; indeed, through a broader consideration, it implicitly involves elements which have been found to be antagonistic to union elsewhere in the account. This type of incongruity occurs once again in the Dark Night of the Soul, and while I think these are significant features that must be dealt with, the broader issues from which they arise must be addressed more in terms of St. John's own historical context than from any strictly epistemological consideration. Our discussion of this apparent inconsistency, inviting though it may be at the present, must wait until our examination of the Dark Night of the Soul where the opportunity will better present itself within another context altogether.

We have already found, much in line with our previous analyses, that the memory must be negated of all knowledge, form, and figure in order to be transformed into its corresponding theological virtue of hope which is explicitly negative:

> "For all possession is contrary to hope, which, as St. Paul says, belongs to that which is not possessed. [5] Wherefore, the more the memory dispossesses itself, the greater is its hope, and the more it has of hope, the more it has of union with God ... and it hopes most when it is most completely dispossessed, and when it shall be perfectly dispossessed, it will remain with the perfect possession of God in Divine union." [6]

This is a somewhat misleading passage, for one gets the impression that when the negative moment is actualized in perfect hope, this alone is sufficient to effect union with God. But we have clearly seen that this is not the case. There is no 'causal' connection between attaining the state of negation and the realization of union, still less a necessary transition logically implied, as we shall later see. For the moment let us simply say that in achieving the state of perfect dispossession which St. John calls hope, the soul is not for that reason, and at once, brought to union with God. Rather, as we had seen in the case of love (will) and faith (understanding), it is only brought into a state of proximity to God – the state of absolute negativity not only relative to nature, but to itself as well.

This persistent emphasis on the negative dimensions of experience within the several 'nights' that we have examined is, in this concluding chapter of the Ascent, clearly explained as ultimately having one purpose:

> "... all means must be proportioned to the
> end; that is to say, they must have

some connection and resemblance with the
end, such as is enough and sufficient
for the desired end to be attained through
them." [7]

Now, we have seen that no positive
commensurability is capable of being established
between metaphysically incommensurable
categories, between the means and the end – how
then, we must ask, is this statement to be
understood? This passage, I think, is extremely
interesting in several respects, and before passing
on to a consideration of our own immediate
question, I think it would be worthwhile for us to
consider another issue, not entirely tangential from
our present purpose; an issue that really ought to be
addressed, if only briefly, in light of what St. John
has said above. Understanding this first will provide
us with a broader perspective of the constant
dialectic that occurs throughout the text. And it is
this: a kind of teleology is suggested in the account
which, positively considered, ultimately finds its
ground in what, for St. John, is man's essentially

reflective ontology in relation to the Absolute, as image of the Absolute – an Absolute itself understood in terms of love. We had addressed this point briefly earlier. While some degree of commensurability is capable of being established between man and God through love, love itself – through which alone this commensurability is possible – is not an inherent metaphysical feature of man's essential ontology independent of the Absolute. Love in fact is the essential ontological feature of man qua image of God, but for St. John, as we shall later see, man's essential ontology is of itself the mere possibility of reflection – given the Reflected. And this is to say that the soul is, substantivally considered, not in itself an autonomous being, but rather, being-contingent-upon-the-Absolute – that is to say, being heteronymously derived, and not self-subsistent apart from the Absolute. And this, of course, is not merely entirely consistent with a traditional theological understanding of the nature of the soul – but in fact is an expression of it. In other words, it is not the case that the soul of itself is understood to be commensurable with God, but that the soul as the image actively reflecting God is, and it is seen to be commensurable only insofar as it does in fact reflect the Absolute. And this, in turn, is essentially to say that man's being, fundamentally considered, cannot, for St. John, be established independently of God. Consequently, the authentic nature of man's being is only teleologically actualized through his participation in God – and this direct participation is what St. John ultimately understands in the notion of union. We will discuss this in much greater detail the second part of our commentary.

Means and Ends

Returning once again to the point from which we departed, we had said that since no positive commensurability can be established between metaphysically incommensurable categories, between the means and the end, how are we to understand St. John when he insists that the "means must be proportioned to the end", and sufficient for the desired end to be attained through them? It would appear that the 'means' of which St. John is speaking are, after careful examination, the three theological virtues that we have been addressing in one form or another all along. And St. John has been unequivocally clear about the negative nature of these virtues. The sort of proportion, then, that St. John appears to be calling for might well be more appositely described as negative commensurability; a commensurability achieved through abolishing all contrariety to God in the *via negativa*, and simultaneously positing at each successive moment in the account a theological virtue, explicitly negative in nature, through which alone, he has repeatedly insisted, the soul attains to a state of proximity to God. And this is further to say that what we confront here, in effect, is a kind of teleological negativity; a movement toward establishing commensurability negatively; not so much, as St. John inadvertently misleads us here, in the form of resemblance, as in the absence of contrariety.

Let us take a different tack. Through these various negative moments, or 'nights', the soul only becomes commensurable with the Absolute inasmuch as it is no longer incommensurable with it. It is not so much commensurability understood as rendering the soul to be what God is – this is not possible, for God is infinitely inexhaustible – but not to be what God is not. In other words, the soul achieves proximity to God negatively. It proximates, is commensurable with God, not in that it possesses characteristics in common with God, but in that it does not possess certain characteristics that God also does not possess – and this essentially is the concept of negative commensurability. Implicit, of course, in the concept of negative commensurability is the logic of negative predication. According to this logic, we are unable to derive logical warrant for ascribing a community of properties or attributes, positively considered, to intrinsically different things simply because they

299

share identical predicates negatively considered. Not-red can be yellow or blue. Given something characterized as Not-red, we have no logical warrant whatever to understand this as indicating blue rather than yellow, or any other color in the spectrum for that matter. In fact, we have no warrant whatever of predicating anything at all of it, outside of the fact that it is Not-Red. Negative predicates, in other words, provide us with no information whatever about being positively considered.

Perhaps we can shed more light on this fundamental feature of mysticism by considering another dimension to the problem. It is very difficult to see how hope as a virtual state of negativity on the one hand, can be proportioned to God who, on the other, is the plenitude of being. To attempt to answer this in terms of negative commensurability is not to establish proportion or resemblance, as we have just seen, but merely, and at best, non-contrariety. How then is 'proportion' or 'resemblance' effected? To answer this we must return for a moment to our previous understanding of the virtue of hope. As the opposite of possession – which for the memory consists in the retention of created (natural) knowledge, form, and figure – hope may equally be seen to be the implicit opposite of nature. And as we had seen earlier, the opposite of nature in the metaphysical understanding of St. John is spirit – which is both proximate and similar, and therefore, proportioned to God. This very clearly follows if by spirit we understand not-nature as synonymous with spirit – and this synonymy is unmistakably implied throughout the account. Whatever not-nature understood as spirit is, it is something positively predicated of God. St. John, then, argues consistently when he maintains that the three theological virtues are in fact proportionate to God, and therefore the only proximate means to mystical union with him.

A Matter of Form

At this point, the memory has been negated of all created knowledge, form, and figure; it no longer archives, reproduces, or synthesizes the store of data it initially acquired through the senses, but rather assumes an attitude of totally passive receptivity. But what, precisely, is the memory receptive to in this state of negation? On the one hand it cannot be phenomena delivered by reason or sense, both having been antecedently abolished. And yet, on the other hand, what are we left with if all figure and form have been categorically abolished along with reason and sense? But, St. John argues, they have not been so – except relative to matter and reason.. It is not the case that the concept of form itself has been abolished – indeed, it is a fundamental principle of the scholastic reasoning with which St. John was so well acquainted that God himself is, in the words of St. Thomas Aquinas, "of His essence a form, and not composed of matter and form." [8] What has been

302

abolished, rather, is form as limitation – a limitation specific to nature and coterminous with matter or co-conceptual within reason. It is, to extrapolate upon Aquinas's own argument, form that is not self-subsisting, but dependent upon matter as the individuating principle of the form.

But the notion itself of form, as preeminently exemplified in God, is not limited to matter and reason. And it is this type of form which, St. John argues, is passively received either as purely spiritual intuitions, or, in the case of those mediated by sensuous form and figure, received not according to their various sensuous configurations, but rather, according to the spiritual form [9] latent in these impressions. The soul, St. John tells us, remains indifferent to the accidents, or accidental qualities if you will, that attend these essentially spiritual perceptions, for the memory has been effectively negated to all capacity for (natural) form and figure. Regrettably, St. John does not – perhaps by the very nature of the experience, cannot – elaborate on the nature of these spiritual forms. I think that the latter case is most likely, for in themselves they appear to be, from the general drift of his argument, absolutely pure intuitions, immediate experiences that, as such, are essentially recalcitrant to language – which, we had said earlier, presumes shared experiences to its intelligibility. I also think it unlikely that the term form relative to spirit, in the way St. John conjoins the two, denotes the type of specificity and distinctness we ordinarily associate with our sensible apprehension of material compositions. It is, I think, much more likely that the term form, at least in the present context, denotes something a good deal more ambiguous, something more in the way of a 'distinct spiritual impression' or a distinct intuition entailing nothing more in the way of perceptible phenomena.

This interpretation seems to be borne out by St. John's insistence that the memory in the state of negation is nevertheless capable of recollecting these spiritual forms of uncreated knowledge as simple noetic intuitions:

"Now, after the soul has experienced one of
these apprehensions, it can recall
it whenever it will; and this not by the effigy
and image that the apprehension
has left in the bodily sense, for, since this is
of bodily form, as we say, it has no
capacity for spiritual forms; but because it
recalls it intellectually and spiritually,
by means of that form which it has left
impressed upon the soul which is likewise
a formal or spiritual form ..." [10]

These forms, then, of which St. John speaks, appear
to be sheer noetic intuitions containing nothing
analogous to the clear, distinct, and determinate
phenomena apprehended by the senses and which
we characteristically understand as instantiating
form. The intuitive character of these specialized
forms is most clearly expressed in the element of
experience necessary to their being recollected:

"... by no form, image, or figure which can
be impressed upon the soul does

the memory recall these [spiritual forms],

for these touches and impressions

of union with the Creator have no form, but

only by the effects which they

have produced upon it of light, love, joy,

and spiritual renewal, and so forth ..." [11]

That St. John has, in this passage, encountered some terminological difficulties as a consequence of his attempt to inflect the rigorous and basically inflexible limitations in language, is obvious, for in attempting to describe these essentially indescribable (intuitive) spiritual forms – that is to say, in an effort to accommodate them, to make them accessible, to reason – he simultaneously and paradoxically describes them as having no form at all. This apparent contradiction seems to result from his having failed to clearly articulate the meaning of "spiritual form" in and of itself; especially as it is to be distinguished from our understanding of the word "form" in ordinary discourse. In fact, the term form in the second sense ("... have no form ...") refers to our understanding of the word as it applies

306

to distinct, clear, and sensuously embodied apprehensions – and not to the noetic intuitions themselves. This contention, I think, is particularly borne out by St. John's insistence that the memory recalls these spiritual forms "only by the effects which they have produced upon it", which he then goes on to enumerate them as light, love, joy, renewal, etc.

Now, implied in all this is a latent connection between recollection, or memory, and knowledge – and not just knowledge, but a particular kind of knowledge: uncreated knowledge. And this connection clearly implicates the element of experience. This uncreated knowledge communicated to the soul and subsequently archived in memory is not retrieved abstractly in the way that, say, geometric theorems are, nor in the remote way that empirically acquired knowledge (which is no longer concurrent with the experience through which it was initially acquired) is. While the form of each of these types remains, in a manner of speaking, resident in memory, the matter to which the form corresponds clearly does not: neither the line which in essence we spatially conceptualize, and from which we extrapolate a purely rational geometric definition, nor yet impressions of sensible objects with which we once had immediate, empirical acquaintance and now retrieve as remote from the material objects themselves. What we recall is the form of the object, and not, obviously, the object itself which is no longer concurrent with the form.

This, however, is not to say that the form and the object can no longer coincide. Clearly they can – but only upon a renewed experience of the object. And this coincidence, or concurrence remains only as long as the experience itself remains. For St. John, however, the recollection of these forms is independent of a concurrent experience of the matter from which these mere forms are derived. In other words, the object is only formally retained in the soul.

On the other hand, the spiritual forms of which St. John speaks appear to essentially produce an effect on the soul, the matter of which is the experience of the effect, which to recall, in turn, is to renew the experience in which the effect consists. And this – a recollection concurrent with the experience from which it evolved – is only possible because it is neither abstractly, nor remotely retrieved from memory; rather, the recollection entails an immediate experience because it is essentially the soul's experience of itself, or more precisely, the self modified by the effects of grace introduced by these spiritual forms which now inhere subsistently in the soul and as such are always concurrent with it as intuitions of itself.

As we now clearly see, it is not the case that will, understanding, and memory are categorically abolished: that the soul no longer wills, or has cognitive activity, or has remembrance (as much of the language we have used thus far appears to imply). The soul in fact is annihilated – but not unto itself; rather it is annihilated relative to the natural exercise of these faculties; faculties which, in the end, are not categorically abolished in and of themselves. Rather, the annihilation of which St. John speaks consists in the transformation of these natural faculties into their corresponding theological virtues which, utilizing the epistemological structures framed by nature,[12] supplants the natural activity (unable to accommodate supernatural phenomena) with supernatural activity which alone is sufficient to it.

An Explication of the Notion of the "Faculties"

Now that we have arrived at a rudimentary understanding of the faculties involved, it is equally important to examine the relation between them. To begin with, understanding and memory, as St. John points out, both in their natural capacities, and in the state of negation, are not of themselves autonomous; rather, he seems to imply, they appear to be unified in their subordination to the will.[13] Here, in this last division of the Ascent, St. John finally concludes his treatment of the soul in its sensuous economy with some closing remarks on that faculty through which the soul, as an organic unity, attains to the consummate state of perfection, or beatitude in God. It remains only to be demonstrated that the three faculties of the soul – will, understanding, and memory – are in fact integrated, unified, in the will's transformation into the cardinal theological virtue of love. In treating of the relation of the four passions – joy, hope, grief, and fear – to the three theological virtues, St. John argues the following:

> "... these four passions of the soul are so
> closely and intimately united to one
> another that the actual direction of one is the
> virtual direction of the others;
> and if one be actually recollected the other
> three will virtually and proportionately
> be recollected likewise. For if the will
> rejoice in anything, it will as a result hope

311

for the same thing ... Wherefore ...
wheresoever one of these passions is, thither
will go likewise the whole soul and the will
and the other faculties ..." [14]

Although at this point he is arguably dealing only
with the passions, a broader understanding of the
dialectic involved is clearly warranted, for
according to the gist of this argument, the nature of
the will is such that the remaining faculties are
unified through the intentionality of the will, and it
is precisely this facultative union through
intentionality which we must now attempt to grasp
before venturing any further. What St. John appears
to be implying at this point is simply this: in the
state of negation into which the contemplative has
entered, we are unable to understand either the
aspirations of hope or the convictions of faith apart
from the object of intention first appropriated
through the will. Through an irreducible act of will
(love), an act divinely inspired, the soul
appropriates to the understanding the articles of
faith relating to the object of its love, and these

312

articles of faith, in turn, are archived in memory to inform hope. And this is simply to say that understanding and memory, faith and hope, acquire a facultative union through the intentionality of the will, relative both to the exercise of each faculty in accordance with the intentionality of the will, and in the object respectively acquired by each faculty subsequent to this exercise. In other words, the soul hopes only for what it loves, and the object of hope is only accessible through faith which is fundamentally appropriated through an act of will. Delete any element and the dialectic is incomplete, the intelligibility of each virtue vanishes. In short, we cannot understand hope apart from love, nor faith apart from hope.

But let us carry this step further; in fact, to its logical conclusion. God, as we have seen, has clearly been equated with love by St. John throughout the account: man is made in the image of God, and this image of God in man is love. These faculties, then, so unified in love, are at least implicitly unified in God. But there are, in fact, two

313

levels of unity corresponding, respectively, to the unity in God only implicit in the state of nature, and the unity in God rendered explicit in what St. John calls supernatural transformation.

Perhaps we can best summarize his line of reasoning this way: As latent in the state of nature, any love is an implicit unity in God through the created participation of the soul in God as the imago Dei. The soul's ability to love derives from, is radicated in, its created nature as the image of God who is love; consequently the unity of the faculties in any love implicitly owes this unity to God. In other words, the unifying nature of love is only latently discernible within and remotely ascribable to, God. The soul, in fact, is unified in its love for anything. That this unifying agency of love derives essentially from the soul's ontological status as the image of God, is only implicit in its nature.

As explicit in transformation, however, love is that reflective resonance become explicit between the Imaged and the image – the unifying nature of love is seen to derive immediately, essentially, from God in the soul's noetic realization of itself as image of the Absolute. In this state of transformation, the soul's unifying capacity qua image, and that in which it is unified, are explicitly one and the same – and this sameness is nothing less than union in God. The soul is no longer unified in its love for the other of God in nature, a love metaphysically constrained from union by the ontological disparity between the lover and the loved, in the absence of that reflection in which the lover realizes his being to be one with the Beloved, a reflective existence inseparably bound to the Reflected. Rather, it has realized itself as the reflection-of-God into God, and it is in dealing with this divine reflexivity to which St. John, on increasingly explicit levels, devotes the rest of his treatises, all of which fundamentally derive from the mystical doctrines and presuppositions which we have examined in the *Ascent of Mount Carmel*. It is, in effect, the soul's ascent to the mount of the transfiguration; the realization of the reflection of divinity lying deeply, profoundly, in the soul of every man and woman. The nature of this union, this reflexivity or resonance that is the apotheosis of the soul in God, now remains to be examined in Part II.

---

[1] AMC 3.2.4

[2] We must not conclude, however, that the notion of *form* does not apply to God. Indeed, it does not apply to God as limitative. But as Self-subsisting and unindividuated by matter, form is, for St. John, as well as for his predecessors in the Scholastic tradition, clearly ascribable to God. Cf. ST Q.3 art.2

[3] AMC 3.7.2 & 3.11.2

[4] AMC 3.2.14 (Editio Princeps, Alcala, 1618)

[5] Heb. 11.1

[6] AMC 3.7.2

[7] AMC 2.8.2

[8] cf. ST Q.3 art.2

[9] AMC 3.14.1 & 2. This rather perplexing notion reappears in *Part II* where it becomes somewhat clearer.

[10] AMC 3.14.1

[11] AMC 3.14.2, emphasis added

[12] Which is simply another way of saying that grace builds upon nature.

[13] AMC 3.16.2

[14] AMC 3.16.5 & 6

THE METAPHYSICS

Part I

Dark Night of the Soul

An Enchiridion to Reality

It should be reasonably clear by now that the *Ascent of Mount Carmel* – and, for that matter, a significant part of the *Dark Night of the Soul* – is not, nor was it intended to be, a theoretical treatise in speculative mysticism. It is, as we had insisted from the beginning, first and foremost an enchiridion, a practical guide for the contemplative. Each of these complimentary treatises were, in fact, written largely upon the insistence of St. John's notable contemporary, St. Teresa of Avila, and were primarily intended for the use of the contemplative nuns of the newly reformed Order of Discalced Carmelites. Hence, St. John's almost inordinate preoccupation with the relevance of such practical issues as the *via negativa*, the relation of the theological virtues to mystical experience, natural and supernatural modes of understanding, diabolical deception, and the notions of judgment and error. I think it is very clearly the case that St. John could have written otherwise and dealt cogently with issues of speculative interest to theologians and philosophers alike, but in a greater sense I think he would have viewed this as an altogether gratuitous exercise. The speculative aspects of mysticism – while of the greatest interest to the epistemologist – are entirely aside from the point. They are, in a very real sense, superfluous to the mystic who has not merely speculated upon, but experienced the Absolute and who, in light of this experience, has consequently been completely reoriented to the priorities articulating his existence. Speculation is

319

well and fine inasmuch as reason is held – among
the tenets of Christian doctrine – to pervade the
universe. This type of speculative enterprise may
indeed result in a legitimate, if limited and remote,
understanding of the correspondence between
constituent aspects of the Absolute – but this type of
speculation is essentially pointless, in a larger sense
even meaningless, before the actual experience
itself. A simple analogy may suffice. To wit: it may
be of the greatest interest to me to endeavor to
explore and synthesize physics, chromatics, and
ophthalmology in order to arrive at an
understanding of the experience of the color purple
which – being color-deficient – I have never seen,
and am unable to see. But were I suddenly to
acquire adequate color perception, I would, I think,
dispense with this exercise altogether in favor of the
experience itself beside which the analysis is only,
merely, academic to my purpose, and in any event
would yield nothing of that unique chromatic
perception to me. Nothing, in other words, short of
the experience itself, would suffice. Now, while my

sudden experience of the color purple will not radically reorient my life, the direct experience of God, I suggest, will. For it involves a good deal more than the characteristically brief experience itself described by the mystics. It effectively serves to validate, to authenticate, everything which faith binds to the existence of God. And this in turn will decisively reorient my priorities subsequent to this experience – a reorientation that will result in an entirely new and different perspective corresponding to no longer a perceived, but an experienced Reality. To the mystic, then, the emphasis is inexorably practical, for it is not merely theory, but reality – in fact the *ens realissimum* that he has encountered vis-à-vis God. Does this, then, abrogate faith? Not in the least. Indeed, for St. John faith has been the indispensable means to this realization.

But St. John's treatise, we must equally insist, is not simply a practical guide to mystical union – although it was written as such. For us, as we had stated in the beginning, it is also a propadeutic to the possibility of articulating a mystical epistemology. And while St. John clearly did not understand himself to be formulating an epistemological doctrine in the writing of his several treatises, there are, nevertheless – and quite necessarily – clear epistemological elements, assumptions, and presuppositions implicit within the texts which lend themselves to the development a coherent mystical epistemology. That they do so at all is no small tribute to the profound insight, the keen intellect and precise reasoning of their author. In fairness we must say that St. John clearly understood his task as being descriptive, and not primarily analytical. He was concerned with describing – as much as inherently is possible – the mystical experience in all its myriad and luminous facets; and when, periodically, he does undertake to analyze the concepts involved, it is done of expedience, and only to supplement the account, to substantiate the description, and to demonstrate both its logical nature and its clear correspondence with orthodox doctrine. And this is to say that since the epistemological elements in St. John's doctrine are implicit only, it is the task of the reader to elicit form from – indeed, occasionally to impose form upon – the various arguments as they occur throughout the treatises if he hopes to arrive at that implicit synthesis which binds the whole of his account into a coherent epistemological doctrine.

The Spiritual Night of Negation

The *Ascent of Mount Carmel*, it will be remembered, dealt principally with the 'night of sense' or sensuous negation, and this was seen to necessarily precede the possibility of mystical union – once again, we say 'possibility' because sensuous negation of itself, as we had found earlier, is no guarantee that mystical union will then follow, in the sense that it should causally necessitate it – and this theme is not immediately abandoned in the *Dark Night of the Soul*. In fact, it necessarily precedes the 'night of the spirit' or spiritual negation as one of the antecedents or premises in the logic of mysticism. Nevertheless it is only addressed transitionally as that residual sensibility prior to the negation of spirit which itself is the complete subjection of sense. As a stage of transition, however, the eradication of sense is not something abruptly achieved; it is more a gradual and centripetal movement away from the superficies of sensibility – toward the metaphysical subsistence of spirit. Moreover, very definite subjective indications accompany this transition: for example, meditation and sensible imagination – which hitherto provided the soul with a framework of orientation relative to God – no longer serve as reliable criteria of the soul's spiritual progress to union.[1] In other words, that residual sensibility to both subjective and objective phenomena, both of which are other to God – and this shall be extremely important later on – which formerly provided the soul with a frame of reference in its relation to God, suddenly and inexplicable fails:

"When they are going about these spiritual
exercises with the greatest
delight and pleasure, and when they believe
that the sun of divine favor is
shining most brightly upon them, God turns
all this light of theirs into
darkness ... and leaves them ... completely in
the dark." [2]

This failure of sensibility to orient the soul to God
effectively brings to completion the night of sense
and inaugurates the night of the spirit. Sensibility,
as an epistemological factor, is thus abolished
relative to God.

This may strike us, at first, as a rather dramatic
conclusion; one which we are initially inclined to
see as essentially both radical and readily
contestable. After all, we well may argue, the very
notion of mystical union essentially – indeed, by
definition –consists in the experience of God. And
does not the very notion of experience itself
presuppose sensibility? This is quite a paradox.

How shall we answer it? To what can we appeal that will not at once involve us in a contradiction? If mystical union is essentially an experience, and if, furthermore, the very notion of experience is radicated in sensibility, how are we to understand the experience, not simply as subsequent to, but as necessarily preceded by, the abolishing of the very sensibility which the experience itself appears to presume? We must, I suggest, look for our answer in a more comprehensive understanding of the key notion of participation, and while we had addressed this notion briefly within the context of several previous discussions, it now becomes critical to examine this concept more closely.

To begin with, in the state of infused contemplation, were the soul's relation to God characterized by a rigorously explicit individuation– that is to say, one in a which a clearly perceived and reciprocal relation of disparity existed – then the notion of union would be meaningless. There would be, not merely an implied, but an explicit distinction between that which experienced, and that which was experienced; in fact, the type of relationship generally understood in terms of the distinction between a subject and an object – that is to say, the subject which experiences, and the object experienced. But it is precisely this type of distinction which the mystic's notion of union cannot admit of. We are faced, then, with an apparent dilemma: on the one hand there can be no union, and on the other, no experience. No union because of the inherent bifurcation of subject and object; and, in the abrogation of sensibility, no experience possible of the one by the other. To further complicate matters, were the notion of union unqualified and absolute – presuming, of course, the possibility of union at all, given this dilemma – it would appear to involve, at the very least, the annihilation of the distinct identity of the one or, subsequent to what amounts to a substantival union, a modification in the identity of the other.

Both alternatives are equally unacceptable to St. John. And not merely because they are alien to the mind of the Church, but simply because they are not consonant with the metaphysics underlying his mystical doctrine. In fact, the apparent dilemma is, upon a closer examination of this metaphysics, found to be essentially spurious, resulting not so much from defective, as from incomplete reasoning, for yet a third concept remains to be addressed; a concept in virtue of which issues involving our dilemma, together with the problem of identity, are ultimately seen to be unrelated to our account – and this is the notion of participatory union. St. John had argued the point earlier, and we will restate it once again: Sensibility can, and must, be abolished in a notion of union through participation. As long as sensibility is retained, then the inherent subject/object distinction is retained as well.

The Central Notion of Participation

As we have suggested, however, an examination of the notion of mystical union as it evolves in the account of St. John reveals that this union is not characterized by the subject/object distinction at all – which is an external distinction, one to which the notion of sensibility applies. Rather, we find, it is characterized by the participant / participated-in distinction – which is an internal distinction, one to which an attenuated notion of identity applies. Subject is eternally other to object in their purely external relation. However, the distinction that obtains between the participant and that-participated-in cannot so readily be rendered into terms that lend themselves to this type of complementary antithesis. It is not a relation characterized by inherent and reciprocal otherness, but rather, by inherent sameness – by an attenuated notion of identity implicit within the concept of participation itself. Let us put this more clearly to our purpose. The very notion of participation itself implies a logical antecedent in the form of an existential proposition in virtue of which alone the notion becomes meaningful: the logically prior element – the participated-in, or unparticipated

329

being – is that in virtue of which the latter – the participating-in, or participated being – assumes certain definite predicates deriving from, and in fact identical with, the former.[3] We find, however, that the notion of participation is generally spoken of in reference not to some form of being, but to some form of activity. We do not participate in "beings" ordinarily understood as discrete ontic existents, but rather, in activities predicated of being. But if this in fact is the case, it is not so much a relation of identity which obtains between the two things to which the predicate activity is attached, as a sharing in identical activities, and this is quite another thing. "Activity" clearly is not in itself a substantival existent; there is nothing apart from the activity which itself is merely a predicate of being, and not in itself a being. Activity, then, is not a being, but something predicated of being. What, then, can the nature of this logically prior element be, such that it admits of the notion of identity – especially inasmuch as it may possibly apply through the concept of participation? In the logic of mysticism

330

there must be an essence which coincides with activity, otherwise participation in this activity would never result in an identity between the two elements involved, merely a sharing in identical activities. In God, however – and here is the crux of the matter – being and activity are held to coincide.[4]

In the Book of Exodus – which is really the *locus classicus* of the conception itself within mystical theology at large – God reveals himself to Moses as the "Ego sum qui sum", or "He who is" .God is a being who is active being, that is to say, being understood not simply as static ontology, but as dynamic activity. In the words of St. Thomas Aquinas, he is the *"quod est esse simpliciter"*, or that which is absolutely. In other words, God is an activity whose essence coincides with his activity – or conversely, God is an essence whose activity coincides with his essence.[5] However one looks at it, since God is the *esse ipsum*, the Being-in-Itself, his activity is, as such, quintessentially substantival, identical and coincidental with his being. So understood, it is not merely the case that we achieve a more adequate ontological perspective of God, but at one and the same time we finally arrive at a coherent understanding of the dynamics of union itself. We had stated earlier that our understanding of the notion of participation was invariably tied up with a conception of activity; that we do not characteristically understand ourselves as able to participate in beings as such, but rather, in activities predicated of being, in which case we may be said to share in identical activities, and not in the being itself in which these activities are enacted. But since God is a Being whose essence is activity – to participate in this activity is to participate in a Being, to participate in God; in fact, it is to assume, participatorily, those very predicates which attach to this Activity which is God – and as a participatory relation, to assume, not the identity of God, but an identity with God. In this state of consummate or perfect participation which we call ecstatic union, the notion of otherness, then, does not, indeed, cannot, coherently apply. It is fundamentally, if only temporarily, abolished in what has become effectively an apotheosized identity.

Participation and the Problem of Identity

Paradoxically, however, this is not to say that a distinction does not yet persist, or is no longer discernible between the soul and God. Unlike the Neoplatonists and other pre-Christian, and for that matter, post-Christian, and Vedantic phenomenologies in which the distinct identity of the soul is held to be categorically annihilated in its union with the Absolute – leaving no vestige of personal identity and, subsequently, no latent notion of individuation – the Christian mystic understands himself to be, even in the most sublime, the most intimate moment of ecstatic union, at least implicitly cognizant of his unique ontological status as a participant in the being of God, and not as constituting the Unparticipated Being Itself. The distinction which remains, however – unlike that

which preceded union, and which, we will
remember, was characterized by an irreconcilable
ontological polarity – is now an internal distinction;
it is a distinction ultimately sublated in what is
essentially a notion of participated identity. What
we mean is this: the soul in the state of ecstatic
union essentially possesses an identity that is
ultimately seen to be at once both inherent and
acquired: it is inherent in that the soul is implicitly
constituted as the *imago Dei*, and this
fundamentally reflective ontology presumes the
Absolute as reflected. In other words, the Absolute
as the imaged is presumed in the identity of the
image. On the other hand, it is no less acquired in
that this image becomes explicit – informed, actual
– only through, and subsequent to – in other words,
in virtue of – union with the Absolute; it is acquired
in that its identity as image can only perfectly
coincide with the Absolute – and so be totally,
authentically, enacted, realized – given the Absolute
in that unobstructed encounter we call mystical
union in which the Imaged is brought perfectly to

bear upon the image. Its identity as the *imago Dei* is no longer implicit in the state of union, and that identity, reflecting the Absolute, now of necessity perfectly coincides with it.

If the distinction between the soul and God so understood, however, still strikes us as tentative, it does so because it is essentially incomplete. Indeed, a casual analysis of this metaphysically nuanced distinction in and of itself is likely to precipitate several problems involving semantic issues that must be clarified first if the distinction we have made is not to be found ultimately spurious. Our most important question, then, is this: Has an adequate notion of distinction really been achieved after all? And while we should find it tiresome to ferret out every possible point of contention – and I am certain there are many in this commentary that I have not begun to anticipate – this particular issue at hand cannot be turned aside without our account suffering needlessly, so let us look at our argument once again. In effect we have said that the soul is the image of God and that its identity as such is most authentically acquired and subsequently enacted when it encounters, in that unobstructed moment of union, God whom it then faithfully images. But here is the problem. If the identity of the soul is exclusively defined by, and is essentially coterminous with, the identity of God, it is very difficult to distinguish any individuating factor through which the unique personality of the soul is preserved subsequent to this union of identities. The ontological distinction we have examined so far yields only an abstract notion of differentiation; one which does not seem to culminate in a preservation of unique and separate identities. The image still appears undifferentiated from the Imaged. It is well to say the two in fact are distinct, but upon what is this notion of distinction predicated if the one is held to be indiscernible from the other; if the identity of the one is equally ascribable to the other?

How are we to respond to this? Are we then, by the logic of our own argument constrained to say that the soul, in virtue of the ontological parameters defining its being solely in terms of its reflective nature *qua* image, loses its unique identity in its union with the Absolute? If so, then we have arrived at a conclusion essentially no different from that of the Neoplatonists. And this is clearly not what St. John intends to argue, nor, in fact, do his metaphysics lend themselves to this essentially abbreviated conclusion. For our answer, I suggest, we must look closely at what St. John says relative to the identity of the soul in this state of union.

In an extremely important passage previously cited, St. John tells us that the soul in the state of ecstatic union "appears" to be God Himself [6], and I think that a closer look at what is actually involved in this notion will prove useful. This apparent identity authentically corresponds to the identity of God inasmuch as it is God's image; it is the perfect, unblemished reflection of God much in the way that a flawless mirror perfectly reflects the object held up before it. The resulting correspondence, we might say, is such that the one is indistinguishable from the other. But while there is no perceived difference, the actual distinction between the two is of the greatest importance – for it is precisely upon this distinction that the difference rests between St. John's account and non-Christian or heterodox interpretations.

But let us carry this analogy – which is fairly common in the literature of mysticism – one step further. The mirror – or the soul as the Divine *speculum* – is essentially incapable of reflecting the totality of the imaged, and while this holds true of a material mirror reflecting finite matter, it is truer still of the finite soul reflecting the infinite God. The frame, if you will, of the image can only to a finite extent circumscribe the infinite aspects of God. This does not make the correspondence in which the reflection consists less authentic, only incomplete. And this is to say that, despite actual union, there is nevertheless an ontological discontinuity inherent in that union – a discontinuity deriving from, and radicated in, the metaphysical inability of the finite to exhaustively comprehend, and therefore to comprehensively reflect, the totality of the infinite – even as it participates within

338

it. And this is to say that the distinction which obtains between the two – between the finite soul, albeit participating in God, and the infinite God – is already ontologically explicit.

Let us now return to our earlier question, our problem, really: if the two in fact are distinct, to what, in our attempt to establish unique identities, can we appeal in distinguishing between them if the one is effectively the undistorted image of the other? Well, to begin with, I think it is clearly arguable that the unique constitutional characteristics of the soul are no more abolished in union with God than the constituent elements entering into the composition of a mirror are abolished in the mirror's being actualized before an object. Nothing in the way of the unique nature of the soul or, for that matter, the mirror, is abrogated as a result of its actualization before its proper object. The soul remains no less a particular soul, and the mirror no less a particular mirror. In acquiring an identity with God, nothing in the way of the unique constitutional identity of the soul is

339

lost – quite to the contrary, it is enhanced in the actualization of its created nature, a nature that was created to be the image of God. It is, in other words, essentially a restatement of the axiom that grace does not destroy, but perfects nature. And this is to say that the unique identity of the soul, however modified subsequent to union, is nevertheless preserved within it. It is not the case that the nature of the soul is transformed – still less abolished – but rather, that the identity of the soul is enhanced; in a manner of speaking, transformed, in that apotheosized realization of its nature as image of the Absolute. The complementary notions of reflection and participation are, then, mutually implicated in the moment of union: the soul's essentially reflective ontology constitutes its inherent identity, an identity that is subsequently enhanced and therefore acquired through participation in God in the state of mystical union.

Participated and
Un-Participated Being

Something more, however, remains to said about

the notion of participation which figures so largely

in St. John's account. The concept itself is found to

embody an implicit ontological distinction that is

not simply central, but crucial to the metaphysics of

mysticism. Participation is essentially a concept

applied to two very different types of being

relatively considered: participated being, or that

which participates, and, by implication,

unparticipated being, or that-participated-in. And I

think that we must be clear at the outset that while

the relationship between these two types of being,

considered as such, is necessarily mutual, it is not

ontologically reciprocal, and what I mean is this:

participated being necessarily implies

unparticipated being as that in which it is said to

participate, and unparticipated being, as a being that

is participated-in but itself unparticipating in any

341

other being, necessarily implies participated being –
given a participated being – as that which
participates in itself. Perhaps a different tack will
illustrate the point better. Participated being cannot
be said to participate in another participated being.
This would be tantamount to saying that it
participates in participation, which is absurd. It can
only participate in being that itself is unparticipated.
But this is not to say that this relationship is
ontologically reciprocal. Unparticipated being in
and of itself subsists independently of participated
being as that through which, that in virtue of which,
the being of the latter is derived through
participation. Of itself it does not presuppose as a
condition to its existence, the existence of
participated being. Participated being, in other
words, is derived being, while unparticipated being,
as totally underived, is totally self-subsistent.
Participated being, on the other hand, is not of itself
independently subsistent, that is to say, separable,
from the being in which it participates and through
which its own being derives. And this is simply a

rather complex way of saying that the soul presupposes God to its own existence, and that God is under no such ontological constraint relative to the soul.

Being, Becoming, and the Paradox of Participation

Deeper implications of a profound ontological nature, however, soon emerge from this reflexive relation between participated-being and unparticipated-being, between the created soul and the Uncreated Absolute, for upon closer examination we find that the indispensable notion of participation itself cannot be abstracted from, because in some way it is fundamentally radicated in, the notion of becoming. Our focus up to this point has been upon Being and the aspectual negation of being through the *via negativa*. Notably absent has been a discussion of the role of becoming in the translation of being. Contemplative union (*unio mystica*) is, if nothing else, a becoming – a becoming one with God, however attenuate the union. Through participation the mystic becomes one with the Absolute conceived as God. All this is well and good … until we are prompted to question two subtle, but deeply profound, ontological assumptions in earnest. What, we must now ask, precisely is the nature of this relationship which so rigorously obtains between the mutually implicative notions of participation in being, and becoming. Is not the inception of the first the cessation of the second? In attaining to being, albeit participatorily, do we not *eo ipso* relinquish becoming? If we have arrived, has not all that was itinerant ceased? In short, is becoming abolished in being?

If this is so, however, it is fraught with perilous implications, not the least of which is profoundly inimical to the doctrine of St. John who is quite clear that despite the soul's union with God, its being is nevertheless distinguishable from the Being of God in the way that the most perfect reflection in a mirror is ontologically distinct from that which is reflected in it. In other words, were the soul to transcend becoming and attain to unqualified being, it would be indistinguishable from God … it would be God. It would also be *contra fide*. How, then, do we respond to this enigma? How do we reconcile becoming with being without conflating the two in an ecstatic subreption? St. John regrettably, does not provide us with this answer … but his metaphysical infrastructure, I suggest, does. Let us look more carefully, then, into the notion of becoming in its relation to participatory being in God. Vital issues are at stake here, issues of such metaphysical proportion that our answer will either repudiate or substantiate the metaphysical doctrine of St. John.

To wit: is becoming an inflection of being, other than an inflection of being, or is it coterminous with being? Unless we can cogently respond to this question, the metaphysics of participation itself – a notion central to understanding the phenomenon of ecstatic union – is deeply compromised, and what we have arrived at is merely a metaphysical synthesis on purely speculative ontological grounds. Fortunately, the general metaphysical schema to which St. John adverts elsewhere in passim provides us with an answer I deem to be at least implicit within the text and standing simply in need of further articulation. We must, then, speculate further upon the notion of becoming within the general context St. John has provided – becoming verging on being --- the bourn at the edge of the Dark Night.

The most summary purview of the Western Mystical Tradition reveals, at least implicitly and with few exceptions, that for the mystic becoming is the created articulation of the uncreated eternal. There is no terminus to becoming vis-à-vis the Absolute, the Infinite, the Eternal, and in this sense it is perpetually parallel to it and only in virtue of it. Even while we may speculate that at any given point of becoming, the soul *in conspectu aeternitatis* subsumes as present all the permutations of its being, in all that has been, and to this extent incorporates being even in the indesinence of becoming; that is to say, if we presume that the soul incorporates as present all that has been up to any given point in the continuum of becoming, we still have not arrived at the soul as being – only as a being-such-that-is-perpetually-a-becoming-of. From this perspective, the soul is indeed the *imago Dei* inasmuch as it embraces as eternally present all that it has been … up to this point in its becoming; however, what lies before it is not yet present, nor can the soul incorporate what it is not yet, into what it has been, into what it is has enacted, up to this point of its becoming. The soul may in fact be understood to exist in a quasi-eternal present – but it is a present that has not yet, and never will, culminate in a terminus of its becoming such that it is a being whose being has been totally and completely enacted and can become no more than it is. But to attain to nothing more, to culminate in nothing more, to become no more than what the soul is, is to understand the soul not simply as having attained to being, but having become

347

distinguishable from it. It would be a being whose essence has culminated in being. But only God's Being is His essence, and only God's Essence is His Being.

Rather than having understood the soul as having spuriously assumed unqualified being, we see the soul as the speculum of this *Esse Ipsum*, this Being Itself, as the finite image of what is absolute – understanding at the same time that the Infinite and Absolute as imaged eternally exceed the boundaries of the finite image. However clear and authentic the image, it is only an image in part, an incomplete instantiation – not only of the Absolute, but of its very own being which is perpetually becoming, and is not yet what it will be, and when it is what it will be, it will still not yet be what it will be, for it remains to be more … to become more than it is, to perpetually verge on the Infinite and the Absolute … but never embrace it in its totality. Since human nature can never attain to the ontological status of Being Itself inasmuch as it can never assume the divine nature (even while participating in it), the perpetuity of its becoming-that-always-verges-on-being remains an indefeasible aspect of its created nature (or its nature qua created) – and therefore remains unchanged – even in eternity. What is more, that is the splendor and the happiness, the felicity enjoyed by the soul in what we understand to be the beatific vision. In a word, Becoming is inexhaustible – because Being Itself is inexhaustible in God; becoming, as such, is a tangent to, because it is enacted in, eternity.

The souls's participatory being in God does not, then, abolish its becoming. The ramifications of this understanding are many, not the least of which is a clarification of the state of the soul before the beatific vision. It is no more static than the vision it beholds; even as God is understood as a Being whose essence coincides with his activity, or alternately, as a Being whose activity coincides with his essence (as we had stated earlier), just so the state of the soul *in conspectu Dei* is dynamic, perpetually becoming in perpetually verging on inexhaustible being; perpetually reflecting, participating in, the consummate being of God which is quintessentially a perpetual enactment.

Identity:
Abrogation or Heteronymy?

This further underscores the fact that the relationship of identity which obtains between God and the soul is not one in which all explicit distinction is sublated in the dialectic of participation: a residual distinction nevertheless clearly remains which is fundamentally an ontological distinction. It is, in fact, a distinction between Being-Absolute, and being- contingent-upon-the-Absolute. And this is precisely the distinction between the Imaged and the image, the latter being understood as heteronymously deriving its being from the former. This distinction, however, does not diminish the fact that the inherent identity of the soul as the *imago Dei* is, subsequent to union, radically enhanced to such a degree that what can only be called a transformation occurs within it in which the soul explicitly acquires through participation what it only latently possessed through nature. It is, in fact, very much along the lines of what the Apostle St. John wrote concerning the identity of the soul before the beatific vision of God:

> "Beloved, we are God's children now; it
> does not yet appear what we shall be,
> but we know that when he appears we shall
> be like him, for we shall see him
> as he is." [7]

In other words, as a consequence of seeing God, the soul shall be rendered like unto him. And this is the metaphysics of participation.

As is often the case in a critical analysis of any aspect of St. John's account, just when we think that we have succeeded in putting a particular issue to rest, another facet of that same issue emerges later on in another and entirely different context, and this is particularly true of St. John's treatment of the notion of sensibility which recurs in the opening Book of the *Dark Night of the Soul*. In a larger sense, this is due, I think, once again to the kind of treatise he writes, the protocols and limitations of which are less clearly defined than had he taken to his purpose the type of examination we have presumed to undertake. And yet we ourselves are constrained to follow the itinerary of this development in his account if our commentary hopes to achieve the coherence toward which we have endeavored from the outset. We had stated earlier that St. John had ascribed the gradual failure of sensibility, which he describes as "... this blessed night of sense ...",[8] to the inexorable transition from the sensuous to the spiritual, a transition in which the soul cooperates but which is, withal and principally, effected by God:

"... the cause of this aridity [that accompanies the inception of this dark night]
is that God transfers to the spirit the good

352

things and the strength of the senses ...

[but] the sensual part of man has no capacity

for that which is pure spirit, and

thus, when it is the spirit that receives the

pleasure, the flesh is left without savor ...

but the spirit, which all the time is being fed,

goes forward in strength ...

[although] it is not immediately conscious

of spiritual sweetness and delight ... [9]

Here, as we can see, we are once again thrown back on the problem of sensibility. It can hardly be disputed that the terms "pleasure", "sweetness", and "delight" which occur in the above excerpt are explicitly sensuous terms, and it appears to be an unpardonable solecism on the part of St. John to have adopted terminology fraught with the very contradictions they appear to engender. But what can be disputed, however, is the interpretation, the meaning which we assign to these terms in light of the gradually unfolding logic of mysticism. In effect, to accept these terms at face value, and not as analogical equivalents, is to accuse St. John of violating the very principles from which he argues, a position very difficult to maintain given the type of close reasoning that we have seen and have come to expect throughout his works. So what in fact does St. John mean by admitting of the possibility of what appear to be sensuous experiences in the state of sensuous negation?

Perhaps this question can be answered by way of analogy and in terms that lend themselves less readily to a sensuous interpretation of the type St. John appears to imply. Clearly there are different kinds of pleasures subsequent to different kinds of activities. The delight, for example, which a mathematician might experience in resolving a complicated differential equation is clearly of another kind to that experienced by a child savoring sweets. The one pleasure derives from the abstract contemplation of an intellectual good, the other from the sensory experience of a perceived physical good. These pleasures are clearly of a different kind; that is to say, the difference is not one susceptible to being quantified – it is not the case that the mathematician derives greater pleasure than the child, but a different type of pleasure altogether. What is more – and apropos of the issue at hand – in not having been initiated into those goods which we have characterized as intellectual, the child is unable to recognize the good otherwise implicit within certain other types of activity. In effect, his inability to participate within activities to which certain goods are intrinsic that are non-sensuous in nature, precludes the possibility of his deriving pleasure from any good not sensuously derived, which alone is the good to which he has been accustomed and to which alone he remains receptive. He is, in a manner of speaking, conditioned to the good (for the moment, the pleasurable) as deriving from the senses, and in order for him to experience the good as intellectual, the physical senses must be held in abeyance as the sole criterion of the good or the pleasurable. And this is very much like saying that the experience of this latter type of good requires a kind of negation of the sensuous. In fact, this understanding of the

problem very closely corresponds to St. John's
subsequent account of this transitional phase:

> "If [the soul in this state of transition] is not
> conscious of spiritual sweetness
> and delight, but only of aridity, or lack of
> sweetness, the reason for this is the
> strangeness of the exchange, for its palate
> has been accustomed to those other
> sensual pleasures upon which its eyes are
> still fixed. Since the spiritual palate
> is not made ready or purged from such
> subtle pleasure, until it finds itself
> becoming prepared for it by means of this
> arid and dark night, it cannot
> experience spiritual pleasure and good, but
> only aridity and lack of sweetness." [10]

Sensibility vis-a-vis Experience: The Problematic

More importantly, what may be said of these pleasures and goods that the soul is capable of experiencing and which St. John briefly describes above? In what, precisely, do these pleasures consist, and why are they experienced? In short, what are they? St. John is very clear in the passage above that such pleasures may be legitimately anticipated subsequent to, though not necessarily as a consequence of, a clearly defined preparatory process – and what is particularly noteworthy is that the requisite preparation consists, paradoxically, in sensuous negation. In other words, the pleasures that the mystic may anticipate are not merely inaccessible, but essentially unavailable until the manifold of sensibility has been effectively abolished. And unless we are able to make a distinction between sensibility and experience, the notion of pleasure abstracted from sensibility will

be a very odd notion indeed. After all, sensibility –
or the ability to be sensibly affected – is, by and
large, not simply a component, but a presupposition,
of experience. It goes without saying that the notion
of sensation presupposes the notion of sensibility.
And the notion of sensation, in turn, while not
strictly tautological with, is more often than not
defined in terms of, experience; to such an extent, in
fact, that we should find it very difficult to
understand an individual, for example, who claims
to have had the sensation of "hot" apart from any
experience of it. Our question then is, while we
cannot understand the notion of sensibility apart
from experience, can we understand the notion of
experience apart from the notion of sensibility?
This, however, is not to say, as I suggested a
moment ago, that the two notions are therefore
effectively tautologous, or interchangeable. We can
be said to experience the sensation of heat, but we
cannot be said to have a sensation of the experience
of heat. We do not sense experiences. We

experience the senses, or more accurately, reports of phenomena delivered by the senses.

There is, then, a very clear distinction to be made between sensibility and experience. Moreover, despite the relationship between sensibility and experience that is, by and large, perceived as being mutual, even this mutuality itself can only be predicated of certain kinds of experience that are explicitly sensuous in nature to begin with. What is more, there are many other types of experiences to which nothing physically sensible corresponds. For example, our experience of delight in being given, say, a relic – is a type of experience that is independent of the tactile, sensible phenomena associated with the relic. It may be said to derive from the relic, but the experience itself is not one of the relic; rather, it is one that arises from our possession of the relic in a sense that is not strictly tactile. That is to say, our experience of the delight of possession is different from our experience of the tactile quality of the relic. Nor is the experience of the one, simply because it is tactile, more real or specific than the experience of the other. And the upshot of our entire argument is simply this: the apparent contradiction engendered by St. John's use of the terms delight, sweetness, and pleasure – terms typically understood in a context of sensibility – subsequent to the soul's induction into sensuous negation, is now seen to be no contradiction at all. But more importantly it means that the notion of experience extricated from a rigorous association with sensibility is in fact a coherent notion relative to the purely spiritual intuition of God subsequent to the abolishing of sensibility.

But let us say something more of the nature of these experiences themselves. It might be argued that these experiences, in and of themselves, appear to be extrinsic to that direct experience of God in which union consists; indeed, that such experiences are fundamentally subjective in nature and as such are merely accidental in a causal way to God's presence. That, in fact, as purely subjective experiences they do not essentially pertain to that direct experience of union which is the participatory assimilation of the soul into God in which nothing explicitly other to God remains. In light of all this, are we really prepared to argue that these experiences, experiences that are apparently radicated in the subjectivity of the soul, constitute an essential feature of the mystical experience, and not, after all, one merely accidental to it? For unless we can come to terms with this objection, it becomes extremely unclear why St. John would advert to these experiences at all – and in so doing occasion this apparent contradiction.

When we consider this objection closely, however, we find that it fails either to discern or to adequately explore two indispensable factors entering into any coherent understanding of the mystical experience: the notion of participation and the nature of God. It is indeed arguable, in fact I shall proceed to argue as much, that these experiences are, in the logic of mysticism, not merely accidental to God's presence, as we might have mistakenly supposed, but rather are logically consequent to a fully articulated understanding of participation – in which the soul's experiences are in fact the experiences of God. Moreover, they are fully experiences of God in a twofold sense: they are the experience of God himself – which is at one and the same time a participation in God's experience of Himself. Now, we hasten to add that this is not to deny the subjectivity of such experiences, for such a denial is clearly impossible – there is no such thing as an "objective" experience, of an experience not related to a subject. But it is a shared subjectivity implicit within, and deriving from, the soul's mystical and participative union with God in which the experience of joy, sweetness, etc., is that felicity which God experiences within himself, and which – as essential to the nature of God – is that in which the soul is understood to be participating through its union with him. The soul, in other words, experiences the felicity of God by virtue of its participating in God – and because it is participatory, this experience is also subjective.

While such an understanding goes a long way in clarifying this particular, if only apparent inconsistency in St. John's doctrine, it hardly serves to exhaust our understanding of this transitional phase to which St. John devotes fully one half of the *Dark Night of the Soul*. It is extremely important to understand that, as phase of transition in an otherwise dynamic development, it is bound to suffer from that characteristic indeterminacy that is always latent in any notion of becoming. Anything on the verge of becoming is neither totally what is was, nor what it shall be. And it is precisely this intermediate penumbra, vacillating between the superficies of sense and spirit in which the soul is at once both and neither, which poses perhaps the single greatest challenge to an understanding of mysticism. Not infrequently, problems encountered in an approach from one of the two perspectives result from suppressed theses answerable only in terms of their alternatives, much as we had found to be the case with the apparently inconsistent notion of the pleasurable relative to union. These apparent inconsistencies – and there are many – demand a place in our account. Some of them, like beads of mercury, may at first elude our grasp until in frustration we hammer them with analysis against the anvil of the text and find, after sorting out the pieces, that when brought together once again the whole is coherent in a way we had not first fully understood. And very much like the bead of mercury, in the end we shall find that reason, after all, may merely touch upon, but never enter into that divine circle penetrable only through faith.

The Imperative of Passivity

St. John, we will remember, has been unmistakably clear that this transition from the sensuous to the spiritual presupposes; indeed, requires, a disposition of total passivity on the part of the soul. In fact, that cooperation with the Divine initiative which throughout has characterized the soul's movement toward union is, from the very beginning, directed precisely toward attaining this state of passivity that is both consequent to, and is now seen to have been the principal goal of, the *via negativa* in each of its multifaceted aspects. And what this essentially means is that all the contradiction and contrariety which has been an impediment to the soul in its quest for union is, in one form or another, ultimately seen to be occasioned by activity on the part of the soul, activity that effectively precludes the activity of God within it:

> "... the beginning of contemplation ... is
> secret and hidden from the very person
> that experiences it; ... [and] the souls to
> whom this comes to pass [must be]
> troubled not about performing any kind of
> action, whether inward or outward ...
> It does its work when the soul is most at
> ease and freest from care ... For in such
> a way does God bring the soul into this state,
> and by so different a path does He
> lead it that, if it desires to work with its

faculties, it hinders the work which God
is doing in it ..." [11]

But let us at once clear up what is really a non-issue
before it culminates in absurdity, and allow St. John
the author a certain latitude that would permit the
type of inexactitude that we should find inexcusable
in St. John the theologian. He clearly is both, and
for the most part integrates the two admirably. An
exegesis, however, of the type we have undertaken
must be as flexible as the text itself and where it
must be unsparing in the criticism of concepts, it
must equally submit to the occasional ambiguity in
literary form. And all this, of course, is apropos of
the opening lines in the passage quoted above. In
effect, St. John appears to be saying that we can
have experiences of which we are unaware – and
since every experience presumes cognition of some
sort, this strikes us as patently absurd. And so
understood it is. But to succumb to this overly
rigorous interpretation is really a failure to come to
terms with the limitations of the text which had
already been set out beforehand. Yes, we can press

the point and accuse St. John of carelessness, but I really think it is unnecessarily punitive, and in the end, quite trivial. St. John simply means that the beginning of contemplation occurs in the soul "secretly", as he would say, or in such a way that the soul is unaware of what God is effecting within it; a point we had addressed earlier in another context. This small matter having been clarified, we can now pass on to what is actually significant in the text.

While it is true that the soul cooperates with God in order to arrive at the passive state of negativity, it is equally and paradoxically true that its achieving this state is not the result of the efforts of its own will – except negatively considered. Were it in fact the case that the soul attained this passive state by its own efforts, then in effect the soul would be subject to no limitations that had not been voluntarily appropriated in the first place, and the subsequent exercise of its will would alone determine the extent to which these limitations were in fact actual constraints. Rather simply put, limitations not independent of volition are really no constraining limitations at all. And it is clearly St. John's argument that it is ultimately God who is leading the soul into these various nights, the conditions of which, once entered into, are no longer subject to the soul's volition. And this is further to say that the notion of volition apparently extends no further than the soul's implicit accession to be subject to new limitations, an assent – already presumed in the soul's ascetical activity described in the *Ascent of Mount Carmel* – to limitations imposed no longer by nature, but by spirit.

Let us sort this out a bit more. In having left the limitations – generally construed in terms of physical laws – imposed on the will by the order of nature (our will, for example, is constrained by laws which prevent us from passing through walls, should we will to do so), the soul has, upon the inauguration of the night of the spirit, simultaneously subjected itself to other limitations constraining the will in the order of the spirit. We have seen, by way of illustration, that the will is unable to engage discursive reason – it is effectively constrained from doing so by the principles of the *via negativa* through which alone the soul gained access to the spiritual order in the first place. It is not the case, then, that limitation is abolished. In one form or another it is metaphysically inherent in the very ontological structure of the soul. But while it is not abolished, the parameters defining the concept of limitation are translated, redefined, to accord with a different metaphysical environment into which the concept itself has been brought. It is a limitation of mind or spirit analogous to the former physical limitations experienced in the order of nature. This seems to be clearly maintained by St. John when he makes such statements as the following:

> "The soul can no longer meditate or reflect
> in the imaginative sphere
> of sense ...[12].. its inability to reflect with the
> faculties grows ever greater
> ... and brings the ... and brings the workings
> of the sense to an end ..." [13]

369

But we must be careful, on the other hand, not to construe this development as depriving the will of its freedom. In every event, in every movement, the soul remains free by an act of will to spurn the divine embrace and to disengage itself from these new constraints simply by rejecting the *via negativa* – and all the limitations subsequent to it – by the same formal act of the will through which it first submitted to them. It is not that freedom of the will has been relinquished, but rather, that freedom has been redefined in light of newly acquired limitations.

Consent, Constraint, and the Paradox of Freedom

But what precisely are these limitations to which the soul has consented, and by what is it constrained? St. John, regrettably, is not clear on this point, but then again, neither should we expect him to be. It is undoubtedly and unavoidably a shortcoming in any type of exegesis that attempts to extrapolate concepts only latent in a text, that the systematic schema toward which it strives as an end, and around which the coherence of its own account evolves, tends to unfairly indict its source as defaulting in a systematic obligation that was never its intended purpose to begin with. In very deed, were this the case our own present study would be altogether superfluous. While it is true that St. John does not elucidate on the nature of these limitations, they nevertheless compel our interest as vital components to our understanding the complexity of the transition in which they occur and the effect on the will as a consequence of it. These limitations, let us say, first of all appear to be relative to the order of nature. From the entire line of argument that St. John has pursued up to this point we may say that these limitations are subsumed under a more comprehensive relation of opposition existing between spirit and nature which we had earlier discussed at length. These limitations, in fact, are readily translated into

371

functions of opposition in which the corresponding and diametrical attributes of each order (finite/infinite, temporal/eternal, etc.) delimit the possible functions of the soul within each respective order. That is to say, the limitations which the soul experiences in either sphere function in accordance with the broader ontological demands of each order. Once introduced into the spiritual order – the demands of which, it will be remembered, required the negation of nature – the soul has necessarily been inducted into that otherness of spirit to nature – an otherness to which the order of nature, apart from divine intervention, effectively forms the limitation to the order of spirit. As such, a phenomenal inversion occurs relative to the will; for in the order of nature the soul was constrained by inherent limitations in the exercise of its will over the order of spirit – limitations clearly defined by, and coterminous with, supernatural realities which were typically unavailable and therefore inaccessible to the exercise of the will. In other words, the spiritual, broadly understood, did not constitute the immediate context in which the will was characteristically exercised; rather the will was seen to have been limited, confined, in its activity to the natural order – and as such to have shared in that otherness of nature to spirit.

This situation, however, is inverted through sensuous negation, or the negation of nature. First of all, we have seen that the spiritual order is achieved explicitly, solely, through the negation of nature. This in itself would suffice to explain new limitations on the will. But what is more, as other to nature through its subsumption under spirit, the will no longer functions in that context which would admit of its exercise over nature. And what this means is that nature forms the will's absolute limitation once the will is subsumed under spirit. This, however, is not to say that the will shall be exercised, merely that such exercise must be subject to implied limitations; limitations which, in this period of transition, the soul experiences relative to meditations, reasoning, and the like. And yet ultimately, as we shall see, the exercise of the will subsequent to negation is understood in terms of the will's identification with the will of God, and the limitations which it presently experiences relative to nature are in the end overcome, St. John argues, when the soul becomes God-by-participation. [1]

Transcendence through Negativity

As we had seen in other and earlier contexts, the notion of the bi-dimensionality of man figures largely throughout the works of St. John. But we must be extremely clear from the outset that this notion in no way implies a dualism of the type we find, for example, in the Zend-Avesta of Zoroaster or in the eclectic and largely Gnostic doctrines of Manichaeism. It is, I think, necessary to emphasize this point simply because St. John's often graphic illustrations, not so much of the incommensurability, but of the contrariety that exists between God and nature, and nature and spirit, at least superficially lend themselves to this sort of misunderstanding. But to misunderstand St. John in this regard is to misunderstand him completely. It is to fail to grasp an entire tradition that coherently spans from early patristic thought to late Scholastic reasoning; a tradition out of which his own philosophy emerges and to which St. John is intensely faithful. The polarity we find alternately between God and nature, and nature and spirit is, in the philosophy of St. John, a metaphysical distinction rooted in ontology, not a dualistic antithesis radicated in cosmology. It is not that matter, the body, finitude, space and time are evil. Quite to the contrary, it is a basic tenet of Christian theology that God – *ex nihilo* – created matter, and the phenomenal framework in which it exists, as good. We do indeed discern metaphysical incommensurability, perceive ontological contrariety, but within the theological tradition to which St. John vigorously ascribes neither is extrapolated to signify an inherent distinction interpretable in terms of a perceived antagonism

375

between the intrinsically good and the irremediably evil. This is entirely outside the perspective from which St. John writes, for in the end, the distinction to be made is fundamentally one not between good and evil, but between Being-Absolute, and every other kind of being, which is being-contingent-upon-the-Absolute.

Since the bi-dimensional nature of man which figures so largely in the thought of St. John is central to the development of our epistemological account, let us look at it a little more closely in the present context. It should be reasonably clear to us by now that the transitional phase that we are currently examining constitutes both a negating and a positing – in fact, it is a negating of the sensuous which is simultaneously a positing of the spiritual; or, conversely, a positing of the spiritual which is a negating of the sensuous. In other words, to transcend the senses is *eo ipso* to enter spirit as the other of sense, an implied other, latent in that very bi-dimensional conception of man around which the entire phenomenology of Western mysticism is essentially constructed. But what is important for us to note here is that such a transition relative to a bi-dimensional nature effectively results in a unilateral negation – a negation of only one of the two dimensions in which the being of man is simultaneously enacted.[15] And while the positing of the one is the negating of the other, it is, for this reason, not the case that the personality of the soul in either event is extinguished in the transition; rather, it is very clearly understood to be preserved within it. Were this transition, on the other hand, understood to entail a bilateral negation, the result, very obviously, would be quite otherwise – it would not be a transition at all, but annihilation. And this is really another way of restating one of the obvious and irreconcilable differences that exists between competing traditions of mysticism: to the Christian mystic, the soul, or the personality, is preserved through what is understood to be essentially a transition; it attains to union with the Absolute, where other and conflicting interpretations see this not so much as a transition, but as an existential terminus in which the soul is effectively annihilated in its absorption into the Absolute. What is of vital interest to us, however, is the fact that the dimension negated subsequent to this transition is precisely the dimension inextricably bound up with time, space, and matter – such that, to pass into its other, is consequently to pass into a dimension that is necessarily atemporal, non-spatial, and immaterial. And it is precisely these categories which are critically important, in fact absolutely indispensable, to the intelligibility of the mystical experience. They form, as it were, the complementary keys to a mystical epistemology.

Of themselves these negative categories merely serve to underscore, to emphasize, those overwhelming aspects of a perceived reality that cannot be comprehended under the positive and limiting categories of space, time, and matter. But what is really of the greatest interest to us is what follows from this negative positing relative to the inherent possibilities of experience. As transcendent to time (atemporal), such experiences are necessarily transcendent to reason [16] inasmuch as a temporal element is implicit within, in being presupposed by, that passing from one concept to another which cognitively characterizes the exercise of discursive reason. Simply put, reason addresses concepts one or a few at a time and moves sequentially, syllogistically through premises to conclusions, the conclusions always being posterior to the premises – all of which, of course, presumes time. Exscind the notion of time from the notion of reason and reason at once and necessarily ceases being discursive – and cognition simultaneously defaults to simple sensibility, or the sheer, intuitive, immediacy of experience; experience from which reason can no longer syllogize nor upon which reason may subsequently comment.

This, I suggest, holds equally true of space. As transcendent to space (non-spatial), such experiences are altogether transcendent to mediation, for mediation is implicitly a spatial conception, inasmuch as it presumes space as the matrix within which the subject is mediated to its experiences – and this, of course, simultaneously and equally implies the notion of otherness and externality. Subsequent to the negation of space, then, any experience whatever will be necessarily divested of otherness, of externality, of distance; which is another way of saying that the experience will be immediate, as it were, perfectly subjectivized through having transcended the medium of otherness in the form of space. And finally, though no less significantly, as transcendent to space, such experiences are necessarily transcendent to matter (immaterial) which itself presupposes space as that in which alone matter is susceptible to configuration. Given this overwhelming transcendence through negativity, all subsequent experience is, in a sense, translated into self-experience since there is no longer an explicit other to the self beyond the post-negative transition.

Epistemological Monism?

Thus the logic of St. John's mysticism inexorably moves toward a kind of epistemological monism characterized by sheer immediacy and self-experience. But does this mean that the negation of sense results in what must then be interpreted as mere solipsism? It would seem, after all, that to pass beyond space, time, and matter is to pass at once and altogether beyond the phenomenal frames of individuation, and therefore beyond plurality into an inevitable monism. For St. John, however, this is not the case, for just as we had found that the soul's induction into the spiritual order entailed a reorientation of the will given the new limitations to which it is was then subject – imitations radically dissimilar from the former – just so, now the previous frames of individuation – space, time, and matter – are abolished in the inauguration of the spiritual order, and new frames in turn are established which are radically and necessarily different from those previously defined in terms of space, time, and matter – to which the soul can no longer appeal in having subsequently transcended them.

Moreover, given what we have called the mystical thesis – that consciousness is unified in God thorough the direct and intuitive participation in the divine existence – this individuation must occur in the context of a unity more comprehensive than the individuation is distinct. In other words, the principle of individuation must in fact be seen to be a function of a more comprehensive ontological unity; a unity in ontology in which the notion of individuation is modalized into terms of the Absolute and the contingent. And these, in turn, are precisely the elements involved in the recurrent notion of participation. The participant qua image (the image which becomes explicit in union) contingently derives his ontological status from the participated-in as Absolute. His being as participant, in other words, derives from the Absolute, and is identical – qua image – with the Absolute – but only contingently, and not absolutely or essentially. And

382

this is why, in participation, we find that experience metamorphoses into an immediacy of identity conceived in terms of the immediacy of self-experience. Ultimately, the one who experiences, and the experienced are one, for the experience itself explicitly becomes self-experience through the notion of participation. It is fundamentally a realization of the self in its primal essence as image of God – and yet not God, for a residual distinction nevertheless and ineluctably remains in ontology. As image and participant, the soul is not other to God, no more so than the reflection in a mirror is other than the reflected – and yet an implicit distinction persists and individuation as latent-only is nevertheless retained. Much of this, as we shall see, is borne out by St. John in later passages.

But turning once again to the text itself, St. John argues that certain subjective experiences invariably accompany the initial stages of this transition to the night of the spirit:

"... contemplation is naught else than a
secret, peaceful, and loving infusion
from God which ... enkindles the soul with
the spirit of love ... [17] This enkindling
of love is not, as a rule, felt at first ...
nevertheless there soon begins to make
itself felt, a certain yearning toward God,
and the more this increases, the more is
the soul ... enkindled in love toward God,
without knowing or understanding how
 and whence this love and affection come to
it ..." [18]

What are we to make of this? How are these, and
other such paradoxical statements, to be understood
in the context of mystical epistemology? If we look
at them once more, but this time in light of the
metaphysics that we have examined so far, a good
deal more is suggested than would superficially
appear. First of all, the absence of certain cognitive
elements in the experience that St. John adverts to
above are seen to both logically and necessarily
follow from the soul's prior submission to the

protocols of the *via negativa*, the demands of which, we must remember, required a total suspension of the faculties, a suspension so complete, in fact, that it resulted in a state of cognitive negativity. Following closely upon this is a realization that the notion of knowing or understanding any subsequent experience becomes not so much superfluous as essentially irrelevant to the account; indeed, the elements constituting any subsequent experience as such are no longer synthesized through reason to be accommodated to understanding – both of which presume definition in the reports submitted to them; a definition (and delimitation) no longer available consequent to the soul's subjection to the *via negativa*. And this is really an unnecessarily complex way of stating that what St. John really endeavors to verge upon is a conception of the simple, immediate, unarticulated experience in which alone the possibility of ecstatic union consists. And this is further to say that, in essence, the attempt to know, to understand, the experience is to subvert it. It is to introduce the very elements of contradiction to which the *via negativa* was vigorously applied in an explicit effort to expunge them.

The Imperative of Experience ... and the Post-Experiential

But how, precisely, does this contribute to our understanding of mystical epistemology? Profoundly, and in two ways, for the consequences of the immediacy of experience are themselves twofold. First of all, that characteristic hallmark of all mystical experience – ineffability – derives in fact from the irreducible immediacy of experience itself which, however exhaustively described, however carefully nuanced, remains not just primarily, but essentially, an incommunicable experience. Comprehending within itself no mediate elements, the sheer immediacy of experience can no sooner be rendered intelligible, than the sheer intelligibility of pure mathematics can be rendered experiential. Much as we are unable to existentially instantiate the purely rational geometric "point" which merely has position but no extension because it is a purely rational concept – and as such cannot be instantiated however infinitesimal the material definition; just so the irreducible nature of experience does not, indeed cannot, lend itself to intelligibility given the most exhaustively nuanced description. We now see that as a consequence of having relinquished reason – and therefore intelligibility – in order to be susceptible to the mystical experience, such experience is, by this very fact, forever disqualified from the descriptive utterances of reason. It is, in a real sense, sheer experience at the cost of reason as mediate, such that the pronouncements of reason will not, cannot, descriptively suffice. Intelligibility, then, is summarily abolished, both by the demands of the *via negativa* in suspending reason, and in the more rigorous demand for immediacy by experience itself.

But this is not all. The second consequence to follow from this imperative of experience concerns the contingency of such experiences. These "fleeting touches of union" as St. John often calls them are occasioned solely by God and depend totally upon the divine will. The mystic of himself cannot produce or reproduce these experiences that are independently and actively conveyed to it by the agency of God that itself is perfectly free and unconstrained by any necessity not self-legislated. In other words, the extraordinary nature of this experience derives from the fact that it is not experience abstractly conceived as pure immediacy as such, a state of mere immediacy to which the soul is necessarily related as to the condition of the most minimal experience – but the experience of God who is not necessarily related to the soul as a condition to its experience – and this is to say that the experience is entirely contingent – contingent upon the will of God – who, moreover, within himself comprehends perfect freedom such that no constraint conceived as external to God necessitates this extraordinary experience independent of the self-legislating will of God. So understood, such experiences are not properly caused, but willed, and as such are not characterized by necessity, but by contingency.

These pure, non-cognitive experiences appear to mark the inception of the Night of the Spirit, which St. John calls:

> "... this night from all created things ... when the soul journeys to
> eternal things ..." [19]

The realm of mediation – sensible and intelligible – gradually recedes until the imperative of pure experience paradoxically asserts itself as the only residual medium between the soul and God, between ordinary cognition and mitigated epistemological monism. And this is a rather surprising result, for the sheer immediacy of experience would seem, by that very fact, to preclude any notion of mediation whatever. Indeed, we had consistently argued all along to experience as in itself irreducible. And so it is – but it is an irreducible medium between that which experiences and the experienced. For upon closely examining the concept we find that it is neither the one, nor the other, but presupposes each as a product of both in mediating the relation of the one to the other. As the last vestige of mediation prior to union, it is, in fact, that proximate relation to God prior to participation which St. John addresses in the *Ascent of Mount Carmel* relative to the theological virtues. [20] It is clear, for example, that the non-cognitive nature of pure experience is very much consonant with that notion of faith which St. John construes as a type of epistemological negation, [21] and both, we have seen, are in turn abolished in the dialectic of participation. We must not for this reason, however, confuse the two: faith is an attitude toward God given the perceived absence of God – experience is the realization of God. And yet we have equally seen that faith is presupposed by the experience as the condition of the very possibility of the mystical experience. There is, then, a certain reciprocity between faith and experience, inasmuch as there is no approaching God, no hope of attaining to this transformative union, in the absence of faith.

Still, at this point in the movement toward mystical union, the soul's relation to God remains, withal, one of proximity – not participation. A proximity in which a distinction is yet implied and evident between the things rendered proximate. And yet the distinction itself, we find, is often attenuate, for the relation that obtains between the two elements entering into experience is often conflated into an apparent identity in which, for example, the distinction between the experience of cold and being cold, or the experience of heat and being hot, is not at all that clear or critical. Now this would equally account for those experiences of sweetness and joy spoken of earlier which, though not properly deriving from participation in any explicit or noetic sense, nevertheless exemplify the typical obscurity of the distinction existing between certain penumbral types of experience. In other words, the nature of experience is such that it is not always possible to draw a hard and fast distinction between that which experiences and that which is experienced – although in fact such a distinction unmistakably exists – especially in this state of proximity which St. John describes, and which must not be confused with participation.

A distinction, then, is always implied in experience; a distinction, as we saw earlier, capable of being rendered in terms of the subject/object bifurcation. So as yet, no kind of monism is seen to result from this transition to the night of spirit: any experience of God so understood is still defined by an explicitly apprehended distinction between the soul and God, the experiencer and the experienced. But the question nevertheless remains to be asked: must the notion of experience always and necessarily apply to the soul's relation to God? And our answer – St. John's answer – must unequivocally be, no. For while our examination of the notion of experience revealed that, at least implicitly, it presupposes the otherness of God to the soul, we had on the other hand equally seen that the soul as the image of God demonstrates an essential sameness deriving from a fundamentally shared ontology. Our confusion, I think, results from an incomplete analysis of the soul's ontological relation to God in the dynamic movement of the soul to the state of apotheosis in union: the distinction between the soul and God (as other) in the notion of proximity relative to experience, is an external ontological distinction, a distinction between subject and object that is, we had found, inherent in the notion of experience itself. But the distinction between the soul and God (as same) in the notion of participation relative to union is an internal ontological distinction implicit in the notion of the union of Absolute with contingent being as we have already seen, and as such becomes, not an absolute, but a relative distinction.

Proximity versus Participation: an Epistemological Vestibule

Proximity and Participation are therefore two distinct moments in the movement to mystical union, to which two quite different modes of relation to God apply. This distinction, I think, becomes somewhat clearer when addressed in a more focused context dealing with the notion of the self – the notion of identity – relative to God as it occurs within these two moments. In the experience of God as necessarily other in proximity, the self is experienced as radically distinct from God. It is essentially a relation between God and the soul mediated by experience in which the soul defines its identity qua subject in opposition to God qua object – hence the identity of the self is derived apart from God; in fact, we may say that it is derived essentially in opposition to God. But this distinction immediately breaks down in the second moment when experience is transformed into participation wherein no radical distinction is discernible, apprehensible, between the soul as participant, as image, as being-contingent, and God as the Participated-in, the Imaged, the Being-Absolute. As a consequence, the very concept of experience that we invoke, especially relative to the notion of apperception, becomes at once and necessarily analogical. The experience of the self is the experience of God – it is the experience of the self as image-of-the-Absolute, and therefore of the Absolute. And the experience of God is the experience of the self – the experience of that in which the self fundamentally consists qua image. Participation, then, generates a relation of divine reflexivity: it is, in fact, the reflection of God into God – either as the Absolute reflected into the contingent, or as the contingent reflecting the Absolute. In other words, there is only God and God's image – and it is self-reflexive from either perspective.

Several very important consequences are seen to follow from this metaphysics. First of all, it is clear in light of previous arguments that the dogmatic opposition of erstwhile diametric categories – finite versus infinite, etc. – essentially breaks down in mystical union, for the realization of God in the self is at once a realization of the infinite-in-the-finite, and conversely the realization of the self in God is in fact a realization of the finite-in-the-infinite. [22] The two categories are not, after all, mutually exclusive in any absolute sense. The infinite as the imaged is found to reside in the finite soul as the ontological condition of the soul's being (image). It is, in fact, the ontological presupposition of contingent being. The unfolding of this absolutely unique relationship reveals it to be characterized not by opposition – still less is it defined by a dialectic arising out of opposition – but it is one which is seen to demonstrate essential relation. The perceived opposition (not, we hasten to add, the actual ontological distinction) between the finite and the infinite breaks down, is abolished in an ontological analysis that demonstrates God's essential relation to the soul as its presupposition in being, as the infinite-in-the-finite. But what is more, this dogmatic opposition is not only abolished – revealing not opposition, but essential relation – but transcended by the identity of the finite soul with the infinite God in the moment of participation. And this is the divine paradox at the heart of the metaphysics of mysticism. Finitude participates in infinitude. In fact, it is seen to be merely *quasi-finite*, for it is no longer dogmatically finite in opposition to the infinite. However, it nevertheless only remains infinite by participation, and that is to say, it is heteronymously infinite – not in itself autonomously infinite. It is, in a word, contingently infinite, and as such incorporates a residual distinction within itself; a distinction deriving from what is essentially a heteronymous identity of the finite with the infinite.

Our argument, so far, appears to consistently follow from principles to which St. John often tacitly adverts without a good deal of elaboration – but inevitably we must come to honest terms with the text. This is not to imply disingenuity. The broad extrapolation often required of a commentary of this sort is, I think, always at least susceptible to forfeiting something of the authentic thought embodied in the text itself in pursuit of a sometimes elusive coherence that was never present to begin with. In an attempt to constrain this speculative impulse, especially at this critical junction in our account, we must now candidly ask, is it in fact the case that St. John himself explicitly equates the experience of the self in mystical union with the experience of God? It is extremely important to be clear upon this point, for no other doctrine in the mystical tradition has been historically more susceptible to confusion and more liable to error than the notion of personal identity as it obtains between the soul and God subsequent to mystical union. So does St. John indeed make the equation toward which we argue? Unquestionably. Consider the following:

> "... from this arid night [of the senses] there
> first of all comes self-knowledge,
> whence as from a foundation rises this other

knowledge of God. For this cause,

St. Augustine said to God [23] : 'let me know myself, Lord, and I shall know thee ...' " [24]

Now, this knowledge of God that derives from and proceeds through introspective self-knowledge, St. John effectively argues, would be impossible were there not, first, some essential ontological connection between the soul and God. Second, an abrogation of the perceived dogmatic opposition between the categories involved. Third, the abolishing of mediation. Fourth, and closely connected with the first, a coherent notion of participation to overcome the subject/object bifurcation if this knowledge is in fact to be veridical. And fifth and last, a relation of reflexivity. Unless these criteria are met, the mystical doctrine that knowledge of God is in fact available through self-knowledge is at best an untenable, and at worst, a meaningless statement. Having uniquely established this notion central to, but not always coherent within, the Western mystical tradition at large, St. John effectively

concludes his treatment of the night of the senses –
the transition is now complete, and the way is
prepared for the Night of the Spirit.

---

[1] DNS 1.8.3
[2] DNS 1.8.3
[3] This is essentially a variation of the doctrine of exemplary
causation used earlier by the Scholastics.
[4] cf. Ex. 3.14, 6.3; Ps. 90.2; Is. 43.13; Jn. 8.58; Rev. 1.4+8,
11.7 Also cf. ST1 Ques.13 art.11, Ques. 3 art.2+8; De Ente.
c.4; Comm. Sent. 2 d.3 ques. 1 art. 1; De Verit. 9.21 a.2,c.
[5] Aquinas puts it in a slightly different way: "The Divine
nature or essence is itself its own act of being, but the nature
or essence of any created thing is not its own act of being but
participates in being from another ... In the creature, the act of
being is received or participated .... To possess being is not be
being itself ... it [merely] participates in the act of being." De
Ente et Essentia, c.4
[6] AMC 2.5.7
[7] I Jn. 3.2
[8] DNS 1.8.4
[9] DNS 1.9.4
[10] DNS 1.9.4
[11] DNS 1.9.6-7
[12] DNS 1.9.8, emphasis added
[13] DNS 1.9.9, emphasis added
[14] cf. DNS 2.20.5
[15] The one, of course, is held to have a direct bearing upon the
other. A reciprocal relation is understood to obtain not only
between the soul and the body, but between the natural and the
supernatural realities simultaneously embraced and enacted in
the being of man. And while reciprocal, it is not held to be
ontologically equal. The existential principle enacted in man
and understood as his being is not equally predicated of the

soul and the body. The being of the soul, while largely enacted within the body, is nevertheless understood as independent of the body. But the being of the body is understood to have no such independence from the soul. The being of the soul is held to continue after the body has ceased to be conjoined to the soul. But the being of the body is not held to continue after the soul has ceased to be conjoined to the body. Despite the organic unity of body and soul that is understood to constitute the total created being of man, their existential disjunction entails the death and eventual nonexistence of the body – but is held to result in the perpetuity of the soul. In a like manner, the consciousness coterminous with identity is acknowledged not to diminish with a progressive dismemberment of the body, but is, in fact, held to remain intact even as the physical locus of that consciousness diminishes. And this is simply another way of acknowledging that the being possessed of the mind – if you will, the soul – is of another and greater magnitude than that possessed by the body. It is essentially, or at least implicitly, a recognition of the subordination of matter to mind, of body to soul, of nature to spirit. Man's being, then – at least from the Christian perspective – is understood to be preeminently radicated in the soul, even as his divinely constituted nature consists in that union of body and soul before which alone the doctrine of the Resurrection is coherent. In fact, and paradoxically, for the Christian, the possibility of union at all presupposes first the Incarnation as we shall later see.

[16] cf. DNS 1.9.8
[17] DNS 1.10.6
[18] DNS 1.11.1 emphasis added
[19] DNS 1.11.4
[20] AMC 2.I-III, 2.6.1-6ff.
[21] AMC 2.1.1, 2.3.1-3, 2.61-2, 2.8.4-5, 2.9.1, 2.10.4, etc.
[22] LFL 3.17
[23] Soliloquiorum 2
[24] DNS 1.12.5

The Metaphysics Part II:

The Night of the Spirit

The Twilight of Reason

The soul, we have seen, has stood at the twilight of reason; it has been brought to the brink of being, beyond which lies the bourne between the Uncreated Absolute and the absolute contingency of all creation. It is filled with a light quenched in darkness, the darkness ex nihilo from which all creation sprang and from which all creation shrinks. The last, most certain guide, experience, blenches before the abyss and, like reason before it, defaults entirely to faith in whose certitude alone remains the unwavering pledge to transition, to transfiguration in the unquenchable light beyond. Night, then, is the chrysalis once burst from which

402

the soul will emerge in unspeakable splendor, in the unutterable beauty of the image of God. This is the plight of the mystic upon the inauguration of the *Night of the Spirit*. But this crucial transition, as we had pointed out earlier, is not experienced by the mystic as a sudden breach in continuity as our narrative might suggest. Still less is it understood to follow causally from, that is to say, as a necessary and immediate consequence to, the negation of sensibility. It is really the culmination of a gradual, often subtle transformation which God alone providentially effects in the soul; a point about which St. John is extremely clear:

> "The soul which God is about to lead onward is not led by His Majesty into this night of the spirit as soon as it goes forth from the aridities and trials of the first purgation and night of sense; rather, it is wont to pass a long time, even years, after leaving the state of beginners in exercising itself in that of proficients ..." [1]

These two entirely distinct moments, then, although methodologically related, are not logically mediated or causally conjoined. Nothing in the way of necessity determines their relation outside of the chronological order in which they must occur according to the metaphysical logic of the *via negativa*. St. John, in this respect, is clearly aligned with that tradition in Western mysticism, the broad consensus of which holds that the mystical experience results from the beneficence of extraordinary grace alone [2] and is, as we had already seen, and as St. John repeatedly points out, entirely dependent upon God's initiative. But what is of particular interest to us here is what follows once this initiative is exercised on the part of God. And here, once again, as in every transition, we find the *via negativa* inexorably implementing the logic of mysticism, for this *night of the spirit* to which the soul is invited is in fact the negation of spirit – the negative moment in which God, according to St. John:

"... strips [the soul's] faculties ... leaving the understanding dark, the will dry,

the memory empty, and the affections in the deepest affliction, taking from the

soul the pleasure and experience of spiritual blessings which it had aforetime,

in order to make of this privation one of the principles which are requisite in

the spirit so that there may be introduced to it and united with it the spiritual

form which is the union of love." [3]

The *Via Negativa*, Annihilation, and Pre-Noetic Transition to Union

The principle of which St. John speaks in the above passage is unquestionably that of the *via negativa* of which we have had ample illustration in the Ascent. But while the role of the *via negativa* in the Ascent was purely predispositional to the possibility of union and rendered the soul merely proximate to God, this multifarious principle of negativity now assumes a significance inseparable from, and in fact coterminous with, the mystical experience itself. It is no longer a factor merely contributing to predisposition and proximity, but is finally seen to be contemporaneous with, and the occasion of, the divine infusion itself:

> "When the faculties had been perfectly
> annihilated ... together with the
> passions, desires, and affections of my soul
> ... I went forth from my own
> human dealings and operations to the
> operations and dealings of God.
> That is to say, my understanding went forth
> from itself, turning from the
> human and natural to the divine ... And my
> will went forth from itself,
> becoming divine; for being united with
> divine love ... it loves ... with
> purity and strength from the Holy Spirit ...

and the memory has become
transformed into eternal apprehensions of
glory ..." [4]

But how, we must ask, is this accomplished through the *via negativa*? Why is it now seen to be invested with the extraordinary significance of being the occasion (albeit not the cause) of mystical experience, such that St. John would be able to state that when the faculties have been perfectly annihilated it becomes one with God to such an extent that its operations may be said to the operations of God? For our answer, we must look closely once again to the text itself – but only after posing a more fundamental question still, a question relative to an earlier statement made by St. John which, I think, carefully considered, will provide us the means around which to formulate the answer to our present question. To wit, how are we to understand St. John's contention that:

> "... [the *via negativa*] is one of the principles which are requisite in the spirit

so that there may be introduced to it and united with it the spiritual form of the spirit which is the union of love." [5]

The principal role of the *via negativa* as an existential application of the logical law of non-contradiction to metaphysically incommensurable categories had, of course, consisted in removing, or more properly, negating, all those elements antagonistic to the soul's union with God. In this role, however, the *via negativa* had functioned merely propadeutically: in rendering the soul proximate to God through eliminating all contrariety with God, it merely predisposed the soul, made it receptive, to the possibility of union. However, we had equally seen that an ontological gap, one interpretable in terms of experience and opposition, nevertheless remained which the *via negativa* of itself could not negotiate. The transition, we had found, implied nothing in the way of necessity such that union with God followed as a consequence – rather, we had understood it to be solely dependent upon the free will of God. If this, then, is the case – as indeed it is – our next question really ought to be this: how, in fact, does God accomplish this transition? That is to say, given the divine will, by what means is this transition effected?

While it is undeniably within the province of God to summarily bring the soul to the fullness of union by a simple fiat, this has been neither the experience nor the testimony of the mystics in general – nor is it that of St. John. Like every other movement that we have observed along the mystical continuum, the transition is not sudden, abrupt, or immediate, but gradual; so gradual in fact as to be at first imperceptible – a phenomena to which St. John has already alluded.[6] So what is the means, what is this secret corridor through which the contemplative is conducted to God across that great ontological divide to which the soul was brought by the *via negativa*, but beyond which, of itself, it could not pass? It is quite simply this: annihilation. Annihilation is at once the end of the souls journey beyond contrariety, and the beginning of the soul's union in likeness. It is the beginning of the end of the one that is the ending of the beginning of the other. In other words, the perfect annihilation of which St. John speaks is at once the pre-noetic transition to union – already! Annihilation for the mystic is the first and darkest moment of union. The last and final vestige of mediation that precluded union – which we had seen to exist in the notion of experience – vanishes in this perfect annihilation; an annihilation that leaves the existence-only of the soul and God as the condition of that existence.

The soul, in effect, is annihilated in every aspect of its being except its being-only, which necessarily is – and implicitly had always been – in union with God as the condition of its existence, a union shortly to become noetically explicit. So understood, annihilation is not a necessary consequence to the *via negativa*. The farthest, in fact, that the *via negativa* can bring the soul is to the sheer immediacy of experience-only which had always implied a distinction – and therefore could not produce union – between the experiencer and the experienced. And this distinction can only be expunged through the annihilation of every aspect of the soul's being with the sole exception, as we had said, of its being-only – which being derives from God, and which then to extinguish is to utterly nullify. If, therefore, annihilation is not a consequence of the *via negativa* – then it can only be effected by the divine will alone, which is to say, by God.

But if the *via negativa* can only carry the mystic so far, to advert to our earlier question, how are we to understand it as concurrent with and the occasion of the mystical experience? Clearly, as we have seen it to function thus far, it cannot, as a principle and without modification, remain in the soul through, and accompany it beyond, annihilation: its function, as we have repeatedly seen, presumes contrariety and therefore distinction – distinction which we had just argued to have been abolished through annihilation. And while this is completely true, it also appears to be true that the *via negativa* itself undergoes a functional transformation. The principle, at least as we had understood it to function previously, is no longer viable – and yet St. John is clear that this principle is nevertheless "requisite in the spirit so that there may be introduced to it and united with it the spiritual form of the spirit which is the union of love." And this is to say that St. John is arguing it to be an integral part of union with God. How can this be?

Well, let us approach our answer this way. St. John effectively argues that the *via negativa* is a principle in the soul. What does he mean by this? Essentially that the *via negativa* itself constitutes a unique aspect of the soul's participation in God; a participation in that nature of God which is the necessary self-separating of God from his creation. In other words, the *via negativa*, we find, is implicit in God's otherness to his creation. It is a divine principle intrinsic to and eternally enacted in God – and as such, it is, *eo ipso*, in the soul as the image of God; the image that is fully and authentically reappropriated through participation. It is the occasion of union because it is already a union with

God in his otherness to nature. What was the separation of nature relative to God, is now the separation of God relative to nature. In exercising itself in the *via negativa* prior to participation, the soul, in fact, was enacting a process intended not simply to remove contrariety to God – but at once to reveal its authentic nature as the image of God.

The Prologue to Ecstatic Union

The night of spirit, then, is in fact the prologue to ecstatic union, a union already marginally effected – but as yet ante-noetic in the negativity of spirit. In other words, it is the celebrated "unknowing" that immediately precedes consciously realized participation:

> "the beginning of ... contemplation ... is secret from the very person that experiences it. [7] ... [for of] this spiritual

night... very little is known ... even
by experience." [8]

And it is precisely because this *night of the spirit* is
pre-noetic that the *via negativa* is held by St. John
to be not only requisite to, but contemporaneous
with, and in fact the occasion of, not simply union –
which, as we had seen, may be "secretly" effected
apart from any awareness whatever – but the
unfolding of conscious mystical union. That is to
say, given this final transition from proximity to
participation the *via negativa* assumes an altogether
different task even while its function remains the
same: it is no longer a principle of absolute
negativity – a negating that results in sheer negation
– as it was prior to the soul's induction into spirit.
Rather, it paradoxically assumes distinct positive
characteristics. It is now a negating that is a
positing: a negating of the superficies of being that
simultaneously reveals the being-essential, the
being-fundamental underlying the superficial strata
of being that has no ontological consonance with
that fundamental being which is being the image of

414

God. In other words, in negating, it discloses– and as such, its movement is in fact contemporaneous with, and the occasion of, fully-realized union with God. What is more, this further means that even prior to conscious participation there is already an effective ontological participation which then, and only then, becomes consciously noetic upon the completion of the work of the *via negativa*. We now can see that it is not the case that the *via negativa* caused this union, but rather, that it made this union conscious, noetic, explicit. It is God, rather, who is the cause of this union through his creation of the soul in his image, an image whose being is ontologically radicated in the Being Imaged.

Preempting the Problem of "Spiritual Forms"

In our eagerness to pursue this point, however, we have neglected to address an equally interesting and relevant concept that St. John brings up in a passage recently cited concerning the notion of a "spiritual form." In order to avoid any subsequent confusion from a misunderstanding of this notion, it is very much worth reviewing:

"... [to be] united ... with ... the spiritual form of the spirit is the union of love." [9]

This spiritual form of which St. John speaks is more clearly and intimately connected with the notion of ecstatic union than would immediately appear, and it is not entirely, or at least immediately clear why St. John chooses to render it with an abstraction that is typically absent elsewhere. We may be inclined to think it entirely likely that he chose to do so simply to emphasize a sense of contextuality in dealing with this increasingly recondite *Night of the Spirit*. In any event, the term unquestionably lends itself to being construed as synonymous with "God", and our question is, is that in fact the case? In a word, yes. It is really a *locus classicus* in scholastic philosophy with which St. John was entirely familiar since Thomism was the dominant philosophy taught at the University of Salamanca at which St. John matriculated in 1564. For example, in refuting the objection that God is composed of matter and form, Aquinas argues the following:

> "... every agent acts by its form, and so the
> manner it which it has its form is
> the manner in which it is an agent.
> Therefore, whatever is primarily and
> essentially an agent must be primarily and
> essentially a form. Now God is the
> first agent, since He is the first efficient
> cause ... He is therefore of His essence
> a form ..." [10]

It is not, therefore, merely highly probable, but virtually certain, that St. John's use of the term "spiritual form" in fact derives from Aquinas's own analysis of divine agency in terms of form – and in fact is identifiable with God who is both form and spirit. [11] This entire development, however, suggests something more than the sense of mere contextuality to which we were inclined to attribute

417

this nominal transition. It is, I think, much more likely – especially in light of what we have recently discussed – that at this stage of the development of his mystical doctrine St. John wishes to emphasize that it is God alone who is the sole agency in the mystical experience, and that this union of pure agency [12] with the passive (the negated) soul is essentially that in which the mystical experience – the state of apotheosized being – consists. We may even go so far as to say that the being of the soul immediately prior to union is essentially a not-being (which is not to say a non-being): it is being negatively considered, or perhaps better yet, being reduced to the primal activity of being-only, to which no other (positive) predicates attach. It is being extensively negated of every other attribute, the *actus essendi* [13] whose activity is merely that of being and not of being thus (or being such and such). As such it is a passive state, for nothing more than being is predicated of its activity, or perhaps better yet, nothing more may be predicated of its activity than this primal act of being-only.

At first appearance this might strike us as somewhat problematic given the sense of ordeal to which the contemplative is subjected in this state, for St. John is very graphic in his description of the suffering of the soul at this point, a suffering which would imply something more than the soul's apperceptive relation to its being-only, but it must be remembered that the unique personal residuum which constitutes the souls being qua persona – that is, a personal being *qua* image of the divine persona – is preserved in the theological virtues as their existential presupposition. But these virtues themselves, we will equally remember, are functions of negativity. And what this means is that the sufferings which St. John describes, far from amplifying the being persona beyond being-only, result in fact from a privation of that being – they are in fact the result of being extensively negated of the persona. And this further means that the being thus left is not being abstractly considered; it is being instantiated in personal being, a being that is a being-suffering–that is to say, being uniquely experienced in the enactment of the dark night of the soul.

Now, St. John, as we have seen, has already argued that this being is passive being. And this is to say that only through participation in union will the soul reacquire active being, and it can do so only insofar as it participates in agency. But we have equally seen that the soul already participates in God ontologically prior to this threshold of transformation in ecstatic union. This participation, however, we had understood to be merely a participation in being-as-such, and not, as we have argued, in being-thus. While it no longer possesses contrariety to God, in its mere being-as-such neither does it possess any similitude with God beyond being as the mere supposition of anything whatever. And this could as well apply to a stone as to a soul. In other words, this type of participation is of the most fundamental sort and really tells us nothing whatever of that of which being-only is predicated, for it is largely being considered negatively. It is the condition, but not the possibility of discourse.

420

Subsequent to the soul's transformation in union, on the other hand, it acquires a being-thus, being positively considered which heteronomously derives from the being of another to which positive predicates beyond being-only not only are ascribable, but in the very concept of which these predicates are implied by definition. Seen from this perspective, the mystical experience is totally dependent upon God as agency: both as the agency alone through which the soul is brought to the state of union, and as that agency in which the soul subsequently participates once union has been effected.

The Empty Vestibule: an Analogical Tangent to Understanding

Some further considerations follow upon our understanding that an ontological participation has, at this point, already been effected, a participation, we have seen, that has not yet culminated in a clear realization that we might otherwise characterize as noetic. The soul has just entered into the first stage of mystical union but curiously its passive awareness remains incognizant of God. Why is this? How are we to understand the soul to be in mystical union with God, while at the same time unaware of it? The answer to this perplexing question is suggested in the text itself, for relative to this inceptive state of contemplation St. John argues the following:

> "The clearer and more manifest are divine
> things in themselves, the darker
> and more hidden are they to the soul
> naturally ... [14] [for] this divine and dark
> spiritual light of contemplation ... [is like] a
> ray of sunlight [which] enters
> through the window which is the less clearly
> visible according as it is purer
> and freer from specks, and the more of such
> specks and motes there are in

the air, the brighter is the light to the eye.

The reason is that it is not the light

itself that is seen; the light is but the means

whereby the other things that it

strikes are seen, and then it is also seen

itself, through its reflection in them;

were it not for this, neither it nor they would

have been seen. Thus, if the ray

of sunlight entered through the window of

one room and passed out through

another on the other side ... if met nothing

on way, or if there were no specks

in the air for it to strike, the room would

have no more light than before,

neither would the ray of light be visible.

Now this is precisely what this

divine ray of contemplation does in the soul

... it transcends the natural

power of the soul ... and darkens ... and

deprives it of all natural affections

and apprehensions ... and leaves it ... dark ...

[and] empty. The soul thinks

not that it has this light, but believes itself to be in darkness ... [15] in this state ...

it is fully prepared to embrace everything ..."
[16]

This passage is remarkable for several reasons. To be sure, there is a clear continuity with an entire tradition in mysticism that is immediately evident not merely in the metaphorical structure of his argument, but in the metaphor itself that he adopts. And while this point warrants pursuit in another context, it is entirely aside from our present purposes. What is particularly noteworthy about this passage is that it essentially constitutes an epistemological summary that properly marks the beginning of St. John's mystical epistemology. It is the first time that St. John explicitly, if only analogically, treats of the noetic element in mystical union.

Before going on to examine the details involved in this cognitive analogy, however, a closer examination of some of the statements he makes will prove helpful in clarifying the critical distinction which St. John maintains between the natural apprehension of God prior to the state of negation, and that intuitive noesis which follows upon the soul's union with God. For St. John – as indeed it had been for the Apostle Paul, who is widely acknowledged as the first mystic in the Christian tradition [17] – all created objects and concepts point to God, or at least in some manner imply the existence of God.[18] Consider the following abstract:

> "... a ray of sunlight [i.e. God: " this divine ray of contemplation ..."] ...
> is the less clearly visible according as it is purer and freer from specks,
> and the more of such specks and motes [objects and concepts] there are
> in the air, the brighter is the light to the eye ..." [19]

In other words, the manifold of cognition is, for St. John, evidential: it somehow implicates or communicates the existence of God. But it does so indirectly; it merely reflects God, communicates God mediately:

> "The reason is that it is not the light itself
> that is seen; the light is but the
> means whereby the other things that it
> strikes are seen, and then it is also
> seen itself, through its reflection in them ..."
> [20]

This mediate knowledge of God, however, has been abolished in the *via negativa* through which the mediating objects – percepts and concepts variously – had been systematically eliminated, and with them, the ordinary mode of cognition which had subsequently ceased altogether. The soul indeed is no longer aware of God, for the objects variously mediating God to the soul – in however inadequate or impoverished a manner – and apart from which the soul has no natural apprehension of God whatever, have vanished, such that:

"The soul thinks not that it has this light, but believes itself to be in darkness." [21]

It is this absence of mediation, then, which ultimately constitutes this "terrible and dark night" of which St. John so often poignantly speaks. It is night from the frames of ordinary reference, from mediation – and hence from cognition. And this would explain why, contrary to what we may otherwise anticipate, this inceptive state of union is not characterized by a sense of the numinous, an awareness of God. It is the empty vestibule of which we had spoken earlier; the room which, to use St. John's analogy, despite its being suffused with light, remains dark – not only because the things with which it was formerly appointed are now absent through the purgative and unsparing apophatic process of the *via negativa* – but because the very walls defining it can no longer be perceived.

While it is certainly true that St. John's analogy affords us little in the way of the close, concise, analytical reasoning that we might in another context expect to accompany a discourse on the first principles of a theory of knowledge, it no less remains that this sort of purely academic inquiry is entirely subsidiary, if not totally irrelevant, to St. John's principle goal which is altogether practical, and consequent to which his task becomes not analytical, but descriptive, illustrative. And while this inchoate epistemological doctrine is only analogically constructed, it is nevertheless sufficient for us to begin a closer analysis of the cognitive elements we find in St. John's description of the actual mystical experience itself. First of all, it has previously been shown at length that the state of mystical union presumes the absence of mediation. And what follows from this absence has particular bearing on our understanding the intuitional noesis in which ecstatic union consists. Take, for example, St. John's statement that:

"... in this state [of negation, the soul] is fully prepared to embrace everything... " [22]

To begin with, how should we understand this very broad but clear epistemological assertion? Initially, I think, we are reluctant to accept it at face value, for the soul of itself – and therefore, of course, its cognitive faculty – we have consistently understood to be finite in nature. It is therefore difficult to understand the sense in which St. John asserts that it is epistemologically capable of comprehending "everything". We are inclined to see such precipitate statements really as endemic to a class of literature only broadly understood as "mystical" and which, regrettably, tend to put the entire mystical tradition into a disrepute of which it is not worthy. Exaggerated statements of this sort – which regrettably but typically abound in the writings of other and less capable authors than St. John – when subjected to even the most superficial examination are likely to result in what may politely be called inexactitudes as likely to derive from faulty reasoning as from poetic excess.

Our question, then, which begs to be generalized but which of necessity we confine to our present inquiry is this: Given the indisputably finite nature of the soul, should we then understand the above statement made by St. John as an instance of this type of hyperbole which even the most scrupulous reasoners occasionally indulge? In other words, is St. John's statement that the soul is "prepared to embrace everything" really meaningful at all in a way accessible to those of us standing outside this closed circle of light? In a word, does this statement coherently follow from the premises that we have understood thus far? And this is really to ask a larger question still, and one which conceivably implicates the credibility of St. John's entire account: how much significance are we to attribute to such utterances – even if isolated – and to what criteria do we appeal in distinguishing between the prima facie value of meaningful statements and their merely hyperbolized counterparts? And this, I suggest, can only be answered in terms of the internal consistency of the text – which is to say in terms of the coherence of the metaphysics underlying it. If this is not forthcoming, if these metaphysical assumptions remain essentially indemonstrable, then the entire enterprise to which we have set ourselves is worthless, or what is worse yet, entirely factitious. So let us look very carefully at this statement which is really paradigmatic of the reasoning of St. John.

I think it is very clear that, for St. John, the soul in this pre-noetic state exists as the sheer potential of no longer limited, but universal cognition inasmuch as the soul in fact is already seen to be participating in the divine essence. And what this means is that when this participation is no longer merely ontological, but is rendered noetic, the soul will equally participate in the divine mind since every attribute of God coincides with his essence – and as such, the soul will share in that knowledge of God which is universal and unlimited. Moreover, and what is of vastly greater significance still, the consequence of this epistemic union has a direct and crucial bearing not only on the soul's cognitive capacity as such, but on the very manner in which this capacity is now exercised.

431

Hitherto, the soul's acquaintance with things in general was mediated to it through sense experience in the case of percepts, or through discursive reason in the case of concepts. In either event, the souls knowledge was always mediate, it was an acquaintance with things through sense or reason; in other words, they were acquired mediatively, and more importantly still, acquired as modified by sense, as accommodated to reason. But now, in virtue of this noetic union with the Absolute, it knows them in and of themselves as purely objective and unmodified realities. Its knowledge is, to adopt Kant's terminology, an acquaintance with *noumenal* reality, with the thing in itself, and no longer as phenomenal, as the thing modified by, to be accommodated to, reason or the senses. And this further means that the soul's perception in the state of ecstatic union will no longer be an indirect cognition of natural objects and created concepts through the medium of experience – which always posited a distinction between the thing experienced and the one experiencing – rather, it will be a cognition of things directly through God. Fully participating in the divine perspective, it will see through the eyes of God, in other words, as God Himself sees. And this, I think, is what St. John understands by the statement that the soul is prepared to embrace everything, for consciousness at this point is no longer the possibility of anything, as it had been prior to union, but of everything, for it is consciousness which has completely transcended all finitude and limitation through its apotheosis in God. The discursive dialectic of reason which discovers the relation among objects and ideas is supplanted by an intuitional noesis in which the distinctions characteristic in perceptions of finite entities are sublated into a type of epistemological monism – not one in which these distinctions evanesce, or are ultimately seen to be illusory, but in which each discrete entity is not dogmatically individuated or existentially isolated, but rather is seen to contribute to, to be constitutive of, the coherent whole of creation which itself not only ontologically subsists through, but is teleologically ordered toward, God. The soul, then, has arrived at this deific knowledge which is both intuitive and monistic because it has transcended the four individuating frames of nature – space, time, reason, and matter – and in having participated in the divine mind it necessarily shares in that single, comprehensive, and universal knowledge which is properly predicated of God alone.

The Vertical and the Veridical: the Problem of Knowing

From a purely epistemological point of view, two distinct vertical moments are therefore observable in the mystical doctrine of St. John: the movement up to God (and consequently to a veridical knowledge of God) in union, and the movement back down to nature (and consequently to a veridical knowledge of nature) in participation. And this last is indeed a surprising consequence, for it is tantamount to asserting that the only veridical knowledge of anything is to be found in God alone. Moreover, it is equally to assert that the authenticity of man's knowledge is, in the most fundamental sense, directly dependent upon the possibility of his participating in the knowledge of God through mystical union with God. And it is precisely a misunderstanding of this contention that piques the critics of mysticism, skeptics and faithful alike, who embrace a more conventional, if democratic approach to knowledge, for the notion of the authenticity of knowledge has, at this point in St. John's account, taken an apparent, if decidedly esoteric turn. Not only is God not veridically cognized outside the state of union [23], but neither is nature – our knowledge under the best of circumstances remains necessarily truncated by our finite nature. That monistic whole, alone in which veridical knowledge may obtain, is, for the mystic, available only through participation in the infinite and uncreated knowledge of God. And where the skeptic would maintain that while such knowledge is clearly conceivable, no such knowledge is possible, the mystic would retort that not only is it conceivable, but it is, through divine dispensation, actually available. The contention really revolves around, not so much a lack of consensus concerning the definition of knowledge, but its possible scope, and this question – very much an indispensable part of our own epistemological analysis – would require a generalized summary that is clearly apart the modest purview of our present inquiry – although we shall attempt to address some of the more pertinent objections arising out of this question a bit later on in our commentary.

It nevertheless remains extremely relevant to our own purposes to explore this question further within our own present context. While it is very clearly arguable that the knowledge we acquire in ordinary states of affairs is a matter of the most practical importance and therefore demonstrates some genuine correspondence with the phenomenal world at large, to the extent that we conceive our claims to knowledge to be confirmed within and therefore validated by experience – a point which, I hasten to add, the mystic does not contend – and even if incomplete, inasmuch as it is nevertheless partial, it is at least partially true, or in some at least limited aspect authentic, the implicit mystical indictment of purely human knowledge – knowledge acquired either solely by empirical acquaintance through the senses or as conclusions drawn from syllogistic reasoning– remains no less valid. Human reason in and of itself cannot discover, perceive, penetrate to causes, for it cannot perceive the first, the uncaused Cause, which is God; it perceives an orderly concatenation of events despite the remonstrance of reason that no nexus is discoverable between them; it perceives in part what is essentially a whole, and what it perceives, moreover, it modifies in acquiring, it subjectively invests with qualities essentially extrinsic to the object; it never escapes itself so it never achieves, attains to, objectivity. At best, man's knowledge is incomplete, and nature, while not sharing that same degree of opacity with God, is nevertheless and at the very least recalcitrant to human knowledge given man's inherently finite approach to every conceivable datum. But this cognitive recalcitrance, both to nature to a lesser degree, and God to a greater, is, St. John argues, overcome in mystical union – and it is overcome precisely because the soul is enabled to participate in the infinitude of God.

Certainly one of St. John's premises is a philosophic commonplace, for it is widely agreed, by skeptic and mystic alike, that man's knowledge, however extensive, is necessarily incomplete. The very notion of complete knowledge implies exhaustive cognition, universal in scope, and of infinite intension; and while we hold ourselves, or the object, or both, either incapable of, or unsusceptible to, this type of exhaustive scrutiny relative to a single item in experience, still less do we presume it possible of that organic unity constituting the world at large. But where the skeptic on his own resources has merely stumbled upon the threshold and has pitched forward into what he finds absurdity, the mystic has abandoned his resources altogether, and along with them the contradictions and absurdities they entail, and has stepped across the threshold; he has then turned and looked back and has reacquired in toto what he erstwhile had only been able to appropriate in part. It is very suggestive, in fact, of certain elements in Hegel's Logic where all the contradictions have been aufgehoben, the quarreling and competing absurdities sublated into a unity greater than their disparity, a harmony perceived in apparent discordance. But it is much more than this superficial summary conveys. The point of the matter is that for St. John such knowledge is only available in mystical states, and this knowledge alone qualifies as totally veridical, for this type of knowledge alone is singularly complete. And what this further means is that the knowledge, the entire truth, of a single item in experience ultimately implicates the entire universe of experience, and that until these latent implications are fully borne out, entirely realized, our knowledge concerning any one item will always be in some way, and necessarily, deficient.

But let us look to the text one again relative to our interpretation of this intuitional noesis which appears to be characteristic of the mystical experience. St. John describes this cognitive transition in the following way:

> "... the soul is to attain to the possession of
> ... a Divine knowledge... with respect
> to things divine and human which fall not
> within the common experience and
> natural knowledge of the soul (because it
> looks on them with eyes as different
> from those of the past as spirit is different
> from sense and the divine from human)
> ... this night is gradually drawing the spirit
> away from its ordinary and common
> experience of things, and bringing it nearer
> the divine sense which is a stranger
> and alien to all human ways ... it goes about
> marveling at the things that it sees

and hears, which seem to it very strange and
rare though they are the same that
it was accustomed to experience aforetime."
24

The problem we confront, I think, is very evident
from the text itself: what in fact constitutes not just
adequate, but veridical knowledge? If on the one
hand we define knowledge in terms of the
limitations inherent in human cognition, what we
really have arrived at is a definition of the scope of
what is knowable and not a definition of veridical
knowledge. And much as we might desiderate
otherwise, in the ordinary state of human affairs we
can hope to achieve no more. But at the same time,
these limitations are, after all, only temporal or
spatial or both: it is not the case that the type of
exhaustive knowledge that we have denominated as
veridical is not at all possible, that is to say, in and
of itself, intrinsically impossible; rather, it is the
case that it is not possible given specific
circumstances, in other words, in a temporal sense –
either given human longevity, for we shall never

live long enough to acquire that type of exhaustive knowledge – or, for that matter, in the more significant temporal sense in which we find ourselves incapable of excogitating an infinite number of complex concepts simultaneously, and in so doing grasping the relations that obtain between them, relations which essentially contribute to a comprehensive understanding of them, for this we do discursively, as we have already argued.

Nor indeed is it possible, inasmuch as we are constrained by spatial limitations to which we are perceptually subject, to grasp any given object of experience in its totality, together with all its dimensions simultaneously; in other words, to perceive or to grasp anything at all in the totality of its being in which alone we may be said to know it, and not merely to know it in part, or aspectually. The problem, then, is this, if we accept the human perspective not merely as phenomenologically descriptive, but as normative, there is no place for the epistemological assertions of the mystics and their utterances. The scope of knowledge has been

442

dogmatically defined a priori – and despite the testimony of disconfirming instances to the contrary. The threshold the mystic has crossed, in short, has brought him not so much beyond the bounds of reason as beyond the limits of accepted experience, and the transition becomes not a transformation in truth but a descent into a preposterous, if elaborate, fiction. The skeptic, in other words, in light of the perceived impossibility, holds the type of knowledge to which the mystic testifies as really no knowledge at all, let alone veridical knowledge of reality. On the other hand, if we take the divine perspective as normative it becomes increasingly untenable to maintain that what we call human knowledge really qualifies as knowledge at all; indeed, given the subjective impedimenta we bring to our perceptions, it is very difficult to assert that our knowledge is at all veridically related to its object beyond its most superficial aspect. If we maintain both, we are unable to account for the apparent disparity which exists between them. Let us put it plainly. If indeed

things are cognized as different in the mystical
state, and if moreover, it is only in the mystical state
that unqualifiedly veridical knowledge is at all
available to man – then what are we to say of the
epistemological condition of man humanly
considered? That the so-called knowledge of man is
in fact no more than the mere apprehension of
appearances to which realities beneath the
appearances do not correspond? Shall we then
argue, as indeed Kant has before us, that given the
kind of constitution we possess we are condemned
to appearances only, appearances beyond which we
cannot conceivably pass to das ding *an sich*, the
thing in itself secreted behind our own subjective
projections? Ironically, these competing
perspectives, I think, both have a place in the
thought of St. John, especially in light of his own
basically Thomistic natural epistemology which is
thoroughly empirical. But I would find the point of
divergence between the objections outlined above,
and St. John's own view on the subject, in two
essentially dissimilar interpretations of the nature of

man inherent in each account.

Empirical Considerations

The first objection we encountered essentially interprets man solely, that is to say, exclusively, in terms of his natural being, and indeed, from the point of view of those who hold this position there is no other provable, empirically available, and scientifically verifiable, dimension to his being – man is neither more nor less than an aesthetic (*aisthetikos*) being, a sensible organism endowed with the faculty of reason and circumscribed by the limitations inherent in the exercise of each. Any other purported dimension of man's being that falls outside the province of either is conjectural at best, or fictitious at worst – in any event it would be beyond the pale, and therefore outside the competence, of the empirical sciences.

To a large degree St. John would undoubtedly have endorsed at least the empirical assumptions in this objection. But he would also have carried the issue further. Recognizing the supernatural dimension of man, a dimension with which he had first hand acquaintance, direct experience, experience as forceful as any delivered by the senses – and even more compelling, more cogent still – he sees man's essential nature to consist in something more than the merely natural and the sensible. And for the Christian mystic this recognition, it is important to understand, in no way implies a denigration of nature and the senses which are simultaneously perceived as indispensable components of man's total epistemological make up. It is a recognition, rather, of an ultimate and irreducible ontological reflexivity underlying the mere superficies of man's being, the superficies beyond which sense and reason alone cannot penetrate, and which, for St. John constitutes the very hypostasis of man's being – a being that is being the image of God, a being-in-itself only possible through its unique ontological status as a being-of-another. Given this metaphysical realization a unique epistemology evolves from this experience, the logic of which is every bit as coherent as that emerging from natural epistemology in the context of its own phenomenological environment – and this is to say that the entire universe of experience, both natural and supernatural, is fundamentally and profoundly rational from an epistemological perspective. The distinctive epistemological contribution of mysticism derives from, and consists in, its relation to the very categories before which natural epistemology defaults, despite the corroboration of experiences it finds itself unable to accommodate. The principles have not changed, but the environment in which these principles now operate has: as a consequence they no longer function in relation to natural, but to supernatural realities. In short, just as the supernatural dimension of man is suppressed in the development of a natural epistemology treating of man in his relation to the natural order, so now the natural dimension of man is suppressed – explicitly through the *via negativa* – in the development of a mystical epistemology treating of man in his relation to the supernatural order.

While St. John's metaphysical assumptions about the essential nature of man have been discussed here and elsewhere largely as logical conclusions drawn from his own descriptive analysis of the activity of the *via negativa*, the question nevertheless remains to be asked: are these assumptions in fact, not just dissimilar, but radically different from those encountered in natural epistemologies of the type previously examined? In short, does St. John have an explicit doctrine to this effect? If we anticipate an answer in the form of an abstract epistemological excursus, we shall be disappointed, for this type of philosophical introrsion is entirely aside from the purposes of St. John. However, it nevertheless becomes unmistakably clear that such a doctrine is not merely implied in, but is essential to, the coherence of St. John's account. Consider the following:

"This purgative and loving knowledge or
divine light acts upon the soul in the
same way as fire acts upon a log of wood in
order to transform it into itself ...
[for the wood] has in itself the properties
and activities of fire... [25] [This] divine
fire of contemplative love, [then,] ... before
it unites and transforms the soul
into itself, first purges it of all its contrary
accidents." [26]

Now, these "accidents" of which St. John speaks are
unquestionably those very elements within man
exhibiting contrariety to God and which we had
seen to have been removed by the *via negativa* prior
to union. We needn't enumerate these contrarieties,
merely to note that among them discursive reason
and sensibility – among the chief factors in a natural
epistemological account – are seen by St. John to be
merely "accidental" to man's essential nature *qua*
image of God. [27] Beyond these mere accidental
qualities, and inaccessible to reason and sensibility
alike, lies a likeness ("it has in itself the properties

and activities of fire [God] ") to God, an image or reflection capable of being elicited and made explicit which we have seen to constitute man's created ontology. As we have said, for St. John, man's ontic being is being-image, and it is this most fundamental metaphysical assumption that distinguishes St. John's account from all others. In fact, strictly speaking, given the several attributes St. John holds to be merely accidental to man's being, his account, otherwise substantially in agreement with, nevertheless in certain aspects differs significantly from, the theological tradition out of which his own epistemology arises and to which both Augustine and Aquinas belong, a tradition in which the *imago Dei* is perceived in terms of the intellect and reason. [28]

A Parenthetical Problem of Accommodation

We hasten to add, however, that this unique metaphysical perspective does not exempt St. John from a clearly defined tradition to which he himself belongs, a tradition that is both mystical and scholastic. His vivid analogy of light entering a dark room [29] for example, has its *locus classicus* in the Pseudo-Areopagite's opening chapter of *De Mystica Theologica*, while his natural epistemology, as we have already mentioned, derives from St. Thomas Aquinas's own analysis some three centuries earlier, an analysis which in turn borrowed heavily from Aristotle sixteen centuries before that. This is in no way to diminish St. John's unquestionable originality; it merely serves to indicate, as E. Allison Peers has pointed out, [30] that a tremendous philosophic and mystical tradition has been brought into focus in the creative mind of St. John.

On the other hand, this is not to gloss over some very real difficulties which arise when St. John attempts to align his own mystical doctrine with the tradition out of which his own theology arises and to which he otherwise so tenaciously holds. There are several passages within the text which leave us with an ineluctable feeling of incongruity, the sense that a hiatus has abruptly occurred in the treatment. It is as though some factitious element that does not readily accord with the whole has been inserted into the metaphysical framework and has corrupted the text. Moreover, when these, what can only be called interpolations, do occur, they are brief and clearly parenthetical to the account. It is as though St. John is giving voice to some alternative perspective to which he himself is not wholly committed. The most notable example of this in dealing with his epistemology occurs in the second book of the Dark Night. After providing a brief summary of his own epistemological account of mystical union, St. John quite suddenly – and, we must add, very problematically – inserts a passage which appears to

generate nearly irreconcilable tension between what
are essentially two distinct and competing
interpretations: the one dealing with the immediate
and veridical cognition of God which we
understand to be the central mystical thesis, and the
other an illumination theory constructed around a
widely accepted model of the hierarchy of being. [31]
In this problematic passage St. John states the
following:

> "... this dark contemplation infuses into the
> soul love and wisdom ... [and]
> the very wisdom of God which purges the
> souls and illumines them, purges
> the angels from their ignorances, giving
> them knowledge, enlightening them
> as to that which they knew not, and flowing
> down from God through the first
> hierarchies even to the last, and thence to
> men. ... each one passes it on and
> infuses it into the next in a modified form
> according to [its] nature ... [32]
> Hence it follows that, the nearer to God are

the higher spirits and the lower,

the more completely are they purged and

enlightened ... and that the lowest

of them will receive this illumination very

much less powerfully and more

remotely. Hence it follows that man, who is

the lowest of all those to whom

this loving contemplation flows down

continually from God, will ... receive

it perforce after his own manner in a very

limited way" [33]

The problems, of course, resulting from St. John's attempt to simultaneously accommodate both theories are obvious at once: the mystic either has direct and immediate access to God through ecstatic union – a point which until now, St. John has vigorously argued – or he does not: his union with the Absolute is, in the end, accommodated through an ascending hierarchy of intermediate beings.[34] In any event, it cannot be both. And yet both conceptions figure largely in medieval thought, the former most prevalently among the Schoolmen, and the latter among the mystics, although as we see, this division is by no means exclusive. How can this be?

To answer this, we must look briefly to the historical context in which St. John writes and attempt to grasp something of the long-standing theological tradition from which this hierarchical conception derives; a conception which, as we shall later see, beginning with Ammonius Saccas of Alexandria, first found its most systematic expression in Plotinus, Porphyry, Iamblichus, and Proclus in the anti-Christian tradition, and which subsequently came to be adopted – with obvious revisions – by Dionysius the Pseudo-Areopagite, Maximus Confessor, John Scotus Erigena and St. Thomas Aquinas within the Christian tradition itself – to say nothing of the emphasis placed upon this theory in the extremely influential philosophies of Avicenna (Abu Ibn-Sina) and Avicebron (Salamo Ben Jehuda Ben Gebirol) outside the tradition of both. For the moment it suffices to simply note the broad historical matrix from which this doctrine emerges in the way of establishing the sense of continuity to be found within widely disparate traditions; traditions which in sum form the basis for this metaphysical conception of hierarchy to which St. John now almost parenthetically adverts. Our immediate interest at this point, however, is not the historical development of this doctrine as such, but, as we have said, lies in what appears to be its blatant incongruity with the mystical thesis St. John had been so painstakingly careful to establish and which, as a result, has become quite suddenly problematic.

Here, for the first time – and for reasons that we shall soon discuss – we find a statement made by St. John which I do not believe to be an authentic aspect of his real agendum, or at least authentically descriptive of his actual thought. To begin with, it is very difficult to understand how an epistemology which until now has dealt expressly with the unmediated, unmodified, and therefore veridical cognition of God as the most central thesis of the mystical doctrine, can abruptly incorporate into

456

itself elements no less expressly mediative and modificatory. Indeed, the most casual examination of the epistemological implications involved in this hierarchical doctrine of being relative to mystical union reveals a divergence so great between the two apparently competing interpretations as to preclude altogether the possibility of an immediate and veridical apprehension of God – consequently, the mystical conception of God, together with the entire mystical thesis itself, is seen to break down under the contradiction of conflicting metaphysics. It is, moreover, equally troubling and extremely difficult to understand how so manifest a contradiction could go utterly unobserved, or at least unresolved, in so careful a thinker as St. John has proven himself to be. Is it really the case that he is guilty of so egregious an oversight?

The evidence available would seem to suggest otherwise. To begin with, we have already noted that a kind of thematic incongruity is clearly observable within the account; a precipitate, obvious, and awkward incompatibility which would seem to suggest something in the way of a perfunctory gesture toward prevailing trends in theological thought on epistemological issues to which St. John remains uncommitted in light of the conclusions drawn from his own epistemological analysis; conclusions, we will remember, which were not speculatively derived, but based upon his own first hand experiences. Within these passages, moreover, the logical coherence that consistently obtains between, and is always observable within, the mystical dialectic that culminates in union – a coherence which otherwise characterizes the writings of St. John in general – is signally absent. Unlike every other significant concept which St. John invokes in developing his mystical doctrine, the most central of which are characteristically treated at great length and in much detail, this one doctrine concerning the hierarchy of being is only accorded an elliptical treatment which is essentially isolated from the overall mystical context, a context, we have said, into which it appears to have been parenthetically inserted. This, I think, is particularly noteworthy and deserving of further consideration. So marked is this deviation, and so uncharacteristic of St. John that, except for the mutual corroboration of even the earliest extant manuscripts, coupled with St. John's own distinctive style, we might too readily be persuaded that this passage was in fact an interpolation insinuated into the text in an effort to make it more closely accord with orthodox theological thought on this subject which, at least within the tradition of Christianized Neoplatonism, extended as far back as the unknown 5th century author of the Areopagitica.

Given the internecine and sometimes rancorous opposition to the reform of the Discalced Carmelites which had been initiated by St. Teresa of Avila – herself a mystic and contemporary of St. John who had closely collaborated in her efforts – together with the greater historical context in which St. John wrote his treatises and of which the Reformation was the most significant feature, [35] to say nothing of the characteristic suspicion with which the writings of the mystics in general were regarded (and quite often with good warrant), it would appear to be virtually certain that the citation in question is, in fact, a conciliatory, if perfunctory gesture to orthodoxy – an orthodoxy, ironically, which St. John never repudiates, even implicitly in his most abstract metaphysical statements. This contention, I think, is further borne out by the fact that the Holy Office – more popularly known as the Inquisition – sat in tribunal to formally condemn some forty propositions taken from the 1618 Alcala edition (*editio princeps*) of St. John's works – only some 27 years after his death. The condemnation, however, was never effected due in large part to the vigorous defense of his works by the noted Augustinian scholar Basilio Ponce de Leon who systematically demonstrated the orthodoxy of each of these forty propositions against the charges of the Office, most of which stemmed from a confusion of St. John's doctrines with those of the Illuminists who held that due to the soul's passivity in the state of contemplation, it was incapable of sin regardless of any act or omission. It is then all the more likely in this theological climate fraught with suspicion that, despite St. John's unwavering adherence to orthodox doctrine, he would find it necessary to reaffirm his alignment with orthodoxy.

While this, of course, would explain the apparent lack of contextuality that we find in this and some other statements of the sort, it does not resolve the metaphysical conflict the statement generates. One cannot have the immediate intuition of God mediately rendered through a descending hierarchy of being. And while I am not suggesting that St. John was intentionally disingenuous in formulating this contradiction, the apparent interpretation would be equivocal enough to conveniently mollify the suspicious temperament of the age while at once allowing an alternative interpretation more in line with his own reasoning on the subject. To put it more plainly, I do not think that St. John consciously contrived this contradiction out of expedience, still less out of duplicity. But as a matter of interpretation it conveniently served both purposes. It was in fact an accurate description, and

it completely aligned with traditional doctrine – and
it was, in fact, St. John's own epistemological
position! But how can this be? Simply in this: what
St. John describes in this problematic passage is not
the extraordinary illumination accompanying
mystical union [36], but rather, the ordinary
illumination accorded man in the state of nature [37],
for St. John is clear that:

> "... this dark contemplation infuses into the
> soul love and wisdom jointly ... [38]
> [and that] From this we shall also infer that
> the very wisdom of God which
> purges these souls and illumines them,
> purges the angels from their ignorances ...
> flowing down from God through the first
> hierarchies even to the last, and
> thence to men ... for ordinarily [this
> illumination] comes[s] through the
> angels ... " [39]

That is to say, this wisdom that accompanies union,
a wisdom co-infused with love, is in fact the self-

identical source of that wisdom with which God illuminates men, through the angels, in the unnegated state of nature. What St. John is saying, in effect, is that the knowledge of God ordinarily given to man through the agency of the angels according to the accepted scholastic epistemological schema, does in fact constitute knowledge of God – but only as it is acquired mediately in nature, and not intuitively in union. By permitting this type of equivocal interpretation, St. John is able to accommodate both without compromising the integrity of either. It is extremely important, however, not to be misled by this passage. We must clearly understand that this mediating and modifying series of intermediary agents – to which St. John adverts out of expedience and in a manner sufficiently equivocal for the purpose at hand – is by-passed in mystical union through the soul's direct and immediate apprehension of God, unimpeded by any hierarchy whatsoever.

This confusing and clearly parenthetical treatment occurs nowhere else in the text and contributes

nothing essential to our understanding; on the
contrary, it serves only to obscure that pervasive
theme to which St. John immediately returns in
concluding his treatment on the dark night of the
soul, the dark night which has finally receded
through the soul's noetic participation on God, for
in these final stages of infusion,

> "... the soul become[s] wholly assimilated
> into God by reason of the clear
> and immediate vision of God ... when it goes
> forth from the flesh ... this
> vision is the cause of the perfect likeness of
> the soul to God, for as St. John
> says, we know that we shall be like Him [40]
> ... not because the soul will come
> to have the capacity of God, for that is
> impossible; but because all that it is
> will become like to God, for which cause it
> will be called, and will be, God
> by participation... [41] In this last step ... there
> is naught that is hidden from

the soul, by reason of its complete assimilation." [42]

The Divine Reflexivity

In these last stages of mystical union, that relation of divine reflexivity, the intimations of which we had seen to occur earlier and elsewhere, is at last finally explicit. The mystical deduction becomes complete. It is clear that there is an ontological connection between the soul and God which is more comprehensive, more fundamental still than the being-only of the soul that derives from the Only-Being of the Absolute; a connection in virtue of which alone a relation of reflexive identity is possible such that " the soul becomes wholly assimilated into God by reason of the clear and immediate vision of God " the nature of which is such that "this vision is the cause of the perfect likeness " subsequently generated. And this remarkable statement, I suggest, can only be understood in light of a metaphysics constructed around man's fundamentally reflexive ontology – his being the *imago Dei*, the reflection of God who is now clearly seen to be not simply the ontic condition of the mere being of man – but the exemplary cause of his apotheosized identity.

This unique mystical conception is not, as we had seen, merely constructed ex hypothesi; it is fundamentally radicated in, emerges from, experience; an experience, moreover, that is seen to accord not only with reason, but with the most incontrovertible theological canon of all – Holy Scripture – for the conclusion drawn by St. John of the Cross is essentially no different from that drawn by St. John the Evangelist when he states that "when he [God] appears we shall be like him, for [because, in virtue of the fact that] we shall see him as he is." [43] Apart from this mystical conception it is, I suggest, impossible to understand how a "vision", a seeing, a standing-before, can produce, result in, "perfect likeness", "assimilation". This vision appears to be the exemplary cause inasmuch as it presupposes a unique ontological matrix in which the perfect likeness to be elicited already exists in posse, as fundamental to, as essentially constitutive of, man's irreducible ontological being as the being-image-of. In other words, a vision, a standing-before, which generates reflection already presupposes a reflective ontological nature in virtue of which this vision is transformative. And this is to say that the soul is already the possibility of this reflection as the unarticulated image of the Absolute. In the state of union, then– which consists in this divine reflexivity – this vision necessarily, inexorably, results in a transformation in the essential ontology of the soul – the soul qua image, qua reflexive – into the explicit reflection of God, and to such a degree and so completely, that the soul in seeing God sees itself, and similarly, God in seeing the soul, in effect, sees himself. St. John describes this resonating dialectic in the following way:

> "... such a manner of likeness does love [union] make in the transformation

of the two ... that it made be said that each is the other and that both are one." [44]

Otherness, then, conceived as a dogmatic distinction, is totally abolished in this state of reflexive identity; it is sublated in that participative union that essentially consists in the reflection of God into God. And this is the paradigm of the mystical paradox. Through transcendence the soul has arrived at immanence. In having gone utterly outside itself, the soul has discovered God within itself. In having relinquished all, it has acquired the All; not in the way of some vague poetic desideration, but as a distinct existential realization. The resulting "oneness", or the becoming one with God, which is a characteristic feature of virtually all mystical phenomenologies, is, in the mystical philosophy of St. John, quite different from every other competing system essentially in this: not that it attains to oneness, but the oneness to which it attains preserves even as it abolishes – and in so doing apotheosizes, and not abrogates. In that it derives, not from the mystical impulse itself in which we discover only synapses of random intuitions that evidence little agreement either among themselves or with reason at large; still less is it capable of being indexed among the theosophical systems which, syncretistically formulated in imitation of reason or imposturing as logic, conclude to a whole that is inevitably opaque to logic, and dissonant with reason. Rather, the oneness to which St. John adverts is the logical terminus to which reason deductively attains through clearly defined and discernible copulas within the logic of the mystical account. And this is to say in a broader sense that it derives from a coherent metaphysics; a metaphysics out of which it arises much as the conclusion to a sorites that has brought us through the *via negativa* to the night of sense, the night of spirit, and finally to the light of union – to the face of God.

We thus find the mystical epistemology of St. John to have culminated in that ontological resonance between being-contingent-upon-the-Absolute and Being-Absolute, between the Imaged and the image, the soul and God. Our understanding of this mystical state, despite the consonance with reason that we have discerned within it, remains abstract, remote, and at best only proximate. Discerning the internal logic, we are, withal, unable to penetrate to the substance. We hold it to accord with reason, but it only affords reason perspective, and not understanding, for, in the words of St. John, not only is:

> "... this dark contemplation secret... [45] not
> only does the soul not understand it,
> but ... the soul is unable to speak of it ... the
> soul cannot speak of it ... it can
> find no suitable way or manner to describe it
> ... and thus, even though the soul
> might find many ways in which to describe
> it, it would still be secret and
> remain undescribed ... it is like one who
> sees something never seen before,
> whereof he has not even seen the like ..." [46]

The intelligibility of the mystical experience, then, presupposes as a condition of that intelligibility – the very experience itself. It is, in the last analysis, a circle into which one cannot break, but to which one must be admitted; hence we find the relatively esoteric nature of mysticism to derive essentially from the inherent limitations of language, language which, as we had discussed earlier, presupposes shared experiences to its intelligibility.

The Perennial Problem of Induction

We must insist, however, that although our understanding of this mystical state is only remote and proximate, the external rationality of the experience is nevertheless available to us; and this accessibility to, this consonance with, reason is a compelling testimony in itself to what is at the very least the probable authenticity of the mystical account. Let us look into this further. It has been seen, by way of illustration, that given certain statements made by St. John concerning the mystical thesis, certain other statements that he subsequently makes about specific types of experience, not just follow, but necessarily– which is to say, deductively – follow. For example, that such states are consistently experienced in abstraction from time is both a universal and uniform feature of the mystical experience. But unlike ordinary facts or features of experience, it is necessary consequence of, and is therefore deducible from, certain existential premises antecedent to the experience – in other words, this experience of abstraction from time is seen not just to follow, but to necessarily follow – to follow as a consequence, as the logical outcome, of certain premises embodied in the *via negativa*. That such experiences are characteristically atemporal in nature follows of necessity from the fact that the suppression of time is the condition of such experiences. Whatever the ensuing experience may be, positively considered, we cannot say – we cannot say that such experiences will be of such and such a nature, for necessity – as Hume has vigorously, and I think correctly argued – cannot be logically ascribed to such assertions. The experience, in effect, may always be otherwise than anticipated, for there is no inherent, that is to say, no logical contradiction engendered in assuming so.[47]

At this vital point we now find that our account has culminated in what is essentially a convergence, an extremely critical juncture between epistemology and metaphysics. Before we can so much as begin to presume to say anything more coherent about the mystical experience described by St. John of the Cross – that is to say, if we presume to pass beyond what is more than merely speculative – we must examine the mystical doctrine of St. John in light of the very serious Problem of Induction. If the mystical philosophy of St. John of the Cross can offer us nothing more than what contemporary philosophy to date has been able to proffer in response to this enigma then our own account has ended on terms no less satisfactory than its secular counterparts, and our own epistemological endeavor has resulted in the same dismal conclusion, which is to say, that we can have no certainty whatever concerning states of human affairs. It is my contention, however, as I had stated at the beginning, that the philosophy of St. John of Cross offers a unique and substantial contribution to the resolution of this recurrent problem. Let us examine this further and very carefully, for in the mystical experience alone, I suggest, we find the one disqualifying instance of the problematic.

---

[1] DNS 2.1.1
[2] Which, by no coincidence, is held to denote an extraordinary sharing in the life of God.
[3] DNS 2.3.3 emphasis added
[4] DNS 2.4.2
[5] cf. footnote 140 (DNS 2.3.3) emphasis added
[6] DNS 1.9.6-7
[7] DNS 1.9.6
[8] DNS 1.8.2
[9] DNS 2.3.3, also AMC 3.14.1+2
[10] ST I Q.3 art. 2, also cf. art.7
[11] cf. Jn. 4.24
[12] ST I Q.44; art.4; De Potentia Dei Q.3 art.15 + ad.1, ad.2
[13] the act of being

[14] DNS 2.5.3
[15] DNS 2.8.2-4
[16] DNS 2.8.3
[17] 2 Cor 12.2-4
[18] Rom. 1.20
[19] DNS 2.8.3
[20] ibid.
[21] DNS 2.8.4
[22] DNS 2.8.5
[23] cf. SC 6.4 ff.
[24] DNS 2.9.5
[25] DNS 2.10.1
[26] DNS 2.10.2 emphasis added
[27] This, incidentally, is not to say that the soul does not reflect that consummate reason which is to be found in the Divine intellect, much less that God is not rational. This reason exhibited in God which the soul reflects participatorily is the ratio of St. Augustine (cf. Solil. 1.12-13; De Immort. Anim. 6.11; 7.12; also cf. De Trin. 15.14 [Patrologiae Latinae 42 1077] and St. Thomas Aquinas (ST I Ques. 14 art. 7). It is intuitively exercised, and is not, therefore, to be confused with its discursive counterpart in man which, while a function of that same reason, is only finitely applied.
[28] cf. Aquinas, ST I Ques. 3 art.1 rep. obj. 2; Ques. 45 art.7; Ques. 93 art.1-9; and Augustine, De. Genes. Ad Lit. 6.12; De Trin. 14.16; De Civit. Dei 11.26
[29] also cf. DNS 2.5.3 and SC 13/14.16
[30] E. Allison Peers, Ascent of Mount Carmel (Garden City, New York: Image Books, Doubleday & Co., 1958), 48, Intro.
[31] The passage which follows. incidentally, derives from Aquinas (cf. ST I Ques. 106 art. 1 ad.1) who adopted it from the Pseudo-Areopagite (De Hierarchia Caelesti), who in turn borrowed it from Plotinus (Enneads 5.1-11).
[32] DNS 2.12.3 emphasis added
[33] DNS 2.12.4
[34] Specifically, the choir of angels.
[35] That St. John was acutely aware of this burgeoning conflict is clearly reflected in certain other passages, for example AMC 3.15.2
[36] cf. AMC 2.24.2

475

[37] cf. AMC 2.24.1

[38] DNS 2.12.2

[39] DNS 2.12.3 emphasis added

[40] 1 Jn. 3.2

[41] DNS 2.20.5 (also cf. AMC 2.5.4+7; SC 11.6+7, 17.3, 27.2+3; LFL 2.30) emphasis added.

[42] DNS 2.20.6

[43] 1 Jn. 3.2 emphasis added

[44] SC 11.6, also cf. 18.4

[45] DNS 2.17.2

[46] DNS 2.17.3 (cf. 2.17.6; AMC 1.3.3, 2.3.2-3.) This doctrine, incidentally, closely corresponds to the Pauline conception that "Eye has not seen, nor has ear heard, neither has it entered into the heart of man what God has prepared for those who love him." (1 Cor.2.9)

[47] This forceful line of reasoning has some rather interesting corollaries, not the least of which concerns the phenomenon of miracles. If the reason for the uniformity of the events we observe is not discoverable; that is, if we can perceive nothing in the way of necessity linking putative causes to supposed effects – and if, therefore, the succession of observed events can always be otherwise than we observe without implying contradiction, then while we have not answered why miracles occur, we have nevertheless arrived at an explanation of how miracles are able to occur. Miracles, by this reasoning, are not understood to occur in violation of laws inherent in nature – for there are in effect no laws to be violated; only observed uniform events. From this perspective, what we call miracles are no more than a reordering of an anticipated sequence of events that were never necessary to begin with. And this is simply another way of saying that in effecting a miracle God merely suspends – but does not violate – what we construe to be laws at work in the universe. If, moreover, the suspension of "laws" is attributable to God in the occurrence of miracles – and such miraculous events are (insofar as reason can discover) at least as likely to occur as the effect we have come to anticipate – then what is to prevent us from ascribing the uniform events that very clearly occur to God as well, and simply because God wills them? It is, I suggest, at least as

cogent to argue that God is the cause of this uniformity as to argue that there is no cause at all.

The Problem of Induction as Pseudo-Problematic:

Mysticism as Metalogical

Within the mystical experience itself we can no more prescind from the problem associated with the notion of causality than from any other state of human affairs. In other words, mystical experience is no more exempt from logical problematics – simply because it deals with the individual in relation to the Absolute – than any other type of experience, and any epistemological attempt to render this account coherent must sooner or later come to terms with the Problem of Induction.

Let us first, however, be clear about the problem before we begin to address it. The sequence of events within which we are accustomed to discern any causal relation, such that the effect perceived is construed to be in necessary relation to a perceived cause – which is to say as invested with the same type of logical cogency that obtains between premises and conclusions – essentially result from what David Hume in his Enquiry Concerning Human Understanding had called a "customary conjunction", a kind of psychological reflex conditioned by the perceived regular succession of contiguous events. The implications of this type of putative association are profound, and critical to our examination of the concatenation of events we find occurring within the mystical experience.

Let us be more to the point. With no disconfirming instance occurring within our experience of any sequence of events that appear to instantiate a regular succession, we interpret what are essentially two separate and unrelated events – or events related only through observation – as causally

conjoined and therefore necessarily related. A
simple analogy will, I think, suffice. Suppose that
each time I flip on the light in my study, a car is
heard to backfire somewhere in the street. The
coincidence at first strikes me as odd … but I find
it recurring again and again, that is to say, without
exception. Further suppose that, beginning to
suspect some causal relation between these two
otherwise completely unrelated events, I begin to
consciously examine this phenomenon by turning
the switch on and off at both regular and irregular
intervals – and each time, without failure, a car is
heard to backfire. It is extremely likely at this point
that I will posit what I interpret to be a causal
connection to exist between the two, even though I
find myself utterly unable to discover the nature of
this apparent, but elusive, nexus between two
otherwise discrete and unrelated events – if indeed
there is one to be discovered at all – and we have no
warrant, at least none served by logic, to believe
that there is. Even one disconfirming instance will
suffice to disabuse me of this notion, but none is

foreseeably forthcoming. In other words, it is no less the case in ordinary states of affair, than it is in mysticism, that we cannot state a priori and therefore with apodictic certainty what course of events will follow those which precede them.[1]

The implications of this assertion, together with the problematics inherent in it, have a direct and significant bearing upon mystical epistemology. While we are unable to say, in any event, what a particular experience will be, especially as it pertains to union with the Uncreated Absolute– whatever it can be, it cannot be temporal, for this possibility has been categorically eliminated by the *via negativa* as a condition to whatever type of experience will ensue, although we cannot positively say what this type of experience will be. One cannot, for example, experience participative union with the Timeless and Eternal God without experiencing the timelessness and eternity of God in that union which transcends time. And this is to say that the negative logic of the *via negativa* invests certain types of experiences subsequent to union with a negative necessity. In a sense, while it cannot prescribe certain experiences, it proscribes others. It informs the nature of subsequent experiences as no positive principle can. As David Hume had correctly pointed out, our experiences subsequent to a given event may indeed always be otherwise – but not when the conditions informing such experience, that is to say, as prerequisite to the possibility of that experience, preclude some clearly defined and distinguishable phenomena from it. In this sense, it is very much analogous, from a purely negative perspective, to the argument that Kant articulates in his attempt to answer essentially the same the question but within a positive context: "How are a priori synthetic judgments possible?"; a question to which he first formulates his answer in terms of the Transcendental Aesthetic, the principal features of which are what he calls the "two pure forms of sensible intuition serving as principles of a priori knowledge, namely space and time." [2] These Kant saw as necessary features of any possible experience, and therefore could be posited a priori of every conceivable experience. While we cannot explore Kant's argument in depth, a brief aside may prove helpful in illustrating our own point.

Mystical Transcendence and Transcendental Aesthetics

For Kant, every possible experience is necessarily invested with temporal and spatial aspects which he describes as the two forms of sensible intuition that are the a priori , the necessary, conditions of all appearances; time as universal to every intuition, and space as relative to every outer intuition. Every possible percept, every conceivable concept, Kant argues, is not just invested, but necessarily invested with at least one of these two forms of sensible intuition precisely because they are what he calls the "subjective conditions" of sensibility: they are the only way that we can apprehend data given our subjective constitution as such, in other words, given the inherent epistemological apparatus with which we have been constitutionally endowed by nature. In effect, the data delivered by sensibility acquire these spatio-temporal aspects precisely because our subjective constitution invests them with these features in order to make them available to us. As a result, we can state *a priori* that all possible experiences will be spatio-temporal in nature because space and time are the conditions under which alone data may be received given our unique subjective apparatus which synthesizes data through the forms of space and time through which alone they subsequently become intelligible to us. In the words of Kant, they are the very "condition of the possibility of appearances." [3] And this, in effect, is how synthetic a priori judgments are possible. Within the terms outlined by Kant in the Transcendental Aesthetic, we can say, *a priori* (that is to say, with certainty) that the nature of any possible experience – even without being able to say what that experience will be – will at least be temporal or spatial, or both.

The resulting problem – the penalty, if you will – involved in acquiring this type of certitude of course, is that we subsequently acquire knowledge of what are essentially appearances, or phenomena, and not what Kant calls the *nouemna*, the objective realities concealed behind the forms of space and time; forms, we had seen, imposed upon the noumena of subjective necessity. For Kant, then, whatever our experiences may not be, the matter is that Kant's thesis, as we can now see, is essentially diametric to that of St. John. But where Kant had asked the question "how are a priori synthetic judgments possible?", or in other words, how does necessity – and therefore, in light of the trenchant objections of skepticism, certainty – not simply obtain relative to our experiences of the natural order, but deductively follow from epistemological considerations deriving from man's subjective constitution as such – St. John now asks, at least implicitly, how are epistemological considerations necessarily related to metaphysics in the mystical experience, such that the conclusions drawn by mystics about states subsequently to be experienced, not just follow, but deductively follow from previously defined mystical premises? In other words, how are the mystic's epistemological presuppositions necessarily related to claims about metaphysical realities encountered in the mystical experience – so that the mystic's purely negative claim, for example, concerning the ineffability of this experience, is validated? In short, are these claims merely analytical propositions that necessarily follow from epistemological premises to which no metaphysical reality necessarily corresponds– or do these premises themselves derive of necessity from the metaphysical features outlined by St. John? In a word, does, indeed, deductive certainty obtain – and if so, what does it say about the nature of the mystical experience that St. John describes?

To begin to answer this question, we must once again turn to the most fundamental epistemological feature deriving from the *via negativa* itself, namely that, unlike a positive or prescriptive principle which purports to eliminate an infinitude of other possible features or elements in the act of positing one, the *via negativa* does not dictate that certain types of experience will follow – to the exclusion of all other possible types of experience – but that certain clearly defined types of experience will not follow – and will not follow of necessity given the conditions under which alone these experiences may occur; conditions themselves dictated by the *via negativa* acting in conformity with the metaphysical parameters to which it is applied. In other words, the *via negativa*, not merely as a negative logical principle, but as a conditioning factor – a presupposition – of certain types of experience, invests each movement in the progress to mystical union with a deductive necessity relative to the type of experience that it will not be. We can apodictically assert that certain experiences will not be of such and such a nature simply because these types of experience are otherwise unavailable except through the *via negativa* which not simply abolishes ontological incommensurability, but in so doing establishes an epistemological correspondence grounded in the negativity of this metaphysical logic such that statements concerning any subsequent experience whatever will not simply be true, but be necessarily true. And this necessity clearly does not derive merely from relations obtaining between logical propositions, but from relations that obtain between ontological realities. That two of the terms negated by this negative principle of metaphysical logic, then, are precisely those terms which Kant posits as necessary to our apprehension of natural phenomena (to which Kant alone confines himself as the only legitimate province of reason) – space and time – is no coincidence.

In this regard, it turns out, St. John is in substantial agreement with Kant relative to the limitations of reason. But St. John would continue on where Kant defaulted, by appealing to knowledge not acquired through reason and relative to experiences that are not sensuously endowed. By a continuation of this inexorable logic, the descriptive utterances of the mystics are understood to deductively follow as so many conclusions from – if you will, consequences of – premises contained within the *via negativa* itself; for example, that certain experiences are unavailable except under certain clearly specified conditions, and that these conditions determine a priori and deductively that only such and such experiences can possibly follow. And it is precisely this type of deductive certainty relative to this unique type of experience which, I suggest, strongly corroborates the authenticity of the mystic's claim to a type of experience that is, at the same time, also validated by the demonstrable coherence of what he utters. Nor must we think that the type of certainty that obtains between the mystic and his experiences in any way compromises the acknowledged autonomy of God, for as we had seen, the *via negativa* does not necessitate that a particular experience follow from the mystical protocol – merely that should an experience follow (solely contingent upon the will of God), it will in fact be invested with certain negative features according to the inexorable logic of mysticism.

The *via negativa*, then, is not simply a practical propadeutic to, but in fact is the logic of mysticism. But what are we to make of the *via negativa* itself? How are we to establish the validity of this negative principle of applied logic – not merely in its negative, logical function which, as we had seen, is essentially an existential application of the law of the excluded middle, or the principle of non-contradiction–but relative to the metaphysical assumptions in which we see it exercised by St. John in particular, and, for that matter, mystics in general? And our answer to this, of course, involves the entire metaphysical infrastructure of mysticism. While, from a purely phenomenological perspective, the *via negativa* presupposes the existence of the Absolute, the infinite, the eternal, etc., it is nevertheless a presupposition held to be verified in the mystical experience – which in turn validates the *via negativa* as corresponding to, if not a metaphysical reality, then at least a coherent claim to a perceived reality. In a word, there is an undeniable correspondence between the metaphysics and the experience – and while we may argue from the premises implied in the metaphysics to conclusions drawn from these premises – that is to say, find the conclusions to be implied in the premises and therefore deducible from them, we cannot argue from premises to experiences. And the existence of this type of correspondence between the premises implied in the metaphysics and the experience itself, I suggest, strongly supports the authenticity of the mystic's claim.

The reality which the metaphysics purports to describe, and the reality actually encountered by the mystic, correspond too exactly and too consistently to be considered less than strongly evidential. And this, in turn, brings us to a clearly related issue that will be examined in greater detail later on but which at the moment is extremely pertinent to the present inquiry: if experience substantiates the negative claims embodied in the *via negativa*, then this means that not only are statements about certain

491

types of mystical experience logically and metaphysically consistent with the principles from which they purportedly derive, but that such statements deriving from these principles are in fact empirically substantiated in experience. The metaphysics of mysticism, then, is at least logically consistent. But what is more, its strictly logical claims are existentially instantiated in the mystical experience itself – which is to say that the principles correspond to realities. And unless this claim is discredited, the mystic is able to offer the skeptic at least two complementary credentials requisite to any science: correspondence with reason and compatibility with fact. Of course, the skeptic will demand much more of the mystic in the way of complete accountability, but, as we shall find, no more than the mystic would require of the skeptic in the demand for equal accountability.

Three arguments, then, are essentially brought to bear upon the credibility of the mystical experience. It is one thing to state from a metaphysics that some dimension of reality exists *qua* rational; in other words, to conclude to some aspect of reality from purely rational premises. It is quite another thing to say that such a dimension has empirical reality. But what is more, it is something else altogether to find that a clear, coherent, correspondence exists, is demonstrable, between what are essentially rational premises and empirical conclusions. It is not merely to say, as in the first case, that the rational is real, but in light of the latter two cases, that the real is rational. In most sciences, for example, the empirical verification of a rationally consistent hypothesis suffices to at least conditionally validate the hypothesis as purporting to say something authentic about reality, and inasmuch as it does, it is held to have made a coherent claim upon reality. In other words, in light of the confirmation of the hypothesis, warrant is derived to make certain statements about, to predicate certain things of, reality in a way that is both rationally and empirically consistent. In short, the correspondence between the hypothesis and the empirical evidence is of such a nature as to be mutually corroborative, and where this corroboration occurs we are generally agreed that sufficient evidence exists to allow our claim of making a meaningful statement about some aspect of what is real. But what is more, in many cases certain aspects of the reality affirmed to exist by the physical sciences are characteristically unavailable except through an extremely sophisticated procedural protocol coupled with equally sophisticated technical apparatus. These aspects are not only typically beyond normal empirical acquaintance, but cannot, moreover, be apprehended unaided by artificial technology – and even when so apprehended exhibit such disproportion to ordinary perception as to appear to constitute something altogether different. It is not that the reality itself has changed or proven illusory – it is that the level of perception has changed. And this is to say that while the methods of attaining to certain ordinarily undisclosed aspects of reality are quite different between the mystic and the scientist, the results are strikingly similar. Too similar, in fact, to be summarily dismissed.

The Model of Science: a Reluctant Analogy

So let us carry the argument further. The reality which science purports to disclose to us is, for all practical purposes, intelligible, coherent, only to those who have submitted themselves to exacting and rigorous programs in the physical sciences covering an abstract spectrum ranging from integral calculus to quantum theory propadeutic both to gaining access to, and to meaningfully interpreting, this otherwise and ordinarily undisclosed dimension of physical reality. We may even pursue the point further and say that these aspects of reality at which they arrive are typically unavailable to the ordinary man inasmuch as he lacks the basic aptitude requisite to the type of extremely abstract thought requisite to these disciplines. This is not intellectual arrogance – it is simply a candid assessment that could be equally turned upon the point of artistic ability. Nor am I persuaded that a specific aptitude is a democratic endowment that can be cultivated through education and that, therefore, all men are latently Heisenburgs or Pascals given the proper tutelage. But neither am I implying that there is a mystical aptitude in the way that there are other clear aptitudes within individuals for the arts or sciences. I am simply suggesting that certain dimensions of reality are no more democratically accessible through science than through mysticism.

Our basic distrust of this argument, I think, stems from our inclination to believe that, in the case of science, while we ourselves are unable to enter into its mysteries, other men, better able than us, are, and therefore can confirm the realities – described by others – which we ourselves cannot.. But in the end this is either a restatement of the argument, or a deferment of the conclusion. In any case, the layman by and large trusts to the authenticity of the reality described by scientific specialists; specialists who, as we have said, had undergone long, arduous years of training in order to gain access to, and to coherently interpret, dimensions of reality available exclusively through special equipment presumed to authentically disclose elements of reality that in turn are interpretable only in terms of the most abstruse and recondite hypotheses. There is much more to the objection of science than this, but for the moment the analogy, I think, between mysticism and science is fairly obvious. The realities, then, defined by Heisenburg and St. John are in this respect equally opaque to the uninitiated.

Considered from this perspective, then, metaphysics is a statement about the ultimate nature of reality much in the way that physics is a statement about the ultimate nature of reality – and these essentially are not so much competing statements as complementary insights. It is not that there is a conflict about what constitutes the nature of ultimate reality – for this issue is entirely outside the speculative interest and competence of physics – as much as a divergence concerning what is ultimate in the nature of reality, and we arrive at divergent, even complementary, but not intrinsically conflicting answers to this question precisely because the one, physics, delimits the scope of its inquiry and establishes the limits of its competence relative to matter considered as the ultimate constituent of physical reality – a claim with which the mystic would not quarrel within its recognized and legitimate province – where, on the other hand, metaphysics resumes where physics leaves off and sees not the being of matter, but being as such, together with the relations obtaining between modes of being, as the ultimate nature of reality; a reality that clearly does not preclude physical being, but which is nevertheless not constrained solely, or even principally to it. In a real sense, the one appeals to that from which the other essentially prescinds inasmuch as neither, in and of themselves, purport to provide a universal and exhaustive schematic of reality *in toto*, but only a general understanding of the principles underlying it. On the one hand, it would be both unproductive and fatuous to argue that only what is sensible is real, for this would leave a good deal more than pure mathematics and formal logic out in the cold. Or that states-of-mind alone are real – a statement neither entirely congenial to, nor likely to be endorsed by, mystic and physicist alike. Nor yet as the Platonists and Neoplatonists would contend that reality is quintessentially suprasensuous and that our empirical acquaintances are either entirely illusory or at best only impoverished representations of a sensibly inaccessible reality. St. John no less than the physicist would find each of these three alternatives unsatisfactory, and for reasons remarkably similar; reasons pointing to more than a casual correspondence between theory and fact, metaphysics and reality, which in turn strongly suggests that authenticity, in fact, is the copula between the two.

Our question then becomes this. If the logic and the metaphysics of mysticism rationally and consistently explain the mechanics of the mystical experience and, in effect, account for uniform and significant features of that experience – which as such has an empirical basis – then on what grounds are we to reject the mystical experience as non-veridical? The objections to which we have adverted – its characteristic unavailability to the majority of men, the unintelligibility of its utterances to the uninitiated or to layman, the lengthy and rigorous propadeutics required to have access to ordinarily undisclosed dimensions of reality, its inability to be comprehended except by an apparently select few – without exception equally apply to science. And while it may be argued that one scientist can confirm the observations of another, we may equally argue on these very same terms that one mystic can confirm the experiences of another. And this is to say that the notion of personal testimony is a significant feature in both accounts. In short, it is very difficult to understand how the mystical experience is to be rejected offhand without at once rejecting not simply some extremely significant features of the scientific protocol, but science itself as purporting to both veridically and meaningfully convey the physical aspects of reality to us. And this really places us in a skeptical posture that few of us would choose to assume.

This is not to say, of course, that very clear differences do not exist between science and mysticism, but it nevertheless remains that the notion of credibility as it pertains to both accounts is too similar to be glossed over or simply ignored. And while we may be inclined to see reason as superordinate to science as a more comprehensive principle beneath which scientific theory is subsumed – and therefore more clearly evident within, and more confirmatory of, science than mysticism – some philosophical retrospect, I suggest, offers another and quite different perspective on the matter. In fact, the notion of reason, or better yet, specific features of the type of deductive reasoning from which a notion of necessity follows are, I suggest, much more strongly supported by the mystical account than by science, and for this simple reason: science is essentially unable to extricate itself from the problem of induction. It cannot forge, because it cannot discover, the vinculum that binds effects to putative causes. It cannot argue with the type of certainty that is apodictic, or implies necessity, that, for example, what so far has been the case relative to specific observations, will in fact continue to be the case; that given identical circumstances, the implementation of a specific hypothesis will necessarily yield identical results: in short, that the future will conform to the past.

Ex-Huming Hume

Let us assume that B has always – that is to say, historically – followed, accompanied, every observed instance of A. If we are then asked to justify our expectation that the next occurrence of A will be accompanied by the occurrence of B we will very likely say something like the following: "every time, without exception, that I have observed A, it has been accompanied by B, and I have never known of an instance of *B* that was not preceded by the occurrence of *A*: therefore *A* and *B* are so consistently, so uniformly conjoined that the occurrence of *A* is understood not simply as antecedent to *B* but necessarily antecedent to *B*. There is an observable sequence of uniform events to which no disqualifying instance can be appealed, so *A* therefore is the cause of *B*; there is, then, a necessary connection between *A* and *B* that can therefore be scientifically legislated as a (physical) law which admits of no exceptions." And this, of course, is quite a subreptive leap from a history of a uniform sequence of events, to the necessity of the continuing uniformity of this sequence. And in the end, the justification of this argument will always be circular: it will always appeal to experience which will only disclose the sequence of observed events – but not the necessity presumed within them. In other words, there is no discoverable reason why *B*, and not *C* or *Y*, should follow an instance of *A* – it is simply the case that *B*, in our experience, always has. Now, of course we can argue, as indeed Russell has [4], that the discovery of uniformities alone, to which no disqualifying instances have thus far been observed, suffices for the rehabilitation of science through extreme probabilities that are quite nearly tantamount to certainty, and that this is really the best that we can hope for since nothing whatever in the way of necessity binds what we construe as effects to events we interpret as causes.

Now, the implications of this argument extend well beyond science and I think, relative to our own position, it will be necessary to examine Russell's objection more closely, for it rather neatly summarizes the objection from skepticism in general. Russell essentially argues [5] along with Hume that our belief in causation results merely from the consistency, regularity, and uniformity of observed events. This much, I think, we are fairly clear about. But the interesting question relative to this line of reasoning is simply this: what are Russell's grounds for stating that uniform events cause our belief in causation? Is it that hitherto uniform events have always caused our belief in causes? And who is to say that tomorrow these same uniformities will not cause our belief in causes, as they have in the past? To advert back to experience is to reiterate the very argument which Hume and Russell have discredited. And this is to say that if the premises upon which the argument is constructed are not true, then neither is the conclusion. If we consistently hold that we cannot argue from causes to effects except inductively, then the grounds upon which we make this statement today – our experience of uniformity in events is the cause of our belief in causes – may not (do not necessarily) hold true for tomorrow. If nothing in the way of necessity binds effects to causes, in either event the result is the same: the discreditation of the notion of causality both as it applies to events observed among phenomena, and as it pertains to the construction of the argument by which the notion of causality has been discredited. If this argument is valid, then Russell is correct in stating that we can achieve no more than probabilities. But by the very argument itself Russell cannot argue to this conclusion consistently from his premises. If, then, we have grounds for neither necessity nor probability, we have no grounds for either claims to knowledge or skepticism. Both are equally discredited.

If, on the other hand, this argument is not valid, if this line of reasoning is not sound, then either the premises or the conclusion, or both, are false. And I suggest that the premises are false while the conclusion remains true for this reason: Russell cannot explain the problem with believing in causes without appealing to a cause (of the problem). In other words, he argues against causes by using causes. And this really is to say that we cannot talk about the problem without invoking causes – and this would suggest that the notion of causality is necessary to any discourse on causality. In other words, even if, as Russell argues, we cannot discover it in events – we cannot dispense with it in discourse. And that with which we cannot dispense, we understand to be necessary – it is what we mean by necessary. The relation, moreover, between my expectations and certain uniform events cannot simply be a matter of inference: we do not infer that uniform events cause our belief – our belief is a direct result of, in other words is causally related to, these events. It is not the case that we conform our expectations to events; it is, rather, that our expectations arise from, are caused by, these events – whether or not this expectation in and of itself is warranted.

There is, it turns out, a necessary relation, not between the uniform occurrence of B subsequent to A, but between my belief and the events that have caused my belief. We should have no expectations at all, no belief whatever, apart from the events which informed these expectations. Beliefs and expectations, then, are necessarily related to uniform events. While there is no necessary reason for the sun to rise tomorrow, there is a necessary reason for my expectation that the sun will rise, and it is that I should have no such expectation except for the observed uniformity of the sun having risen every day. Nor can we argue that the conditions for our belief may not be the same tomorrow; that is to say, that the conditions from which alone the development of expectations derive may be different tomorrow from what they have been today, or that tomorrow the uniformities we observe will no longer cause any expectations regarding them whatsoever. For this would mean that we can have no expectations. But we do have expectations. Whether or not they are legitimate expectations – which is quite beside the point – is another question entirely, but the expectations that we do in fact possess are necessarily connected, arise out of, derive from, uniform sequences of events, and are unintelligible apart from them as the necessary condition of the formation of expectations. There is, in short, no other way that expectations are formed; they are necessarily derived from consistent and uniform sequences of events and cannot be understood apart from them.

Equally important, I suggest, is that the argument – essentially the Problem of Induction itself – is subreptive upon its own terms. It indicts what it holds to be a circular argument upon circular terms. It arrives, pseudo-syllogistically at a conclusion from, but in violation of, its own premises. What do I mean by this? Quite simply this: to hold that we have no logical warrant to posit a necessary connection between what now appear to be two discrete and unrelated events (say the occurrence of B invariably following each and every occurrence of A with no disqualifying instance) because we have hitherto been unable to discover such a connection – is to make the subreptive leap to the very proposition which the argument holds to be untenable: that the future will conform with the past: in other words, because we have not been able to establish a necessary connection up to this point in time, does not warrant the conclusion that we will not be able to establish such a connection in the future. Yes, nothing in the way of contradiction results if we hold that B will not immediately follow the occurrence of A simply because it always and without exception has. But by that same token, nothing in the way of contradiction results if we affirm that what we have been unable to establish today, we will be able to establish tomorrow. Upon what basis can we maintain that the argument (to wit, against causality) which now holds today, will hold tomorrow? Inevitably, ineluctably, we invoke the same premises, adduce the same terms that the argument has already repudiated. In the end, we can make no claims whatever, logical or otherwise, upon the terms invoked by the Problem of Induction, not even the problematic posed by the pseudo-problem itself.

It would appear that both Russell and Hume have made something more in the way of a psychological observation than an epistemological claim, and if this in fact is the case then their argument is of little interest to us from a purely epistemological point of view. Their argument essentially appears to be more along the lines of operant conditioning than epistemological analysis: in effect, they appear to be conflating two entirely separate issues: our conditioning to observed uniformities, which is a

psychological claim, with our inability to discover
necessity between expectations and the events that
precipitate them, an epistemological claim which in
the end, I argue, is a mistaken claim. What they
really seem to be talking about is, fundamentally,
the provenance of certain types of belief. And this,
in the end, is all that the skeptic is left with if
nothing whatever in the way of necessity obtains in
our experiences. But I am not persuaded that this is
the case relative to all our experiences, and I
suggest that it very clearly is not the case relative to
mysticism in particular. The point from which we
had departed in this rather long, but I think
necessary, aside is this: the pronouncements of
science, widely accepted as paradigms of reason,
are ineluctably subverted by the problem of
induction, and as a result, the type of deductive
certainty toward which it strives, it cannot attain.

We had further argued that as a consequence of this
disability, reason of this deductive type finds a more
consistent paradigm in the metaphysics of
mysticism than in the physics of science, and

essentially for this reason: within the phenomenology of mysticism, there is no way of stating without contradiction that, for example, subsequent to the negation of time, temporal experiences may nevertheless follow. To presuppose the negation of time as the condition to a certain type of experience is to be able to assert not simply with certainty, but with deductive certainty that, whatever subsequent experience will be, it will not be temporal. In other words, as metaphysical logic, the *via negativa* binds it premises to its conclusions with a deductive certainty that is clearly analytical in nature. As an existential principle – a condition – it also connects certain types of experience mystical in nature, to certain other types of experience negative in nature which the former presupposes. In either case the conclusions are understood to be implied in the premises, and as such, to deductively follow from them. The mystic, therefore, can appeal to the type of certainty to which the physicist cannot – but it is a certainty only negatively descriptive in nature and will yield no knowledge whatever of what subsequent experiences will be; only what they will not be. And while the scope of this knowledge is confined to negative assertions, they are at least deductively certain relative to the nature of future experiences – an assertion to which no law of physics can lay claim. And the deductive nature of this certainty itself , I suggest, coupled with the testimony – together with the consistency, uniformity, and agreement with reason that we had examined earlier – puts the burden of proof not on the mystic, but the burden of disproof on the skeptic.

There remain problems of another type, however, which must be discussed before concluding our analysis; problems relating to the authenticity of the mystical experience in light of several of the more significant objections commonly brought to bear against it. In attempting to substantiate the mystic's claim upon reality, if we find that the criteria to which we appeal is conceded to substantiate other types of experience as genuine, and not illusory – if this same criteria, in other words, holds true for the mystic's claim as well, then at the very least the probable authenticity of the mystical experience must be conceded also. In the following prolepsis, then, we will consider some of these objections which, if a coherent epistemological account of mysticism is to be achieved, must ultimately be answered.

---

[1] This, of course, is the Problem of Induction forcefully stated by the skeptic David Hume in his Treatise of Human Nature (Bk. I, Part III, Sec. 1-6).

[2] Immanuel Kant, "Transcendental Doctrine of Elements, First Part, Transcendental Aesthetic," Critique Of Pure Reason, translated by Norman Kemp Smith (New York, NY: St. Martin's Press, 1965, 67 A 22.

[3] op. cit. B 39

[4] Bertrand Russell, The Problems of Philosophy (Oxford University Press, 1978), pgs. 64-65

[5] op.cit.

The Prolepsis:

Objections to the Mystical Experience

The Plight of the Mystic and the Occasion of Animus

It is inevitable that the claims of the mystic, even within the very ecclesiastical community through which his aspirations had been nurtured, will often be met by reproach, disdain, and hostility. True sanctity – the most fundamental prerequisite to union with God conceived as Most Holy – has seldom been greeted by less. And if there is one unerring mark of the authentic mystic, it is indubitable sanctity. The mystic is set apart. As everything deemed holy, he is understood as set apart not merely for God – but by God. This simple

515

observation alone, I think, suffices to explain a good deal of the hostility with which the mystic has historically been greeted. We are, by and large, indefeasibly democratic in nature, and when this sense of democracy has been violated, our response, to a greater or lesser degree, has been similar to that of Cain before God's predilection for Abel, expressing itself in hostility in having been disfranchised. We are indignant that prerogative, access, has been accorded another, while it has been denied to us. This appears to hold equally true for wealth, power, and knowledge – in fact, for the possession of anything from which we feel ourselves arbitrarily excluded. Anything whatever, exclusive in nature, is repugnant to our ingrained democratic sensibilities. In a larger sense, it is the same animosity, but on a much grander scale, encountered by the Church in maintaining Herself to be the indispensable means to salvation. No one likes being left out in the cold, understood either as outer darkness or invincible ignorance – especially when it is through no fault of their own. The perspective enjoyed by the mystic – or, for that matter, the physicist – from which one is excluded either by predilection or aptitude, is at least as likely to arouse resentment as to stir admiration. The question, in the end, inevitably becomes this: why this man and not another? Or more often than not, why him, and not me? And this, I think, is simply a candid assessment of human nature.

And then there is, of course, the discredit, even disrepute, into which mysticism has occasionally been brought by individuals uttering the most abhorrent and remarkable nonsense that in one way or another had come to be mistakenly associated with mysticism, but which really belong within the phenomenology of occultism, such as thought transference, metempsychosis and the like. I think that the problem, in large part, is due to the name which lends itself to such wide abuse, and for this reason should probably be dropped entirely and replaced with something much less general and altogether more specific. Too much in the way of undeserved but nevertheless common association with altogether discreditable notions accompany the term "mystic", and I suggest that the term "infused contemplation", which St. John frequently uses (he seldom uses the word "mystic", and never "mysticism") would be much more appropriate to the purpose. I think it entirely likely that a mystic would blench at being called a mystic, and would more probably consider himself a contemplative if he were forced to consider the point.

What we are really considering, then, is the larger problem of the broad and often indiscriminate interpretation applied to what is essentially a clearly defined phenomena concerning man's relation to Absolute Being in the person of God. Nor is the problem confined to those who have merely a superficial understanding of the subject. William James, for example, includes in his understanding of mysticism "voices and visions and leadings and missions," [1] no less than the noted skeptic Bertrand Russell who apparently includes in his own understanding of the subject, visions of angels and saints.[2] I suggest, however, that such visions and the

518

like are "mystical" in another and more ordinary sense, and really do not compel our interest insofar as a coherent mystical epistemology is concerned.

This regrettable tendency, I think, results not simply from too broad an application of the term which suggests a fundamental misconception about the nature of authentic mystical experiences. It also appears to follow from an impulse to subsume too disparate an array of mystical interpretations under a single rubric and one general accounting. Mysticism – at least of the Christian variety with which we are dealing – however, does not readily lend itself to this rather facile subsumption. While most varieties of mystical experience undeniably share certain common features – which itself implicates something universal that in turn suggests something authentic about this experience that cuts across cultural and phenomenological lines – the disparities within the several accounts are often too metaphysically inconsistent, if not contradictory, to be ignored. Quite obviously, certain of these accounts, for example, narcotically induced states of so-called mystical awareness, demonstrate less logical and metaphysical coherence than others; and the account which equates visions invested with apparent corporeity with mystical experiences quite clearly conflicts with another account of the type described by St. John which explicitly suppresses such experiences as not pertaining by definition to the nature of mystical experience at all.

It is, then, patently impossible to ascribe equal validity to competing interpretations without at once becoming involved in numerous logical contradictions. We cannot hold, for example, that the mystical experience is sensuously embodied on the one hand, and at the same time maintain that it is explicitly non-sensuous on the other. Both assertions clearly cannot be true in any univocal sense. And as the criteria to which we appeal in our effort to categorize these essentially dissimilar experiences become increasingly general, they eventually reach the point at which they become altogether meaningless. How, then, do we set about distinguishing between authentic mystical experiences, and other experiences which are held to share similar features but which derive from entirely dissimilar sources, such as those observed in the dysperceptive reflexivity of pathological psychosis, or narcotically-induced states of pseudo-mystical awareness?

Before beginning to answer this question, it is necessary to avoid some confusion at the outset by agreeing upon a clear, if concise, definition of our understanding of mystical union, and I think that the following will be adequate to our purposes while remaining consistent with the text. By mystical union, St. John understands the direct, immediate, and intuitive participation of the finite and created being of the soul in the infinite and uncreated being of God. And while there are a wide variety of objections to an equally wide variety of interpretations, some more cogent than others, only those objections that have a direct bearing upon our understanding of St. John's mystical thesis will be considered. This approach, I believe, will serve us in several ways: first and foremost it provides us with a reasonably clear index of the types of objections to which Christian mysticism is legitimately subject through a critical assessment of its actual premises, and not those commonly but mistakenly associated with it through its subreptive incorporation into essentially unrelated and incompatible systems. And in so doing, it will at once provide the focus necessary to systematically address problematic issues and legitimate criticisms specific to St. John's account without the need to contend with issues only incidental to our strictly epistemological purview. Such an approach, at the same time, equally serves to eliminate a surprising number of objections which more properly address interpretations of experiences construed as mystical and which deny, for example, the reality of space, time, matter, and personality – a denial in which St. John has no part.

Ite ad fontis

While the queue of contemporary philosophers and epistemologists – considered as either skeptical or antagonistic to the mystical doctrine – is long and distinguished, each representative nevertheless appears, in one form or another, to either further articulate or simply reformulate the principle and most cogent objections to mysticism already embodied in the writings of whom I consider to be the two greatest luminaries in this field: Bertrand Russell and William James. Every other contemporary critic, albeit providing valuable, if ancillary, insight, pales before the contribution of these two exemplary thinkers. In scope, insight, perspicacity, and clarity, their analyses to this day stand unrivalled.

The first type of objection which we encounter is rather concisely, if sardonically, stated by Bertrand Russell in the seventh chapter of his treatise on

Religion and Science. Here Russell argues the following:

> "From a scientific point of view we can
> make no distinction between the man
> who eats little and sees heaven, and the man
> who drinks much and sees snakes.
> Each is an abnormal physical condition, and
> therefore has abnormal perceptions."

Let us look at this argument a little more closely. Russell contends that what pass for mystical experiences are directly induced (caused) by presumed physiochemical changes, characteristically morbid in nature, that attend (result from, are incurred by) specific forms of behavior, and that this experience, which is fundamentally symptomatic, is particularly manifested through physical privation. By this interpretation, then, mystical experience is essentially pathological in nature. Consequently, we can dismiss the phenomena as a purely physiological issue as quickly remedied by, as it is answerable in terms of, mere biochemistry or psychophysics. The problem with this argument, however, is that it simply is not the case, for example, that millions of people suffering involuntary privation of this sort throughout the world, and greater privation still, overwhelm us with reports of experiences of a mystical nature. I think it extremely unlikely that there is any genuinely scientific data to substantiate the claim that undernourished people are more likely to have ecstatic experiences as a result of malnutrition, than people who are well-nourished, or that any statistical analysis will prove it. Simply from the point of view of probability, the preponderance of evidence suggests otherwise.

The argument, then, that abnormal physical conditions cause abnormal perceptions, although not entirely spurious in the most obvious sense, is nevertheless largely deceptive. If I have a fever I may indeed hallucinate, but when the fever has subsided I recognize the absurd nature of my perceptions; I do not set about attempting to

construct a metaphysics around this clearly
recognized pathological experience. Fasting,
moreover – and this is unmistakably the point to
which Russell adverts – is neither held to be
necessary to, nor is it an explicit protocol of,
Christian mysticism *per se*. Surely it is a discipline
within the Church, and has been from time
immemorial, but most Christians under this
obligation are, I suggest, more likely to experience
hunger than ecstasy. Nor is there any evidence to
suggest that St. John, or for that matter St. Teresa,
Eckhart, Tauler, Suso or van Ruysbroeck were
anything but healthy, active, and productive
individuals for the greater part of their lives,
experiencing as much or as little in the way of
abnormal conditions as any of their contemporaries,
especially within the religious communities
themselves where the discipline was equally
exercised. In short, any statistical evidence, if
indeed there is any, appealing to pathology upon
which a disqualification of mysticism is held to rest
can be equally applied to a given population at large

and will subsequently yield quite different and essentially contradictory results.

But more apropos of this type of objection are statements to be found within the text itself. Even a cursory reading reveals St. John himself to be extremely skeptical about most reports of mystical experience, and most especially as they relate to embodied visions and the like. [3] But more importantly, we must recall that St. John insists that the majority of those who have gone through the preliminary stages to mystical union – never in fact achieve it. [4] And the reason that they do not, we will remember, was outlined by St. John earlier in his ascribing the cause of this experience to God alone. [5] In other words, the type of causality to which Russell appeals, and from which he elsewhere prescinds entirely – any irony in itself – is signally absent. And more compelling still, I think, is the fact that, with one or two very minor exceptions, the privation and poverty of which St. John speaks as necessary to the state of infused contemplation, are exclusively spiritual in nature. Nowhere do we find emphasis upon the physical aspects of asceticism in the writings of St. John who, at one point, tersely states that "all extremes are vicious". [6] The type of argument, then, that would attempt to establish a causal relation between supposed pathological conditions and mystical states is clearly inconsistent both with the evidence at large and the premises of mysticism in particular.

If the mystical experience cannot be adequately accounted for pathologically, then perhaps its origin can be found elsewhere, specifically in a disordered state of the mind, and there are indeed those who maintain that a similarity exists between certain forms of delusional psychoses and mystical states of consciousness which indicate a common psychological ground in reference to which, like psychoses, mystical experiences are susceptible of explanation. This argument, of course, is a somewhat more sophisticated variation of the first argument we examined if, as some contemporary schools of thought maintain, psychological disorders are physiochemical in nature. In either event the objection remains essentially the same. Mystical experience and pathological psychoses are different in kind, but similar in nature. Fairly representative of this line of thought is William James who argues the following:

> "... religious mysticism is only one half of mysticism. The other half has no accumulated traditions except those which the textbooks on insanity supply. Open any one of these and you will find abundant cases in which mystical ideas are cited as characteristic symptoms of enfeebled or deluded states of mind. In delusional insanity, paranoia, as they sometimes call it, we may have a diabolical mysticism, a sort of religious mysticism turned upside down. The same sense of ineffable importance in the smallest events ... the same controlling by extraneous powers, only this time the emotion is pessimistic: instead of consolations, we have desolations;

the meanings are dreadful, point

of view of their psychological mechanism,

that classical mysticism, and these

lower mysticisms spring from the same

mental level, from that great subliminal

or transmarginal region of which science is

beginning to admit the existence,

but of which so little is really known. That

religion contains every kind of

 matter: 'seraph and snake' abide there side

by side." [7]

Mysticism as Aberration:
A Clinical Objection

What are we to make of this argument? First of all,

it seems to me that it is not at all clear just what

James is arguing here. Is it that certain aspects of

mysticism are analogous to certain aspects of

pathological psychoses? Certainly no analogy

obtains between the content of such experiences, for on this point he is quite clear that the two are not just dissimilar, but essentially diametrical. James, however, has failed to elaborate the point sufficiently, and it is precisely on this elaboration that our contention rests. The one, we have seen, is an experience of escalating unity, increasing coherence, within the universe of perception; the other of amplified disunity, dyscontextuality, and incoherence. For the contemplative, the universe of experiences gradually unfolds itself, reveals itself, as a providentially ordered and harmonious cosmos. Perfect ontological syntony, as it were, discloses itself among the infinitude of existents; opposition yields to complementarity, plurality to unicity – in short, the universe unveils itself to the mystic as infinitely coherent. On the other hand, within the solipsistic ambits of psychoses we find quite the converse to be true: the involuted world of experience is apprehended as incommensurable chaos; ordinarily lucid connections fail to obtain between rhapsodic and isolated perceptions.

Experience is characteristically recalcitrant to order, syntony yields to opposition, coherence to incoherence. And where the mystic's experiences are interpretable in terms of movement toward a coherent objective – and are in fact seen to correspond with a systematic and rational metaphysics – there is no end, no goal, no objective toward which the psychotic strives, or in light of which his behavior becomes subsequently intelligible. There is no discernible purpose toward which these apparently discrete or parenthetical states of mind are directed and in light of which his experiences become susceptible of interpretation beyond the abbreviated experience of the moment. Any meaningful notion of intentionality within a context at large vanishes amid the pure spontaneity of apparently discontinuous perceptions, and all correspondence to any coherent standard of what is presumably real breaks down, disintegrates, in a reflexively constructed dysreality.

Perhaps, then, in arguing that mysticism and psychoses "spring from the same mental level",

James is suggesting that they are analogous in that the two experiences share in fundamentally identical categories? But neither is this the case, for we have seen that the mystic's experience is consistently – and quite necessarily – outside the categories of space, time, and radical individuation. On the other hand, whatever the psychotic perceives, however distorted and incoherent the context, he necessarily perceives as invested with spatial and temporal characteristics, and for this reason: the confusion encountered in this apparently rhapsodic type of consciousness presupposes a clearly defined chronology of erratically indexed perceptions. In other words, the confusion and incoherence which psychology understands as diagnostic of psychosis could not occur outside of a temporal matrix within which alone a sequence of disordered perceptions is possible. However disorganized, there is a temporal priority of one experience to another. Moreover, inasmuch as hallucinatory aspects of these perceptions, ordered in time, are typically embodied as discrete forms, and so are individuated one from another, such experiences are inescapably spatial in nature. Were they not spatially individuated, there would be no discrete perceptions for time to index, and consequently there would be no confusion. It is not merely a matter of psychological, or even pathological interpretation of experiences of a kind, as James suggests, for the categories involved in the types of these experiences are radically dissimilar. And the point is that they are dissimilar not from a psychological point of view concerning the way that the mind organizes, or fails to coherently organize, the data brought to bear upon it; still less from a pathological perspective as causative – but from a metaphysical perspective. It is not so much a different subjective response to essentially identical data, but to data altogether different; data which are outside the possibility of empirical or psychological acquaintance simply because these acquaintances are universally and necessarily defined in terms of time and space. In short, because an individual is psychotic does not exempt him from the conditions governing perceptions in general– irrespective of whether these perceptions are hallucinatory or not.

These rather general observations, however, fail to make an assessment of perhaps the most significant feature to be invoked in distinguishing between these essentially dissimilar experiences: the notion of volition. In his argument, James adverts to what he sees as "the controlling by extraneous powers" to which mystic and psychotic are subject alike. But we must argue in turn that while it is true that the mystic exercises no positive control over the mystical experience – a point upon which St. John is very clear – in the sense that he is unable to occasion, effect, this type of experience into which he is cooperatively inducted, it is equally true that these experiences are, at any moment of his choosing, negatively susceptible to his volition. That is to say, by a simple act of will – for the contemplative is never deprived of his freedom – a turning from God, the mystic may withdraw from the mystical state and terminate the experience at will, although all evidence suggests that he would be strongly disinclined to do so. [8]

But disinclination and inability are two quite different things. And this is to say that while mystical consciousness is not voluntarily attained, neither is it involuntarily imposed. The autonomy of the will is never subverted in ecstatic union. We may discern a coincidence of wills – the soul's and God's – to such a degree that the will of the soul is, as St. John had stated earlier, indistinguishable from the will of God, but it nevertheless remains a freely appropriated correspondence of wills. And this means that the experience, while not solely accessible through the will alone, is an experience preeminently conditioned by will. Psychotic states, on the other hand, are experiences over which the psychotic exercises no control whatever, either positive or negative. He presumably neither wills to induce them, nor to suspend them. He is not free to extricate, to exempt himself from the conditions to which he finds himself subject. He may not choose not to engage in these chaotic states of mind, or to resume at will that integrated state of consciousness associated with a sound mind. Nothing of the pathology of psychosis suggests that the condition lies even marginally within the province of the will. Here indeed there is a "controlling" of the sort that James describes, a controlling in the most rigorous sense through biochemical factors that appear to effectively preclude the meaningful exercise of the will relative to these states.

But let us consider this objection further. Perhaps it may be argued that the sufferings which the soul typically endures prior to union, and which, we had suggested earlier, derive not from a lack of orientation to, but from the complete absence of, every reference to the phenomenal world at large, are in fact similar to those encountered in psychoses in that both are a suffering resulting from the absence of ordinary frames of reference. In other words, these two experiences are identical in certain respects specifically related to suffering and perceptual orientation and therefore have at least a common psychological ground inasmuch as the

537

suffering is causally related to conditions of perceptual reference. This objection, however, becomes decidedly less tenable when we consider that for the mystic, the *dark night of the soul*, unlike the cognitive chaos typical in psychosis, has a constant and coherent frame of reference: God. However dark the night that eclipses sensibility and reason, together with every ordinary frame of reference, the intentionality of the mystic remains singularly intact. He is always cognitively oriented toward and intensely focused upon a consistent and coherent end in the Person of God; an end first acquired and subsequently maintained through what St. John calls the infused theological virtue of faith. This coherent, almost teleological orientation suggests that the mystical experience is too susceptible of purpose, accords too closely, almost seamlessly with widely recognized theological canons, and remains too much in the domain of the will, to allow for anything but the most casual correspondence with psychotic states of the type to which James and others would advert in dismissing the phenomenon. In addressing the problem of suffering, we might better understand the apotheosized contemplative as, in a sense, a victim of his own sacrifice, for in one of the typical paradoxes of mysticism we find that in the prelude to ecstatic union the suffering of the mystic is palliated by the very virtue through which it is embraced. [9]

Given disparities of this sort which cannot be objectively overlooked, it becomes increasingly difficult to understand the analogy which James attempts to draw between two types of experience that in fact become increasingly dissimilar the more closely we examine them. If this type of argument concludes to an assertion of identity (mysticism is form of psychosis) based upon the observation that the two experiences simply appear to invest ordinary perception with certain extraordinary features, albeit radically dissimilar in kind and nature, then the analogy, I suggest, would appear to hold equally well between narcotically-induced states of awareness and mysticism. But this analogy, in the end, is simply a variation of Russell's earlier argument; an argument in which we had been unable to adduce any compelling evidence to substantiate precisely this type of claim; a claim suggesting that psychological states causally related to physical stimuli are equally explanatory of ecstatic union. Ironically, the more appropriate analogy may in fact be between this type of narcotically-induced consciousness and psychosis of the sort adduced by James. For here we find a strikingly similar inventory of evidence in the way of altered consciousness and disrupted cognitive processes, the re-composition of space and time accompanied by perceptual disorientation and the complete interpretive restructuring which James mistakenly sees as typifying both mystical and psychotic experiences. But unlike the relationship between psychosis and mystical experience, here a common ground is clearly distinguishable, and widely recognized, between psychotic states of mind and narcotically altered consciousness inasmuch as both are seen as resulting from, and are therefore explicable in terms of, biochemistry; the one disorder apparently spontaneous in nature, the other narcotically induced. In either event the cause and the effect are held to be identical in both cases. No such observable nexus, however, links the mystic to his experiences. And this brings us to what I think is an extremely interesting question relative to this entire line of reasoning, and it is simply this: why, relative to a discussion on mysticism, was the analogy from psychosis chosen over an analogy from narcosis, when the latter would appear to have served the purpose equally well?

The answer to this question, I think, is particularly illuminating. In the former analogy James could at least plausibly argue that the mystical experience is essentially explainable solely in terms of biophysics and without reference to anything extrinsic; a biological isolation within which alone his interpretation will hold, and which effectively excludes any other principle of causation. Any appeal to Divine causation, then, becomes not superfluous, but entirely unnecessary. Using the analogy from psychosis is clearly more congenial to James's purposes: the mystical experience is more readily dismissed, together with God, if it can be shown that no appeal to a cause outside of man is necessary in order to explain it, and this is perfectly true – but the problem is that James's argument does not offer this proof. He has not demonstrated that these experiences derive from a common source, merely that they are superficially related through the fact that ordinary perceptions sometimes acquire extraordinary features, which is clearly as answerable in terms of narcotics as clinical psychosis. James's type of argument in a nutshell is this: change the biochemistry and you change the perceptions. But arguments of this type adduce no evidence whatever of biological alteration diagnosable in mystics. Moreover, were such evidence produced; even were it proven that the biochemical makeup of mystics is similar or even identical to that of psychotics, this still would not prove the point, for it still fails to account for the radical dissimilarities between these two experiences and the still coherent orientation of the mystic toward an objective as clearly maintained to exist within the experience itself as outside of it.

Mysticism as Constitutive

The type of argument exemplified by James might well be called a theory of psycho-mystical immanence, for James essentially attempts to understand the mystical experience as somehow immanent, albeit latent, within consciousness itself. Given the necessary protocols, the types of experiences associated with mystical states can be induced: ecstasy is elicitable within consciousness. If we ascribe to this theory, however, we confront several significant problems at once. An adequate understanding of the concepts, especially the metaphysical presuppositions involved in Christian mysticism, make this extremely problematic for those ascribing to this theory. First of all, it must be demonstrated that the mind contains certain data in the form of a priori intuitions that are very specific to this to this type of experience, particularly those relating to the transcendence of time, space, and finitude; intuitions which could not, in any event, be empirically derived from experience since all experience necessarily presumes them. But what the mind possesses a priori is necessarily understood in formal and not empirical terms: we speak of them as rational concepts, not empirical percepts. But mysticism, we have seen, if nothing else, is fundamentally an experience, an intuition; and while we can meaningfully argue for the a priority of certain rational concepts, we cannot without contradiction argue for the a priority of empirical percepts, for to do so is to argue that we possess certain experiences prior to experience, which is absurd. Any theory, in a larger sense, that would hold certain experiences to be immanent or innate, awaiting, as it were, the proper conditions to actualize them or to stimulate them from latency, has failed to grasp the immediacy of experience as such. It is unintelligible, because it is contradictory, to argue that we are innately possessed of certain experiences which are not immediately experienced, for in what sense is an experience one that is not experienced? I can argue that I possess the recollection of the experience of "hot", but I cannot argue that I possess the experience "hot" even though I do not presently experience it. To further contend that under the proper stimulus I would reacquire this experience which is latent within me is to have missed the point of the immediacy of experience altogether. The only stimulus adequate to this immediacy is a renewal of the experience itself.

Let us take a different tack, and for the moment hold the entire question of the provenance of such data in consciousness in a kind of methodological suspension. Let us merely assume the point as proven. What would follow from it? What are the logical implications? Well, to begin with (and prescinding entirely from the question of what legitimately constitutes data per se) the data must, first of all, exist prior to experience: since such data are absolutely incommensurable with experience, they cannot derive from it. Such data, then, must be innate. But they are not innate in the way that, say, Plato held our acquaintance with forms to be innate, such that our empirical acquaintance with particularized instances of this form stimulates a recollection of the true form, epistemologically latent, of which the particular is recognized to be only an impoverished representation, a form, in Plato's case, that we possess and had acquired, say, through an ante-natal existence. And while the critique of mysticism that we are presently examining would appear to explain mystical experiences much in the way that Plato endeavored to explain our acquaintance with forms – by maintaining them to be innate – the similarity between the two accounts is too superficial to be exploited. The fact of the matter is that the data we encounter within the mystical experience are entirely unique: they are not mere concepts much as Descartes famous chiliagon; [10] still less the formal protocols of reason we find in the canons of logic. They are, rather, irreducible experiences; sheer intuitions with which the mystic is immediately acquainted. The question, then, remaining to be answered, is this: in what possible sense can an experience be understood to be innate or implicit?

As we had argued earlier, to speak of becoming conscious of an experience is absurd. An experience is a conscious perception. To put it another way, if we understand experiences to be coterminous with consciousness, such that the notion of an unconscious experience is essentially unintelligible and meaningless, how can we hold ourselves to possess experiences of which we are not simultaneously conscious? It would appear to be equally clear that we do not experience the laws of logic; we comprehend them. Nor do we, in any Cartesian sense, experience a chiliagon (a thousand-sided polygon); we conceptualize it. But these mystical data, we have argued, are neither logical functions nor capable of conceptualization: they are experiences, like any other kind of experience, mystical or not, to which we cannot ascribe the notion of a priority without contradiction. James's type of argument in one respect, and Russell's in another, draw illegitimate conclusions from basically defective premises; premises which I suggest are based upon a subreptive association between fundamentally dissimilar experiences. Both, in the end, are too quick to explain the phenomenon of mysticism by an appeal to superficialities.

The Real Contributions of Russell and James

While the types of arguments exemplified by Russell and James fall short of their purpose, it would be an error, I believe, to dismiss their general perspective altogether. And while I am not prepared to grant an inherent disposition on the part of the soul to certain states of quasi-mystical awareness – certainly not within the terms outlined by either – I do not think it is entirely unprofitable to consider some states of awareness to be suggestive of, and in a sense an empirical testimony to, the inherent limitations of reason, and more importantly, to the possibility of alternative modes of cognition. One paradigm which readily comes to mind concerns that state of consciousness we call dreaming. To wit, in dreams it is not uncommon to find ourselves quite suddenly and forcefully illuminated to some obscure connection between the most remote and erstwhile unrelated events, such that we are likely to say with the most profound conviction born of a truth that has suddenly been thrust upon us, "Aha, so that is the nature of such and such!", or "So that is the connection!" And while the wording, obviously, may be different, the sense remains the same. A single object or concept, or perhaps the relation between several, suddenly assumes manifold aspects; a previously unknown dimension, a newly revealed facet, emerges in light of which the relation we perceive is changed instantly and dramatically, unfolding before us as something invincibly true. Connections become marvelously translucent and strike us with the inexorable force of revelation in light of which our previous understanding palls.

These connections, however, these insights, gradually evanesce as we recede from this state of subliminal intuition and as reason gradually, inexorably reasserts itself in waking consciousness. The more that reason becomes explicit, operative– the more it supplants intuition – the less able we are to grasp these erstwhile lucid connections until at last they disappear entirely and reason is left with the awkward conjunction of apparently incongruous, irrelevant, or irreconcilable ideas. Yet often, despite the verdict of reason which pronounces these relations absurd, we are left with an unmistakable feeling of an experience of certitude often more compelling than reason ever delivered us. We are left, momentarily, with a firm conviction in the unity of reality; with the impression that there are not so much alternative, as complementary categories to be discerned within reality. And in a larger sense I think that our perception of reality is enriched by these dreams: we are persuaded that a real and fundamental stratum of unity is at least possible beneath the equally real surface phenomena of plurality and distinction which reason critically divides and apportions to us. That somehow, perhaps, these connections are not entirely chimerical, were we to discover a cognitive faculty superior to reason and through which this iridescent reticulation of perceptions would once again become accessible to us.

However appealing such an alternate might be to consider and while, much like Russell and James, we might be initially persuaded to follow this tenuous skein of evidence to the end of the strand at which point it passes completely through our grasp to no good end, we must, in our pursuit of coherence, be ingenuous enough to come to frank terms with the phenomena from the outset. Dream states are, with few exceptions, characteristically lacking in overall contextuality: in most dreams, no perduring frame of reference consistently orients the dreamer throughout his dream-experiences–indeed, were this not the case, it would be impossible to distinguish between ordinary and somnolent states of consciousness. And it is precisely this incoherence which essentially has no analogue in mysticism. While it is true, as we have already said, that the sufferings which the soul endures throughout the dark night prior to union effectively stem from the absence of ordinary frames of reference, it nevertheless remains equally true, despite this fact, that such experiences are not experiences of incoherence, but of negation. The dark night prior to mystical union is not an incoherence among experiences, but an absence of specific types of experience. Indeed, subsequent to union, these experiences, we find, are transformed into experiences of a markedly coherent and unified nature.

Dreams, unlike mystical states, moreover, are not characteristically ineffable. The difficulty encountered in describing some dreams – by far not

552

all dreams – derives not from any intrinsic incommensurability between the perceived experience and waking reality, but rather, from the attempt to impose contextual coherence upon essentially incoherent experiences. It is, I think, equally clear that dreams invariably contain, instantiate, simply the elements of ordinarily experienced perceptions, however bizarrely arranged, superimposed, and synthetized. Dreams, in other words, are not perceptions of an extraordinary or transcendent reality, but of ordinary reality reflexively projected in unsystematic consciousness; a somnolent consciousness upon which reason exercises only marginal influence. Lastly, of course, but perhaps most apropos of the point, dreams, however extraordinary, are, one and all, perceptions invested with spatio-temporal features. The similarities, then, which we might otherwise impulsively seize upon to prove a relationship between these essentially unlike experiences, are, as their predecessors were in the arguments of Russell and James, at best

553

superficial only. They do, however, suggest something valuable no less: that reason may in fact not be the exclusive arbiter of every type of experience.

Metaphysical Objections

Another and more serious objection yet remains to be considered from an entirely different perspective which, unlike the objections we have previously addressed, questions not the psychology, but the metaphysics itself upon which the mystical thesis stands. And because it is a metaphysical objection to a fundamentally metaphysical issue, it is on this account by far the more potentially discrediting, for in questioning certain ontological features of the mystical experience, it calls into question the very credibility of the metaphysics of mysticism itself. The argument may be formulated as follows:

Given not the relative, but the absolute ontological otherness of this purported mystical dimension, how can such a reality not simply relate to experience in general, but be held to structure experiences with which it is understood to be totally incommensurate? In other words, given the acknowledged categorical opposition in ontology, how is it possible for these not merely apparent, but real, contradictions to be sublated in a mystical and metaphysical unity?

The essentially monistic aspect of mysticism is clearly problematic by this account, for mystical experiences are invariably experiences of unity; a unity, as we had seen, in which opposition is not so much abolished as reconciled, and in which dogmatic individuation yields to the attenuated distinction implied in the notion of participation. The difficulty arises when the principle of reconciliation, the unifying, structuring element in this experience, is not only incommensurable with, but in fact is held to be in ontological opposition to, its counterpart in ordinary experience. In short, it is totally other. What can the nature of this principle possibly be such that it structures and unifies that of which it is essentially the antithesis? If indeed it can structure the universe of experience, then it must in some way be related to the world at large. But as St. John has forcefully argued, it is not related to the world, neither formally nor materially.[11] How, then, are we to answer this?

To begin with, it is, I suggest, equally clear that despite this apparent contradiction there is a connection – for the two dimensions are in fact experienced as structured and unified in the mystical experience; an experience, moreover, that has shown itself to be extremely recalcitrant to being proved illusory. This point was well illustrated in the case of explanations that would summarily dismiss the authenticity of the mystical experience through theories of psycho-mystical immanence. In fact, the psychological models we explored failed to adequately account for the most significant features of the mystical experience precisely because they mistakenly interpreted the phenomenon in terms of immanence; an immanence which could make no account, not merely of an implied disproportion among specific types of experience, but of a clearly perceived and experienced incommensurability between them. And this contradiction– which is central to the problem – is, I suggest, only capable of being resolved if a principle, not of immanence, but of transcendence is assumed in the account. And the whole point is that this is precisely the case with regard to Christian mysticism which posits God as a principle ontologically assumed which not only comprehends the exhaustive plenitude of reality, but is held to be the ground of its existence. [12]

Given this universal ontological presupposition – that God is not merely the cause of every being, but ontologically necessary to every being as such – there is, despite contrariety in nature and categorical polarity in essence, a necessary and fundamental connection between the phenomenal world at large and the ens realissimum of God which is encountered in mysticism. To put it in other terms, there is a transcendent metaphysical nexus between God [13] and every aspect of reality (creation) – which cannot possibly obtain between man and reality. While we cannot argue for the unqualified reconciliation of ontological opposites, [14] it nevertheless remains incontestable that the relation of the one to the other is fundamentally and necessarily ontological if God is posited as the ground of existence.[15] And this ontic relation, we had seen in an earlier context, derives from the notion of being-as-such: the primal, unqualified, and unpredicated ontic state which is only commensurate with God as Being Itself, in its being-only – and not its being such-and-such. However, once formal predicates are attached to this being-only, subsequent to which it becomes informed as a being-such-and-such, then all commensurability vanishes, for every ascribable predicate will be necessarily finite and stand in opposition to the Infinite (God).

Even so, inasmuch as all existents are primally possessed of being-only, some residual commensurability remains, however remote, and an ontological connection is in fact discernible in the account; the one, in other words, is understood to be coherently related to the other. But while we have succeeded in establishing relation, we are still left with the problem of incommensurability and opposition between predicated-being – the being-such-and-such understood in every existent beyond its being-only – and the infinite Being-in-Itself which is God. To complicate matters further, we have argued that this opposition cannot be ontologically reconciled – but indeed, it need not be reconciled, for while these experiences pertain to ontological categories reciprocally and necessarily remote through opposition, they are at the same time experiences transcendentally unified through what is essentially apotheosized consciousness; the consciousness acquired in ecstatic union. It is a transcendental structuring which does not alter, or encroach upon, the respective ontologies, but in which infinite or apotheosized cognition is brought to bear upon finite existents. It is a structuring that does not violate what is finite in ontology, but which elicits infinite epistemological dimensions from it. And it does so, I suggest, in the following way: while it remains a perception of a manifold in existence, it is at the same time a perception of the transcendental unity of relations that obtain between the manifold existents. And this is simply to restate what we had suggested earlier: that the experience of the mystic is that of a manifold not ontologically, but transcendentally unified. One in which the apparent ontological isolation of each entity is not abolished, but transcended through the epistemological disclosure of infinite relations obtaining between – and consequently unifying – otherwise isolated finite existents in a mutually implicative manifold in which the perception of the part entails a simultaneous perception of the whole to which it pertains. This perceived relation then, since it cannot be predicated of any being in isolation, but which obtains only between being, is, then, a transcendental relation deriving its unity not from the manifold in which it is discerned, but from an apotheosized apprehension of that manifold.

Extraordinary as this state of affairs may be, it is not without its analogue in ordinary human perception which is capable of eliciting limited, or finite, epistemological relations from, and in so doing effectively unifying, otherwise discrete and isolated ontological and conceptual elements. One conspicuous difference remains, however: in mysticism, ontology is already totalized in apotheosized consciousness through being transcendentally unified in an intuitional noesis. The entire ontological spectrum is already apprehended, not as unified ontologically, but as totalized epistemologically. And in point of fact, most of the errors involved in the misinterpretation of the mystical experience originate in a fundamental misunderstanding regarding this very point. What is actually a transcendental unity experienced in mysticism is mistakenly interpreted as ontological unity. It is not, however, the ontological aspect of reality that is transformed –

such that the perception of individuation and distinction perceived in the phenomenal order is ultimately revealed to be illusory – it is rather the cognitive faculty itself that has been transformed, and through this transformation has been enabled to simultaneously perceive the multiplicity of relations that obtain between, and therefore mutually implicate, every instance of being, both created and Uncreated, finite and infinite, temporal and eternal. It is, in a word, to possess the mind of God. [16] It is, consequently, cognitive and perceptual limitation which is transcended and abolished – not real distinctions in ontology. It is not the case that being is one, monistic, and ultimately, essentially, unified; but rather that the sum of being, and being in every instance, is capable of being totalized in a cognitive apotheosis.

But this is merely one of two levels of unity discernible within the mystical experience. As finite and temporally-conditioned beings we are, of course. limited in our perception of any given item in experience. Reason, on the one hand, constrained by time, cannot simultaneously entertain the vast multiplicity of relations that enter into any single object falling under its purview, while perception, on the other hand, constrained by space, cannot simultaneously apprehend the multiple facets circumscribing and defining any object acquired through sensibility. And this means that the multidimensionality of being is never simultaneously disclosed to us. In a sense, our access to being, to any being, is dimensionally limited in the way that the geometer is limited to a plane. And the consequence of this limitation is a certain opacity to being finitely considered: from one standpoint certain relations and dimensions obtain which are not accessible from another and as a result, our perception, our knowledge, our understanding of being is characteristically and necessarily incomplete.

The Cubist and the Mystic: A Common Agendum on Limitation

Within the mystical experience, on the other hand, finitude and limitation are transcended and cognition is no longer subject to these limitations, for it is no longer constrained by time and space. Our best analogy, I think, comes from art, and is that offered by certain Cubists who had the perspicacity to recognize these fundamentally spatial constraints inherent in perception and the artistic ingenuity to redefine them. Our first impression upon viewing the cubist's rendering of his subject is that of formal chaos. The subject presented to our consideration is unlike anything that our ordinary perception would be likely to encounter in the world around us, the parameters of which are defined in terms of time and space. But this, for the cubist, is entirely superficial. Beneath what sense can only perceive as chaos, inasmuch as it appropriates data within the limitations of time and space, is the ingenious rendering – and unity – of the subject in terms appropriable only through the intellect. The Cubist, recognizing the totality of his subject, is not satisfied with the single facet, the one perspective, to which perception is limited by time and space – one given particular spatial perspective among a multiplicity of possible alternate perspectives permitted in one particular point in time. Realizing that we cannot attain to the totality and unity of the subject aspectually, facet by facet – as it were, by a process of addition, attempting to arrive at a sum from the parts – he strives, rather, to grasp, to render, the subject in its entirety, from all perspectives and simultaneously. And because he does so at the cost of the organization of space and time – by superimposing perspective upon perspective as so many temporal overlays upon his subject– the product is formally recalcitrant to perspective and strikes us as odd, even grotesque. Prescinding from a presumed aesthetic value, the rendering is perspicuous to the intellect only. In a similar manner, in the mystical experience the multifaceted dimensions of being, of any being and all being, become totalized in an intuitional noesis, and through this totalization become susceptible of being cognized simultaneously. It is a perception of erstwhile unrealized dimensions and relations in being – dimensions and relations latent in ontology and capable of being elicited only through the soul's virtual participation in the Divine Mind, the absolutely illimitable cognition of God. And it is precisely for this reason that mysticism purports to convey to us an unqualified, veridical perception of reality, for it is reality simultaneously and exhaustively considered in all its luminescent dimensions and relations.

Objections from Orthodoxy: Indwelling Unknown

The types of objections that we have been considering until now have largely come from perspectives outside the tradition to which St. John belongs and apart from which his metaphysics are incapable of being understood. The scientific perspective, while not in and of itself intrinsically inimical to mysticism, is nevertheless more often than not critically, if unsuccessfully, invoked in attempts to discredit the mystical experience, while the skeptic, to whom Christian metaphysics in general is not simply insufficient but abhorrent, is openly hostile toward it. In a greater sense we may have anticipated these objections beforehand, for while they are clearly brought to bear against mysticism in particular as epitomizing the religious impulse, we may equally anticipate their critical inquiry into any aspect of religion in general, especially when claims are made about religious experiences, for any experience as such would appear to bring at least certain aspects of putative religious phenomena within the competence, and therefore under the legitimate purview, of science. In any event, a long and often unnecessarily antagonistic association has existed between science and religion which leads us to expect, as a matter of course, at least a critical commentary on topics religious from science in general. This is no especial handicap to mysticism, as we have seen. But there are other types of objections, more critical still, brought against mysticism from the very tradition upon which it is nurtured; criticisms which have sometimes resulted in an internecine conflict between dogmatic elements embodied in orthodox doctrine, and a perceived incompatibility with, if not an outright repudiation of, acknowledged dogma in the sometimes rarefied metaphysics of mysticism. This tension, more often than not, has essentially resulted from either a misunderstanding, or too rigorous an understanding of the sometimes fluid metaphysics subtending the mystical experience. This, coupled with the limitations inherent in language – and not occasionally by concepts carelessly constructed or poorly thought through – had, until St. John of the Cross, combined to create an atmosphere not altogether congenial between Dogmatics and Mysticism.

Nor was St. John himself, as we had seen, exempt from the lingering odor of heresy inasmuch as his own doctrines were called before – although subsequently exonerated by – the Holy Office. [17] Historically this has not always been the case. The Holy Office had good reason, and ample evidence of justification, for its vigilant skepticism. A point in fact, among many others that could be invoked, involves no less a well known and influential mystic than Johann Eckhart who, to his credit, and as an enduring testimony to his humility, retracted several controversial positions before the scrutiny of a panel assembled against him by the archbishop of Cologne in 1326, subsequent to which some twenty-eight of his propositions were formally condemned, seventeen among them being pronounced no less than heretical. St. John, on the other hand, so brilliantly and meticulously synthesized dogma and mystical doctrine, that he earned the title Doctor of the Church Universal by proclamation of Pope Pius XI in 1926 – some 335 years after his death. That is to say, subsequent to 335 years of close doctrinal investigation and the unremitting dogmatic analysis of his work. This is no small achievement, and speaks, I think, extremely well of the mind of this inimitable, if diminutive, Spanish mystic. Even in his most ecstatic utterances, St. John has ground his doctrine firmly in the elements of dogmatic theology. This is not to say, of course, that misunderstandings will not inevitably occur given the often abstruse metaphysics upon which his doctrines rest, and for this reason it appears to me entirely worthwhile to consider some of these misunderstandings in light of a brief Scriptural exegesis from which dogma ultimately derives its own doctrine.

One of the more cogent objections that we encounter involves the doctrine of the resurrection, and the argument may be stated as follows: If the perfection of man, or the consummation of his being, consists in the beatific vision of God, [18] which the Christian understands to be heaven; and if such a vision is, according to mystical doctrine, inaccessible to man in his created and finite nature, then how is this to be understood as compatible with the divine eschatology in which the separated soul is held to be rejoined with the body in the general resurrection when the bodies and souls of the just will be assumed into heaven – that is to say, brought before the beatific vision? For indeed, Job himself in the midst of his afflictions utters:

> "For I know that my Redeemer liveth, and in the last day I shall rise out of the earth. And I shall be clothed again with my skin, and in my flesh I shall see my God." [19] (*"Scio enim quod Redemptor meus vivit, et in novissimo die de terra surrecturus sum: et rursum circumdabor pelle mea, et in carne meavidebo Deum meum."*)

This is equally affirmed by the Apostle Paul in his epistle to the Thessalonians:

"... the dead who are in Christ shall rise first.
Then we who are alive, who are left,
shall be taken up together with them in the clouds to meet Christ ..." [20]
("... et mortui, qui in Christ sunt, resurgent primi. Deinde nos, qui vivimus, qui relinquimur, sumul rapiemur cum illis in nubibus obviam Christo.")

Moreover, the Apostle John in the Book of The Apocalypse reports seeing:

"... a great multitude, which no man could number, of all nations, and tribes, and peoples, and tongues, standing before the throne, and in sight of the Lamb, clothed with white robes, and palms in their hands."
[21] (*"... turbam magnam, quam dinumerare nemo poterat, ex omnibus gentibus, tribubus, et populis, et linguis:*

stantes ante thronum, et in conspectu Agni,
amicti stolis albis, et palmae in manibus
eorum ...")

And again, from the same source, the Evangelist
states that:

> "They shall no more hunger nor thirst again;
> ... for the Lamb, which is in the midst
> of the throne ... shall lead them to the
> fountains of the waters of life; and God shall
> wipe away all tears from their eyes." [22] (*"...*
> *non esurient, neque sitient amplius ...*
> *quoniam Agnus, qui in medio throni est,*
> *reget illos et deducet eos ad vitae fontes*
> *aquarum, et absterget Deus omnem*
> *lacrimam ab oculis eorum."*)

Given such passages, from unimpeachable sources,
it would seem that we shall indeed see God in our
created nature, for it is clearly the body, and not the
soul, which is possessed of hands, and in need of
raiment (Apoc. 7.9); which alone has eyes, and

requires food (Apoc. 7.17). It would then appear that the mystical doctrine which maintains that the beatific vision of God is accessible to man only through the negation of that created nature with which he is providentially endowed, is incompatible with Scripture. But is it really? Consider the following statement by St. Paul in his letter to the Corinthians:

> "... flesh and blood cannot possess the kingdom of God: neither shall corruption possess incorruption. Behold, I tell you a mystery. We shall all indeed rise again: but we shall not all be changed. In a moment, in the twinkling of an eye, at the last trumpet: for the trumpet shall sound, and the dead shall rise again incorruptible: and we shall be changed. For this corruptible must put on incorruption; and this mortal must put on immortality." [23] (*"Ecce mysterium vobis dico omnes quidem resurgemus sed non omnes inmutabimur in momento in ictu oculi in novissima*

tuba canet enim et mortui resurgent

incorrupti et nos inmutabimur oportet enim

corruptibile hoc induere incorruptelam et

mortale hoc induere inmortalitatem.")

And earlier:

"So also is the resurrection of the dead. It is
sown in corruption, it shall rise
in incorruption. It is sown in dishonour, it
shall rise in glory. It is sown in
weakness, it shall rise in power. It is sown a
natural body, it shall rise a spiritual
body. If there be a natural body, there is also
a spiritual body ..." [24] (*"Sic et*
resurrectio mortuorum seminatur in
corruptione surgit in incorruptione
seminatur in ignobilitate surgit in gloria
seminatur in infirmitate surgit in virtute
seminatur corpus animale surgit corpus
spiritale si est corpus animale est et
spiritale.")

And yet again:

> "... our Lord Jesus Christ ... Who will
> reform the body of our lowness, made like
> to the body of His glory." [25] (*"Dominum
> nostrum Jesum Cristum, qui reformabit
> corpus humilitatis nostrae configuratum
> corpori claritatis Suae ..."*)

And finally, the Evangelist John affirms this
eschatological doctrine in stating that:

> "... we are now the sons of God; and it hath
> not yet appeared what we shall be.
> We know, that, when He shall appear, we
> shall be like to Him: because we shall
> see Him as He is." [26] (*"... nunc filii Dei
> sumus et nondum apparuit quid erimus
> scimus quoniam cum apparuerit similes ei
> erimus quoniam videbimus eum
> sicuti est."*)

While the historical development of doctrine
pertaining to eschatology, especially as it unfolds

within the canon of Scripture, is obviously another study altogether, it nevertheless remains pertinent to our understanding that from St. John's point of view, it is not the case that the latter four citations are simply more compatible or more readily accord with his own mystical doctrine – and that therefore Scripture is somehow vindicated or validated by his own metaphysical insight. This would be to misunderstand St. John entirely. For St. John, it is rather the case that his mystical doctrine is in agreement with Scripture – and that therefore his metaphysical analysis is effectively validated in divine revelation. Nor is this relationship to be understood as coincidental in the least since St. John's metaphysics is profoundly based upon Scripture – a fact amply attested to by his constant appeal to Sacred Scripture in elaborating his doctrine. Now certainly it was not the intent, and clearly aside from the purpose, of both St. Paul and the Apostle John to proclaim a metaphysical evangel – but the latent metaphysical implications upon which St. John of the Cross drew are nevertheless conspicuously present within that divinely inspired *kerygma*. The obvious question, then, remains as to how the four previously cited passages are to be understood in light of the latter four statements. First of all, I think it is important to understand that the use of symbolism and metaphors, which is largely a feature of apocalyptic literature in general, is a type of mystical signature in all eschatological accounts; and they are so precisely because these accounts are characteristically eschatological, being narrated either at the margin of, or in fact within, supernatural experience itself. In a very real sense they share in the unique mystical problematic of language: the attempt to communicate what is experienced as essentially ineffable. And as is often the case in mystical experience, only analogies, similes and metaphors can suffice where descriptive language either proves altogether inadequate or completely fails. The canonical books of Ezekiel and Daniel, to say nothing of the Apocalypse, are eminent examples of this type of encounter with linguistic limitations. Here we find a tremendous literal effort to introduce some measure of commensurability into the account of an experience that is commensurable with no other: hence the proliferation of symbols, metaphors, and similes, valuable in themselves only insofar as they intelligibly, albeit remotely, proximate or convey some sense of experiences inherently recalcitrant to the descriptive utility of language. St. Paul's own mystical experience, to which we had briefly adverted earlier, is a good case in point. In his second epistle to the Corinthians, St. Paul, speaking of himself, says:

> "I know a man in Christ above fourteen years ago (whether in the body, I know not, or out of the body, I know not; God knoweth), such a one caught up to the third heaven. And I know such a man (whether in the body, or out of the body, I know not: God knoweth), That he was caught up into paradise, and heard secret words, which it is not granted to man to

utter." [27] (*"Scio hominem in Christo ante*
annos quattuordecim sive in corpore nescio
sive extra corpus nescio Deus scit
raptum eiusmodi usque ad tertium caelum et
scio huiusmodi hominem sive in
corpore sive extra corpus nescio Deus scit
quoniam raptus est in paradisum
et audivit arcana verba quae non licet
homini loqui.")

It is, I suggest, precisely in light of this type of apparent incommensurability that we must endeavor to understand apocalyptic and eschatological symbolism. It is not the case that one part of Scripture is true from a mystical point of view and another part not true – it is essentially the manner in which that truth is communicated. One clear example at hand of the hermeneutic tension likely to result from this type of recurrent symbolism is to be found in the sense in which the Lamb (Christ) is understood to "feed" the souls of just as we had seen described in Apocalypse 7.17, and in the first Gospel where Christ says:

"Not in bread alone doth man live, but in
every word that proceedeth from the
mouth of God." [28] ("Non in pane solo vivet
homo sed in omni verbo quod
procedit de ore Dei.")

And in The Apocalypse:

"... to him that overcometh, I will give the
hidden manna ..." [29] ("... vincenti
dabo ei manna absconditum et dabo illi
calculum candidum ...")

How are we to understand this symbolism? What,
for example, is this "hidden manna"? It is nothing
less than a share in the life of Christ as is evident
from the fourth Gospel where Christ declares:

"I am the bread of life. Your fathers did eat
manna in the desert, and are dead.
This is the bread which cometh down from
heaven; that if any man eat of it, he
may not die. I am the living bread which
came down from heaven. If any man

eat of this bread, he shall live for ever; and
the bread that I will give, is my flesh,
for the life of the world. He that eateth my
flesh, and drinketh my blood,
abideth in me, and I in him." (*Ego sum panis
vitae. Patres vestri manducaverunt
in deserto manna et mortui sunt. Hic est
panis de Caelo descendens ut si quis
ex ipso manducaverit non moriatur . Ego
sum panis vivus qui de caelo descendi.
Si quis manducaverit ex hoc pane vivet in
aeternum et panis quem ego dabo
caro mea est pro mundi vita. ... qui
manducat meam carnem et bibit meum
sanguinem in me manet et ego in illo."*)

Such passages, then, much as we had found in the
Apocalypse 7.17 and the three citations subsequent
to it, cannot, in and of themselves, be literally
interpreted and therefore construed as disconfirming
the mystical thesis. Much as we had found in our
previous examples, the literal meaning – presented
to us in terms that would appear to imply actual

corporeity – inadvertently obscures, if not effectively corrupts, the authentic significance latent within the text itself. And I think that we must see this not as a literary device to conceal doctrine beneath ambiguities – but merely as the result of a certain default in language characteristically encountered before certain types of experience. And this, I think, is particularly true of those references we find to the body. It is virtually certain, in light of the sorts of statements made by the Apostles which we had just considered, that we must indeed assume a radically different kind of body than we now possess in order to accommodate ourselves to that vision of God in which perfect beatitude is held to consist; a body no longer possessed of the limitations to which it is presently subject; in the words of St. Paul, a spiritual body, one in which presently experienced limitations are transcended, overcome, abolished. And this, of course, is an essential element in mystical doctrine: the restoration of commensurability through the transcendence of limitation. And while this mystical

583

contention that man in the state of nature – and by the state of nature we always mean prescinding from grace which is a share in the life of God – cannot attain to the beatific vision, is implied elsewhere in Scripture, [31] the whole point which St. John endeavors to develop is that it is of the essence of the mystical dialogue that we cannot prescind from grace and arrive at a coherent explanation of the mystical experience. St. John, we have insisted from the outset, is writing within a very clearly defined tradition to which an adequate notion of grace is indispensable. And what we understand by grace – essentially, participation in the life of God– is the crucial key to the most central, and at once most enigmatic, paradox of mysticism: the union of incommensurables. And here we enter into the mystery of the Incarnation.

A Two-Fold Doctrine:
Mysticism and The Incarnation

In order to understand how it is possible for man as a finite, created being to come to union with the Infinite, Uncreated Being of God – a union to which, of himself, he cannot possibly attain given an acknowledged ontological contrariety that can be neither breached nor reconciled – we must first understand how it is possible for the Infinite, Uncreated Being of God to come to union with the finite, created being of man; in other words, our answer must be formulated in terms of the Christian dogma of the Incarnation. Briefly summarized, this profound dogma is defined as the hypostatic union of the human with the divine nature in the one divine person, Jesus Christ, in whom, therefore, two distinct natures are held to subsist – the unique ontological integrity of each remaining equally intact – and which are understood to be substantially united and so constitute one substance in the one person. Simply put, the Divine and the human, God and man, the Infinite and the finite, the Eternal and the temporal, are united in the one person of Jesus Christ – arguably the most fundamental doctrine of Christianity.

Now, quite obviously, it cannot be our argument that the Incarnation is an inverse paradigm of the mystic's relation to God. The mystic does not partake of the divine nature in the way that Christ assumed our humanity. It is, for that reason, called a mystical union – and not a hypostatic union. The human nature of the mystic does not become one substance with the divine nature of God. In fact, were this understood to be the case, he would be no different from Christ. But the point I wish to make in the way of explaining the divine paradox embodied in mysticism is that the doctrine of the Incarnation effectively establishes the ability of God – to whom nothing is held to be impossible [32] –to reconcile in His own person two otherwise mutually exclusive and incompatible ontological categories without conflating the two or diminishing the integrity of either. In other words, the reconciliation of otherwise incompatible categories that is impossible for man – is possible for God; and the

586

whole point that is key to our understanding of mysticism is that it is possible only within His own person; the hypostasis, if you will, with whom the mystic is united through infused contemplation. Let us attempt to sort this out a bit.

Because the human and the divine can coexist without contradiction in Christ, the humanity of the mystic through his sacramental incorporation into the sacred humanity of the Christ, is susceptible of being united with God through the divinity of Christ. The participation of the mystic in God – beyond what is only latent in his created ontology as image of the Absolute in terms of his being-only–is only possible through the assumption of humanity by Christ, which is to say, by the Incarnation. Apart from Christ, the mystic has no ontological recourse to God, for his nature is one, created, and finite. He does not embody the terms of commensurability necessary to the union of ontological opposites. But Christ, as the Son of God, does. The mystic's union with God, then, is (only possible) through God's union with man in the person of His Son. Christ is the point of union between God and man, the created and the Uncreated, the finite and the Infinite, the temporal and the Eternal. This is the first point. The union of incommensurables is established in Christ. The second point is perhaps best introduced through the Johannine Prologue:

"... the Law was given by Moses, grace and truth came by Jesus Christ." [33]

There are essentially two vertical movements, then, to be found in St. John's mystical account. The first, as we had seen above, involves the descent of God to man and the union of ontological opposites in the person of Christ through the Incarnation. And while this remains a profound mystery accepted on faith and not susceptible of proof, it nevertheless effectively establishes the basis for the possibility of the union of opposites in the created nature of the soul vis-à-vis the Uncreated nature of God – a possibility so radicated in, as to be inconceivable apart, from the Incarnation. The second movement, then, is of course the ascent of man to God through mystical union. And this is uniquely achieved through Christ – who, in the sublime poetry of St. John of the Cross, is the Spouse, the Beloved, and the Bridegroom, with whom the contemplative ultimately attains to union. Christ alone, as true man, comprehends within himself the created nature of man reconciled with divine nature of God, and as True God the divine nature of God reconciled with the human nature of man. And it is of the essence of our argument that the mystic is only enabled to participate in both through his union with Christ in whom alone these otherwise irreconcilable natures, while yet remaining distinct, are united in one substance in one person. And this means that mystical union is not only unintelligible, but unattainable apart from Christ – who himself said that no one comes to Father except through him [34] who, in his divinity, is one with the Father. [35]

While me may have acquired some insight into certain aspects of the mechanics involved in the movement to union through the *via negativa*, together with some of the metaphysical principles underlying it, the impelling force itself behind this movement is ultimately grace; not simply actual grace as the mystic's subjective response to the invitation, but sanctifying grace through which the mystic already shares in the life of God Himself through his incorporation into the Mystical body of Christ. And this is to say that aside from the purely ontological relationship to God that is understood in terms of mans being-only, which, in the strictest sense, is possessed of an ontic dignity no greater than, and essentially no different from, anything else of which being-only may also be predicated through its participation in the Being-Absolute–a relationship, in any event, which we do not understand as constituting ontological union because of real metaphysical contrarieties in nature – or yet even in the more articulated ontological presupposition that is rooted in man's being understood as a being-the-image-of-the Absolute, of God, which presumes to its being, the Imaged of which, and in virtue of which alone, it is an image –

beyond all these relations which only metaphysically obtain, there is a far greater, a more binding and commensurable relationship that obtains through grace.

Ontology merely defines the terms of the relation legislated in nature. Within it we discern the metaphysical relation, but also the insuperable contrariety that metaphysics alone cannot reconcile. Grace, however, ever building upon nature, redefines the terms in the person of Christ, and specifically through the mystery of the Incarnation. The infusion of the divine, the infinite, the eternal, into the human, the finite, and the temporal, binds, with neither contradiction nor conflation, two erstwhile irreconcilable categories into one substance in the one person in a way analogous to that in which the mystic attains to union with God in Christ. The difficulty that we have, I think, in coming to terms with this notion is our tendency to confuse union with identity. Christ, in assuming human nature, did not make it divine such that it was no longer a human nature, but was transformed into, and therefore identical with, his divine nature. The Incarnation did not abolish his human nature. It brought it into substantive union with his divine nature. In other words, the notion of union, as we had pointed out earlier, presupposes two distinct terms attaining to a unity of those terms, and not a reciprocal transformation of those terms. And this is precisely the manner in which the mystic comes to union with God, while not becoming God. Where the mystic attains to this union through participation, God, in Christ, achieved an infinitely more profound union through the Incarnation – the Incarnation, subsequent to which, and through which alone, the participation of man in God is made possible because God first deigned to come to union with man.

This really brings us to what I feel is by far the most serious objection to mysticism; one that is occasioned by a misunderstanding of the most fundamental mystical doctrine that man not simply can participate in God, but effectively, be God-by-participation. This conclusion is so obviously fraught with possibilities of misunderstanding and so readily lends itself to misinterpretation, it is little wonder that historically it has consistently been the subject of ecclesiastical censure; and for very good reason. From the outset, as far back as Plotinus and Porphry, the third century antagonists to the philosophically naive Christians– and themselves the metaphysical precursors to Christianized mysticism – this doctrine has, in one way or another, either acquired or been tainted with the odor of heresy. This regrettable consequence had resulted largely from heretical conclusions that necessarily, or systematically followed from basically defective metaphysical premises; premises to which the Christian mystic had inadvertently committed himself in good faith, but from which he could not extricate himself without repudiating his own metaphysical doctrine. It is, I think, not so much a case of a lack of critical assessment as a lapse in critical judgment. The conclusions may well follow deductively from the premises, but the premises, and, a fortiori, the conclusions, are in some essential aspect defective, resulting in consequences unacceptable either to reason or orthodox doctrine, or more often than not, to both.

The great thirteenth century mystic Johann Eckhart, for example, in his celebrated *Opus Tripartitum* [36], maintained that man, already possessed of an "uncreated" scintilla (*vünkelin*) as the essence of his soul, is capable of total transformation into God, and that this transformation, because it is total, essentially requires the annihilation of his created nature. John Tauler, another acclaimed thirteenth century mystic, appears to suggest that mystical union is achieved only at the cost of man's unique identity, as well as his own distinctive consciousness, apart from God. In the following century we find the equally renowned mystic, Jan Ruysbroeck, in the third chapter of his *De Ornatu Spiritalium Nuptiarum* [37], describing the union of the soul with God in terms which do not clearly admit of any recognizable distinction, or, for that matter, individuation, from God. Eckhart, it is important to note, submitted to the censure his writings provoked and had subsequently retracted these statements and publicly recanted his position, while Suso – despite his error– was nevertheless beatified by the Church in 1831. Those who like to see these early Dominican mystics as proto-antagonists to the institutional Church will be disappointed to find in their humility not a formal, but an earnest submission to what they recognized as the Magisterium of the Church. These men, in other words, were by and large faithful sons of the Church, even holy men, consumed with a love of God that sometimes led to impulsive, rather than closely reasoned, speculation on the nature of their mystical experiences.

It is against this background that we must begin to explore the objections to the fundamental mystical doctrine that man is capable of becoming God-by-participation, and in the process endeavor to understand how St. John avoided the errors that dogged his predecessors within the same tradition. Let us first be clear about the problem, especially as it is viewed from the perspective of dogmatic theology. That God's nature is absolutely unique and essentially apart from every other nature is fundamental to some of the most ancient canons of Scripture beginning with the first proscription of the Decalogue [38] where God effectively establishes his unique transcendence beyond, not simply man, but everything that has a claim to man's reverence through its transcendence, such that the prophet Isaiah simply states:

> "To whom, then, have you likened God? Or
> what image could you make
> for Him?" [39] ("Cui ergo similem fecistis
> Deum aut quam imaginem ponetis ei?")

Indeed, God Himself speaking through this same prophet, asks:

> "To whom have you likened Me, and made
> Me equal, and compared Me,
> and made Me like? [40] ... I am God, and there
> is no god beside, neither is there
> the like to Me." [41] ("Cui adsimilastis me et

adaequastis et conparastis me et
fecistis similem ... recordamini prioris
saeculi quoniam Ego sum Deus et non
est ultra Deus nec est similis Mei.")

The Odor of Heresy:
God-by-Participation

How, then, can St. John – indeed, any mystic –
claim that through ecstatic union the soul becomes
"God-by-participation" through this God "who has
no like"; this God to whom nothing can be equated?
But indeed, this has been the starting point of the
mystic from the beginning, the very metaphysical
realization that is both the focal point and whole
purpose of the *via negativa*. What we find here,
then, is essentially a restatement of the mystical
problematic; not a contradiction, but an affirmation
of the problem which mysticism takes to itself from
the outset: given the absolute incommensurability,

the categorical contrariety, that is perceived between man and God, how is it possible for man to attain to union with Him? Nor is the question merely speculative in the way of an attempt to define a relationship in terms of possibility only – it is a genuine, an earnest inquiry arising out of actual experiences, equally real experiences of contrariety and unity, that in turn demand coherence, a coherence which the mystic clearly perceives but toward which he must strive through the limitations and liabilities of language and in the context of dogmatic parameters with which his doctrine must accord. Nor are these parameters, at least for St. John, perceived as constraints upon the mystical impulse; to the contrary, as we had explained earlier they are understood as constituting an indispensable index of irrefragable truth in the form of dogmatic certainties derived from no less an unimpeachable source than divine revelation itself to which the mystic subsequently appeals both as a means of verifying the authenticity of his experiences, and in avoiding the impediment of error – the twofold source of which, we will remember, is human and diabolical – that would otherwise frustrate his journey to union. Dogma, in other words, is not something simply subsidiary to the mystical experience for St. John; it is requisite to achieving it.

If we succeed in understanding St. John's mystical doctrine in its clear relationship to dogma, we immediately grasp the context in which his claim that the mystic does indeed become, in a carefully nuanced sense, "God-by-participation", for the possibility of man's participating in God ultimately derives, as we had seen, from man's ontological status as essentially being-the-image-of-God, and Scriptural references to this effect are numerous. [42] At its most basic level, we have understood this participation to relate to man's being-only, or being-contingent-upon-the-Being-Absolute of God. And in this sense, man's being necessarily, but only remotely – in the most minimal sense that unpredicated being-only implies – participates in the being of God, in Whom, unlike man, being and essence coincide. Beyond this merely ontological relation that man shares with virtually every other created existent, a greater dignity obtains in man through the further articulation of his being-only into being-the-image-of-God which conveys a good deal more in the way of proximity than is implied in the remote concept of being-only.

The question then naturally arises, in what does this image consist? And St. John – unlike Aquinas and Eckhart before him, both of whom had understood this to consist in the intellect – answered, as we had seen earlier, that it principally consists in the faculty of love, which for St. John is the only proximate means to union with a God Who is Love. And while we tend to see this as an essentially affective faculty capable of embracing the totality of man's being in the impulse to union with the Beloved – compellingly and beautifully illustrated in the poetry of St. John – love is essentially more than merely affective, at least as we are inclined to understand it in contemporary terms: indeed, a close analysis reveals that it fundamentally pertains to the will in its relationship to the good. In its essence, love simply consists in willing every possible good and no evil. And this, of course, is what we preeminently understand of God. It is not Divinity conceived in terms of power, or being, or intellect, that invincibly compels our affinity to God; it is his goodness, and the divine, the absolute and unqualified love that is the enactment of this goodness – the clearest expression of which, for the Christian mystic, became Incarnate in His Only Begotten Son. Reason, the intellect, only affords us an analogy – not a likeness between the soul and God. Love, on the other hand, is, for St. John, the impress of God upon the soul, the impress of likeness. But we have found that even this impress alone, that is to say, in and of itself, is insufficient to union – a union that can only be effected, not through nature, but through grace which alone is accessible through the Son, even as we had seen earlier in our discussion on the Incarnation. Man indeed can become God-by-participation – because

God in His Son had first become man through the Incarnation.

The mind of St. John, then, is unequivocally the mind of the Church. But the genius of St. John, even beyond his inimitable, even sublime, poetic creativity, lies in his ability not simply to elicit, but to reconcile, a complex multiplicity of metaphysical and ontological antinomies, to submit them to the demands of reason and to the equally exacting demands of doctrine, and to arrive at a coherent synthesis that, without compromising either, is consonant with both. It lies in his capacity to discover not merely plausible but cogent relations between the formal articles of faith and the empirical deliverances of experience, between the cerebral austerity of metaphysics and the resolute passion of dogmatics, between the abstracted Absolute and the virtual real – in a word, between God and man. To view his achievement in terms less than this; to see it merely as the successful conclusion to an endeavor defined from the outset by a preconceived effort to conform doctrine to dogma – a success that his predecessors within the same tradition did not enjoy, and which in large part rightfully earned him the title of Doctor of the Church – is nevertheless to miss the point of St. John's contribution altogether.

It is not the case that St. John modified or scaled down his doctrine as a theological expedience to conform to – in a greater sense, to comply with – the orthodox demands of dogma, and in the process sacrificed the authenticity of his account; much less that he exercised what amounts to duplicity in offering one doctrine while secretly subscribing to another. There is no evidence whatever suggestive of this in any of the Juanistic writings. His genius quite simply consists in his ability to coherently elicit from experience what dogma presents to faith. It is, in a sense, experience infused with theological reciprocity.

From a doctrinal standpoint there is essentially little difference between the Apostle Peter stating that "... you will be able to share the divine nature ...[43], and

St. John maintaining that the mystic in ecstatic union becomes "God-by-participation". And this, of course, is no mere coincidence. St. John was renowned for his profound knowledge of Sacred Scripture, which he deftly quotes, often analogically, to illustrate a point in his own mystical doctrine, and while his writings are free of the scholastic encumbrances of many of his contemporaries – and are for this very reason accessible, as they were meant to be, to the average reader – the tradition within which he writes is unmistakable. One does not find a multiplicity of references outside of Sacred Scripture in the works of St. John, and the appeal to authority in establishing an argument ("... for according to the philosopher ...") which had become somewhat of a hallmark in a good deal of scholastic philosophy, is conspicuously and refreshingly absent in the writings of St. John – but the scholastic stamp itself remains indelible. In any event, any question concerning the tension between St. John's mysticism and orthodox doctrine was definitively settled, at least within the Church, upon St. John's beatification in 1675, and his subsequent canonization in 1726. And despite the animus that motivates much of the criticism of the Church, her scholars, in their critical examination of the mystical doctrines of St. John, have, by and large, been men and women whose reason has been as profound as their faith.

Rewarding as such an analysis of St. John's works has been, it is not unaccompanied by a certain sense of incompleteness. His intuitive grasp of Sacred Scripture, his uncanny and unerring insight into human nature, and, above all, his poetry, have been barely touched upon – the latter most regrettably of all. It is difficult to try to summarize even a few of the many profound dimensions in the thought of perhaps the greatest figure in the Western tradition of mysticism, and it is extremely doubtful that any commentary, however comprehensive, will completely succeed in plumbing their depths or exhausting their amplitude. But this, after all, is St. John's own particular charism, both as philosopher

and mystic. It is, in the end, a fitting testimony to
the depth of one man's being, whose being became
inseparably bound to God's.

---

[1] Varieties of Religious Experience, lecture 17
[2] Religion and Science, Chapter 7
[3] AMC 2.11-12; 2.16ff; 2.19ff; & 3.2ff
[4] AMC 1.1.5; DNS 1.9.[9]
[5] AMC 1.1.4-5; DNS 1.1.1 & 1.9.7
[6] DNS 1.6.2
[7] The Varieties of Religious Experience, Lecture 7.
[8] The freedom implied in this possibility, incidentally, was
apparently overlooked by the Illuminists mentioned in an
earlier connection. Freedom is generally conceded to be a
perfection in man; hence, the Illuminists, while holding man to
be essentially impeccable in the state of union, inadvertently
deprived man of this perfection. And this, of course, is
incompatible with the notion of union with God as constituting
man's highest perfection. In other words, the highest, or
consummate, perfection cannot be achieved through a
privation of that very perfection.
[9] i.e., faith (cf. AMC, 2.4.2 ff.)
[10] The thousand-sided figure that we can conceive but not
apprehend. Meditation VI
[11] AMC 1.4.4, 1.5.4, etc.
[12] Ex.3.14; Jn. 1.3, 8.58; Col. 1.16-17; Rev. 1.8 Also cf. ST I.3
Ques. 44 Art.1-4

[13] And, *eo ipso*, man understood as participating in God.
[14] Such an argument, were it successful, would in effect
demonstrate this opposition to be, not real, but apparent only,
and the ineluctable consequence of this line of reasoning
would be a pantheistic interpretation of the universe; an
interpretation which, beside being clearly outside the pale of
Christianity, entails myriad contradictions within its own

terms.

[15] While we cannot offer proof of this assertion within the limited scope of our present inquiry, this presupposition constitutes the first principle apart from which nothing further intelligible in the mystical account may follow. God, in a word, simply must be taken as the sine qua non of Christian mysticism.

[16] In the words of St. Paul, arguably the first mystic in the Christian tradition: "Nos autem sensum Christi habemus." 1 Cor. 2.16

[17] cf. page 191

[18] cf. DNS 2.20.5; 1 Cor. 13.12; 1 Jn. 3.2; Aquinas, Sum. Cont. Gent. 4.1.1; Augustine, De Civit. Dei 22.24

[19] Job 19.25-26

[20] 1 Thess. 4.16-7

[21] Apoc. 7.9

[22] Apoc. 7.17

[23] 1 Cor. 15.50-53

[24] 1 Cor. 15.42-44

[25] Phlp. 3.21

[26] 1 Jn. 3.2

[27] 2 Cor. 12.2-4

[28] Mat. 4.4

[29] Apoc. 2.17

[30] Jn.6.48-56, emphasis added

[31] Ex. 33.20; Deut 18.16 (also cf. Gen. 32.30; Dt. 5.25 + 18.16; Jg. 6.22-23; Is. 6.5)

[32] Mat. 19.26

[33] Jn. 1.17

[34] Jn 14.6

[35] Jn.10.30

[36] Work in Three Parts

[37] Adornment of the Spiritual Marriage

[38] Ex.20.1-5

[39] Is. 40.18 (also cf. Dt. 3.24; Ps.86.8, 89.8, 113.5; Jer. 10.6)

[40] Is. 46.5

[41] Is. 46.9

[42] Gen.1.26-27; Ps. 17.15; Rom. 8.29; 1 Cor. 11.7, 15.49; 2 Cor. 3.8; Col. 3.10; Jas. 3.9

[43] 2 Pt. 1.4

Being, Becoming, and Eternity

As a final note, something further must be said about the permutations of being as they touch upon our attempt to arrive at some kind of epistemological synthesis. In the writings of St. John of the Cross, any attempt to seize upon a coherent notion of being immediately brings us to the ineluctable realization that for St. John the ontological is deeply radicated in the eschatological. Being in its utter immediacy is possessed of identity, and therefore history. The historical nature of being, embracing, as it does, all the antecedents that culminate in present being, being not merely verging upon, but enacted within the telos of becoming, is, within the mystical context, without terminus; it is eternally enacted because God is eternal. Ultimately, beyond the eschatological chrysalis, being is epiphanous, a perpetual epiphany in perpetually becoming. What I mean by this is that God's autonomous perpetuity is in Being. Man's heteronymous perpetuity is in becoming. Let us take another approach..

Becoming, I at least suggest, is the created articulation of the uncreated eternal. There is no terminus to becoming vis-à-vis the Absolute, the Infinite, the Eternal, and in this sense it is perpetually parallel to it and only in virtue of it. Even while we may speculate that at any given point of becoming, the soul (in eternity) subsumes as present all the permutations of its being, in all that has been and to this extent incorporates being even in the indesinence of becoming; that is to say, if we presume that the soul incorporates as present all that has been up to any given point in the continuum of becoming, we still have not arrived at the soul as being – only as a being-such-that-is-perpetually-a-becoming-of. From this perspective, the soul is indeed the *imago Dei* inasmuch as it embraces as eternally present all that it has been …

. up to this point in its becoming; however, what lies before it is not yet present, nor can the soul incorporate what it is not yet, into what it has been, into what it is, has enacted, up to this point of its becoming. The soul may in fact be understood to exist in a *quasi*-eternal present – but it is a present that has not yet, and never will, culminate in a terminus of its becoming such that it is a being whose being has been totally and completely enacted and can become no more than it is. But to attain to nothing more, to culminate in nothing more, to become no more than what the soul is, is to understand the soul not simply as having attained to being, but having become indistinguishable from it. It would be a being whose essence has culminated in being. But only God's Being is His essence, and only God's Essence is His Being. Rather than having understood the soul as having spuriously assumed unqualified being, we see the soul as the speculum of this *Esse Ipsum*, this Being Itself, as the finite image of what is absolute – understanding at the same time that the Infinite and Absolute as imaged eternally exceed the boundaries of the finite image. However clear and authentic the image, it is only an image in part, an incomplete instantiation, not only of the Absolute, but of its very own being which is perpetually becoming, and is not yet what it will be, and when it is what it will be, it will still not yet be what it will be, for it remains to be more, to become more than it is, to perpetually verge on the Infinite and the Absolute but never embrace it in its totality. Since human nature can never attain to the ontological status of Being Itself inasmuch as it can never assume the divine nature (even while participating in it), the perpetuity of its becoming-that-always-verges-on-being remains an inviolable aspect of its created nature (or its nature *qua* created) – and therefore remains unchanged even in eternity. And that is the splendor and the happiness, the felicity enjoyed by the soul *in conspectu Dei*, that is to say, in the beatific vision. Becoming is inexhaustible – because Being Itself is inexhaustible in God; becoming, as such, it is a tangent to, because it is enacted in, eternity.

A Biography of St. John of the Cross

While it might appear odd to append a biographical sketch as a postscript, I have done so deliberately. In an effort to isolate the logical and metaphysical elements in St. John's mystical account from any biographical overview whatever, I have attempted to subject his doctrine to a philosophic inquiry specifically upon its own terms. In approaching the works of St. John as a purely epistemological enterprise, our primary focus has been a rigorous examination of the internal consistency of the doctrines that evolve from a close and critical reading of the text. A doctrine, however, which simply evidences no inconsistency among the terms through which it is articulated, while persuading us of its cogency, or even its consonance with reason, leaves us with something not so much epistemic, as doxastic in nature. Specifically, the quantum leap from the hypothetical if to the existential is – in other words, from the conditional to the existential, from $<P....$ to $\exists x$, is nothing less than a leap from the qualified hypothetical to the unqualified ontological. However splendid the architectonic that we observe in the metaphysical edifice, the predication of being remains another matter altogether, often attaining to something merely speculative, tentative or altogether elusive. To complicate matters further, the canons to which we appeal in our attempts to qualify or disqualify such phenomena as authentically ontic in nature are themselves notoriously fluid. In this sense, philosophy is a propadeutic to something beyond itself. It brings us to the brink of the chasm dividing the hypothetical from the ontological, but is not itself the bridge over which we pass. Yet if we hope to attain to something more cogent, more compelling, than mere speculations delivered *ex hypothesi*, we must earnestly acknowledge, take

into account, and attempt to respond to, some very rigorous criticisms of the epistemological credentials we have presumed to proffer, especially philosophical critiques that emerge outside the tradition of which the mystical doctrine of St. John has subsequently become part. We find in the end that we have arrived at neither a contention, nor an accommodation, so much as a confluence of ideas that contribute to an understanding of that sublime phenomena we have come to know as mysticism. Whether these have crystallized into something coherent I leave to the judgment of the reader. The point I now wish to emphasize is that in making every effort to allow St. John's account to stand upon the integrity of its own arguments – and apart from the personality behind the mind that forged this remarkable doctrine, I have sought to bring impartial and objective focus to the consistency of the doctrine – independent of the undisputed sanctity of the man. I think that this is quite necessary. Holy men do not necessarily make sound doctrine, as clearly was the case with Blessed Henry

Suso. There is no binding vinculum between sanctity and perspicacity, because in large part the latter is unessential, and in the end ultimately superfluous to the former.

Let me take another tack: the culmination of every Christian life is the attainment of holiness, and if erudition attends this achievement it is admirable but largely beside the point. I am a great admirer of Russell; his perspicacity and often trenchant, critical, insight are refreshing both in their candor and clarity; but I decidedly esteem Mother Teresa of Calcutta, or for that matter, Blaise Pascal, as having arrived at something more estimable through, rather than having merely articulated sterile abstractions in, the pursuit of truth. Perspicacity, in a word, is engaging – but sanctity is compelling. And this really brings me to the point of this preface. Sanctity, I think, is often so compelling that we are loath to subject it to any association with error. We are inclined, in effect, to extrapolate from sanctity to inerrancy, as the though a defect in the latter vitiates the former, which is not at all the case.

Christ's stinging rebuke to Peter is a sober reminder of this. [1] But the fact remains that it is likely in some to attenuate the genuine and unsparing critical impulse necessary to the objective analysis of a Saint's work – and as a consequence to forfeit truth; a defection no less antagonistic to good philosophy than to religion. Truth itself, it has been suggested, must be esteemed as holy – and any defection from it a defection from the very holiness toward which we strive. And this is simply another way of saying that we cannot hope to attain to a consistent end through inconsistent means. And while we must be careful of a susceptibility to this type of critical latitude in dealing with the Saints, we must, on the other hand, and quite obviously, recognize that sanctity and critical acumen, while not allied of necessity, have quite often found common ground in the lives of the Saints. Even the most cursory perusal of the voluminous *Patrolgiae Latinae Cursus Completus* or the *Patrologiae Graecae* – to mention nothing of the great multiplicity of philosophical and theological works within the

Church that extends to the present day – clearly attests to this. And this is simply to say, on the other hand, that sanctity no more precludes critical acumen that critical insight precludes sanctity. Nevertheless, it remains a common, even a persistent misconception that a Saint's commitment to doctrine – which, from the Catholic perspective, is at least an integral aspect of the imputation of sanctity – precludes, or at least impedes, hampers, confines, even compromises the disinterested dedication to truth. But the fact of the matter is that the sanctions incorporated into that very body of doctrine are more far-reaching, and far more stringent, relative to a commitment to truth than those which are selectively and subjectively appropriated outside of it according to the individual inclination of the skeptic. This is not to disparage the moral integrity of the skeptic, but merely to place it within existential perspective. The historical and often heroic commitment to truth on the part of many Catholic philosophers is, I suggest, exemplified in a way seldom encountered by their skeptical counterparts in a given culture– whether we consider the ancient martyrology beginning with the early Christian philosopher St. Justin Martyr who, rather than equivocate the truth, was scourged and beheaded in 165 AD; or in our own times, and within the great Carmelite tradition itself, in the case of St. Teresa Benedicta of the Cross, who as Edith Stein, the German philosopher and colleague of the twentieth century phenomenologist Husserl, perished at the Nazi death camp at Auschwitz in 1942, both as a Jew and a Nun, renouncing neither and suffering for both – despised by the Nazis as a Jew and forsaken by her family as a Catholic Nun. Both, I maintain, are paradigms in the sense that each had clear existential alternatives, the extreme consequences of which turned exclusively upon their uncompromising relation to truth. These, and the many examples to which we can appeal, evidence a commitment to truth often supremely enacted; and that commitment, I suggest, which does not blench before the prospect of death is much less likely to be compromised in matters decidedly less final in nature.

Of course, such commitment can be, and frequently is, dismissed, or worse yet, trivialized as 'fanaticism', but I think, by and large, that this explanation is much too convenient, for we invariably see little of this trait, and much more in the way of balanced reason evidenced in the lives of the Saints. And this essentially brings us to the second reason that I have chosen to append St. John's bibliography in the way of a postscript. Bibliographies, especially within the twentieth century, are seldom read without a good deal of psychological conjecture, and a parallel, often narrative form, conceived in terms of the doctrine with which we are first acquainted, accompanies and superimposes itself upon our assessment not simply of the personality behind the doctrine, but more importantly, of the doctrine itself which is then held to be, by extension, an interpretation of the personality. As a result, we frequently do not allow the doctrine, the philosophy, to be interpreted solely, objectively, in terms of its own consistency, but rather in light of bibliographical features presumed as contributing to, often in a psychological way, the development of the doctrine; features which are then seized upon as an explanatory of it. We are all familiar with one account or another in which the personality, or more specifically, perceived defects in the personality, are held to be explanatory of the doctrine. Interpreted psychologically in terms of a symptomatic, rather than philosophically in terms of its intrinsic coherence, the focus shifts altogether from philosophy (the doctrine as logical) to pathology (the doctrine as pathological). At times this would appear to be explanatory of at least some aspects of a given doctrine – but seldom the entire doctrine. Nietzsche, I think stands as one example of this, and so does Schopenauer. But one will be hard pressed to detail this type of psychological association between St. John of the Cross and his doctrine; in effect, to see his doctrine emerging from his personality, and not out of his experiences. Those who would seek such an explanatory are bound to be disappointed in the life of St. John.

Beginnings

Born Juan de Yepes y Alvarez on what is likely the 24th of June 1542 in Fontiveros, Spain, St. John of the Cross was the youngest of three sons born to Gonzalo de Yepes and Catalina Alvarez. John's father, from a proud Toledo family which had accumulated some considerable wealth, had a bright future before him in the silk trade from which the family fortune had been amassed, but his marriage to Catalina, who was of humble origin, was considered by his family an unpardonable misalliance, and Gonzalo was effectively disowned and subsequently disinherited by his family, leaving Gonzalo with his wife and three children in great hardship. The callous disregard of Gonzalo and his family, now reduced to poverty, is stunning, especially in light of the untimely death of Gonzalo in 1543, two short years after the birth of John, subsequent to which the family turned a resolutely deaf ear to the pleas of the now destitute widow on behalf of her small children, one of whom, the second eldest, died within a few years of Gonzalo, leaving Catalina with John and his eldest brother Francisco. The poverty that John was later to embrace as a religious, was cruelly thrust upon him in childhood. Catalina's meager earnings from silk-weaving were not enough to feed and clothe her children who in large measure, and out of necessity, relied upon the beneficence of a catechetical orphanage in Medina del Campo to provide not simply the education, but the substance as well necessary to her children. During this period, John had acquired some instruction, but no great proficiency, in several trades with an eye toward some practical vocation, but it was really in his youthful office as acolyte at the Convent of Augustinian Nuns, where he served in the sacristy each morning, and not infrequently elsewhere among other duties in the afternoon, that John's lifelong love of the Church very likely began. The often long and solitary hours spent in obligations within the sacristy undoubtedly imbued the young John with a keen sense of the sacred and an early formative acquaintance with an atmosphere of introspective contemplation.

The Divine Summons

At sixteen, and now working at the nearby *Plague Hospital de la Concepcion*, he had matriculated at the Jesuit College at Medino del Campo where after four years of a liberal arts education, he entered the Novitiate of the Carmelite Order in 1563 and, as was the custom, assumed a new name, that of *Juan de Santo Matia*, or John of St. Matthias. Upon professing solemn vows he undertook further study at the Carmelite College at San Andrés which, rather auspiciously, was located at Salamanca. Here Fray John had the opportunity to study under some of the finest minds of late medieval Europe at the great University of Salamanca whose reputation as a center of learning equaled, and in some respects surpassed, the renowned medieval Universities of Paris and Oxford. Both at the College of San Andrés and at the University of Salamanca, John had acquired an apparently outstanding grasp of both Scholastic philosophy and theology, and in general excelled in his studies to such a remarkable extent that, while yet a student, he was appointed to the post of Prefect of Studies at San Andrés. In 1567 Fray Juan de la Cruz took Holy Orders and entered the priesthood. On the auspicious occasion of the celebration of his first Mass, which brought him to back his hometown of Medina del Campo, he met Madre Teresa de Jesus – better known as St. Teresa of Avila.

This acquaintance – not entirely fortuitous, for St. Teresa had sought out the young priest who had been recommended to her as a likely candidate to assist her in her efforts to reform the Carmelite Order at large, friars as well as nuns – evolved into a lifelong friendship and alliance, and was to prove momentous to both the 52 year old Carmelite Nun, and the young 25 year old priest whose deepening spirituality and strong sense of interiority had compelled him at this point to consider transferring from the Carmelites to the more austere and reclusive Carthusians. But St. Teresa in short order succeeded in persuading the diminutive but intense young friar that his vocation lay in the white mantle that presently stood upon his shoulders, and not elsewhere; the Order of Our Lady, she insisted, must not be abandoned, but reformed. And she had quite definite plans for effecting the reform which the Mitigated Rule stood in such desperate need of, and John would be instrumental in restoring the venerable Order to its Primitive Rule among the friars in the way that St. Teresa had tirelessly labored to effect it among her nuns at Valladolid. In 1568, in the company of three other Carmelite friars, St. John changed his name at Duruelo from *Juan de Santo Matia* to *Juan de la Cruz* – and effectively entered upon the reform of the Order. The mutual vision and reciprocal commitment,

626

coupled with the deep and holy affection that bound the younger John to the older Teresa, would sustain this collaborative effort for many years and through much hardship.

It was not long before the exemplary lives of the small community of reformed friars and nuns that had gathered around St. John and St. Teresa respectively began attracting vocations, and with the burgeoning reform, in which St. Teresa had been indefatigable, it was inevitable that the friars and nuns of the Mitigated Rule who wished to retain the individual latitude to which they had grown accustomed should respond sometimes acrimoniously, even violently, to the vigorous threat which the zeal of the reform had posed. From a larger perspective, however, the ensuing turmoil – and it was considerable – cannot be laid entirely at the feet of St. Teresa and St. John, though neither were loath to come to terms with the consequences of their zeal, for the call to a general reform of all Religious Orders had been issued by the Council of Trent a year earlier in 1568, and was already in the process of being implemented by King Philip II in that same year – a reform, we must remember, itself precipitated by the Counter-Reformation which had begun a mere 8 years earlier in 1560 under the Papacy of Pius IV.

Reformatio in Capite et in Membris:
The Counter-Reformation

Some brief overview of this period is necessary, I think, to understanding the historical context from which the reform efforts of both Saints took their impetus. The lax and reproachable state of affairs, especially concerning discipline and morals, into which highly profiled segments of the Church had fallen, had, of course, precipitated the Reformation some years earlier, and what had been experienced by the Church on a much larger scale had no less been the occasion of the lapse in discipline in the religious orders in Spain as well. The formation and training of the clergy at large had been seriously neglected in favor of the decidedly more immediate and provincial interests of higher ecclesiastical dignitaries and this regrettable state of affairs was often not unaccompanied by moral turpitude. Members of the Papal Curia, no less than local bishops and abbots, had come to understand and so exercise their authority in increasingly secular terms, to the neglect and detriment of the primary spiritual offices with which they were entrusted; offices which, at least as often as not, were as instrumental to augmenting their income as to their acquiring the perquisites of secular power. Entire cathedral chapters, whose ecclesiastics were beneficed through endowments established to maintain the clergy, would often spuriously combine prebends – salaries intended to be distributed among the clergy attached to the Cathedral – within one individual, increasing his leverage in both power and wealth. And conditions, regrettably, fared no better with the Religious

Orders themselves. Not infrequently, monasteries of religious women were largely congregations of the unmarried daughters of the nobility, and for many Orders, the original charism upon which the community had been founded, and which had provided its raison d'être, had been entirely lost in this lapse of orientation, or the rule so seriously mitigated as to be unrecognizable. A recognition of the impendence of this sorry state of affairs had existed for some time and in fact dated at least as far back as the 14th century where the call pro reformatio in capite et in membris [2] had begun slowly gathering the initial momentum that would culminate in the Counter-Reformation in 1560. St. John and St. Teresa, while confining their efforts at reform to the Carmelite order in particular, may in fact be seen not simply as the product of the Counter-Reformation, but as two of the most brilliant, articulate, energetic and successful figures that the Counter-Reformation had produced. The influence of their efforts extended well beyond the cloisters of Carmel; indeed, well beyond the border of Spain and continues to exert itself to the present day within the whole of Catholicism at large. In any event, the reform which the two Saints had collaborated in effecting resulted in some particularly bitter consequences for St. John who, taken captive by the Calced Carmelites – the friars of the mitigated rule, who, unlike the newly reformed Discalced Carmelites, wore sandals, the latter going barefooted, or discalced – and refusing to renounce the reform, was subsequently imprisoned at the Carmelite Priory in Toledo in 1577 for the better part of a year. The room – a closet actually – that served as his cell, was a meager 6 foot by 10 foot area, unheated, unventilated, and effectively unilluminated except for a small crevice in one wall well above the head of the spare and diminutive friar who, standing erectly, barely attained to five feet. Subsisting only on bread and water and an occasional sardine, he was routinely scourged, not by one, but by every present member of the Calced community following their evening refection and returned to the darkness and cold – or stifling heat – of his cell. Having nothing but the tattered clothes on his wounded and unhealing back, no breviary, and probably most painfully, nothing with which to confect the species through which he could celebrate Mass, St. John was left with the outer darkness – and the gathering inner light, a combination which crystallized in the sublime poetry that has made the works of St. John of the Cross not just classic in Spanish literature, but among the most beautiful poetic works ever written.

Chronology of St. John's Writings

After six months closely confined and in great privation, St. John was providentially assigned a new jailer, Fray Juan de Santa Maria, who was much more kindly disposed toward the gentle St. than his previous incarcerator. He appears to have allowed him oil and a lamp, and more importantly, paper and ink upon which to write, and in general seems to have made every effort to alleviate the condition of the straitened friar as much as was within his power to do so, despite the severe sanctions, under provisions of the Order's constitution, that would have been applied against him, and with the same severity and exactitude with which St. John himself had become intimately acquainted. At this time, St. John composed the first thirty-one verses of his magnificent Spiritual Canticle, and several less well-known poems. Two months later, in August of 1578, and under circumstances deemed by some to have been miraculous, St. John managed to escape his captors and found refuge in Toledo with the reformed Carmelite nuns who sheltered him from his pursuers, bringing him south to the greater safety of El Calvario in Andalusia where he began composing the *Dark Night of the Soul* and the *Ascent of Mount Carmel* upon which he worked sporadically until their completion in 1585.

St. John's poetry, the magnificent and inimitable style of which contrasts so sharply with his dense and often redundant literary treatises, is widely considered among the most beautiful and preeminent in all of Spanish literature to date. In fact, it is among the most beautiful, most evocative of poetic literature in any language. As Fr. Kieran Kavanaugh, O.C.D. correctly observes,

> "St. John of the Cross has received the title, "the loftiest poet of Spain", not on account of his books of poetry, but with some ten or twelve compositions. These compositions, however, display such variety that it can almost be affirmed that each of them represents a completely distinct poetic vision and technique, a singular accomplishment in Spanish literature." [3]

There are ten poems of indubitable authenticity, all composed within a 14 year period preceding St. John's death in 1591. Regrettably, none of the original copies are extant. The copies which do exist are incorporated into what is known as the Codex of Sanlucar, which, while not in the hand of the Saint himself, were nevertheless unquestionably reviewed and revised by St. John as attested to by glosses and additions to the text which appear in the handwriting of St. John. The authenticity of four other poems is also very likely. It is, I find, an extreme irony – even a paradox – that one is more likely to arrive at a much clearer intuition (not understanding) of something verging upon the experience of *unio mystica* through any of these 14 poems, than through all the protracted, carefully nuanced, and often involuted explications which St. John offers us through the treatises we have examined in this work. Here we have attained to consistency. In his poetry we attain to sublimity. The poems of unquestionable authenticity are as follows:

- The Spiritual Canticle (*Cantico Espiritual*)

- The Dark Night (*Noche Oscura*)

- The Living Flame of Love (*Llama De Amor Via*)

- I Entered in Unknowing (*Yo No Supe Dónde Entraba*)

- I Live, but Not in Myself (*Vivo sin Vivir en Mi*)

- I Went Out Seeking Love (*Tras de un Amoroso Lance*)

- A Lone Young Shepherd (*Un Pastorcico Solo Esta Penado*)

- For I Know Well the Spring (*Que Bien Sé Yo la Fuente*)

- The Romances (*Romances 1-9*)

- On the Psalm: "By the Waters of Babylon" (*Romance Que Va Por "Super flumina Babylonis" (Ps. 136)*)

The remaining four poems, the authenticity of which cannot be definitively established but which very likely were composed by St. John are:

- Without Support and With Support (*Sin Arrimo y con Arrimo*)

- Not for All of Beauty (*Por Toda la Hermosura*)

- Del Verbo Divino (*Del Verbo Divino*)

- The Sum of Perfection (*Suma De Perfeccion*)

These poems are faithfully reproduced in Spanish and meticulously translated into English by Fr. Kieran Kavanaugh O.C.D. and Fr. Otilio Rodriguez, O.C.D. in "The Collected Works of St. John of the Cross" [4], which I highly recommend.

Death and Canonization

St. John, in the years ensuing, was extremely active within the newly reformed order, holding a variety of positions as confessor, vicar, Prior, Second Definitor, Vicar-Provincial, Definitor and Consiliario, and Deputy-Vicar General – to say nothing of the great administrational skill he demonstrated as founder and rector of the Carmelite College for the students of the Reform at Baeza. This activity, however, was balanced by the contemplation he had patiently and diligently acquired through spending long hours in prayer. As is often the case with great saints no less than great men, the end of his life would find him persecuted by the very cause for which he gave of himself entirely, patiently enduring the spite of lesser men resentful of his irrepressible sanctity. Deprived, for his conviction, of every office within the Reform, and in failing health, he repaired to La Peñuela in 1591 only to learn that efforts were already under way to expel the holy friar from the Reform itself which he had founded, and for whose sake he had willingly suffered so much. This must have been a bitter disappointment to St. John – not to find himself despised and put to naught; indeed, it was his wish to die alone, without title, and in obscurity – but to find his brothers in Christ at such a great distance from the heart of God, the mind of Christ, in their enmity not just to him – but to any man. It has indeed been well put that in the Church where the lights are brightest, the shadows are also deepest. St. Teresa, who had died some nine years earlier in 1582 would probably have come closest to understanding the heart of St. John at this crucial and final point in his life, but was providentially spared the pain of this ignominy. John, whose health continued to decline, and still under the vow of obedience, was ordered to seek medical assistance which was available both at Baez and Ubeda, and when presented with the choice opted for Ubeda where, he felt, he was unknown and would be accorded no more consideration than any other friar in failing health. But even in Ubeda, St. John's reputation preceded him, and despite his ill health, those both envious and suspicious of his sanctity received him coldly, brusquely assigning him the poorest cell available while taking pains to make clear to him the inconvenience and expense incurred of necessity by his stay at the monastery. This must have troubled St. John as much as the festering ulcerations that had by now progressed from his legs to his back, and before long it became apparent that the small friar in the most dismal cell was dying. Without reproach, and in the most earnest humility, he begged pardon of those to whom he had become such an unwelcome burden, and parting his lips finally, uttered the words of

Christ on the Cross: "Lord, into your hands I commend my spirit", and with this, died. He was forty-nine. Within eighty-four years of his death on December 14, 1591 St. John of the Cross was beatified by Pope Clement X on January 25, 1675, subsequently canonized by Pope Benedict XIII on December 26, 1726, and finally declared a Doctor of the Church Universal by Pope Pius XI on August 24, 1926.

Something more must be said of this great luminary, something vitally important to any adequate assessment of the life of St. John. And it may be summed up simply in this: St. John was a good man. For all the austerity to which he subjected himself willingly and without murmur, his heart was singularly inaustere. Embracing poverty, and the son of poverty from his earliest childhood, he was nevertheless pained by the poverty he saw in others, even in the sometimes desperately poor nuns of the Reformed and Primitive Rule for whom he himself would beg alms as a father for his children. Knowing the needs of others, he never humiliated those in want, but anticipating their need, set about to secure what was necessary for them, knowing that they would never ask it for themselves. His concern, it is important to note, did not extend simply to the spiritual welfare of those with whom he came in contact: he saw the whole man, the entire woman, not just the imago Dei sequestered behind the ephemerality of the flesh, but the Sacred Humanity of Christ which ennobled the humanity of every person. His eyes, St. Teresa tells us, were large and dark, and in St. John they were not merely the portals to his own soul, but the lamps of compassion that burned with a love that seemed to embrace the totality of the person who stood before him. The hunger that gnawed at the stomachs of his penitents was just as real as the cancer of sin he sought to excise from their souls in the holy tribunal of penance. The illness that racked the bodies of men and women was every bit as real as the spiritual sickness that plagued their souls, and he sought to remedy both as much as it was in his power to do so. His life, in short, was conformed to the life of Christ who not simply forgave sins, but healed the sinner, and who, in the succinct words of the Apostle Peter, went about doing good.[5] St. John, in a word, was the faithful steward whose will was to do the will of the Master. And these who gathered around him, Carmelite and lay, would in the end be called home through the same night to the same House by the same Father, in the one same unquenchable light that, consuming all else in a holocaust of love, ultimately reveals the face of God.

---

[1] Mk. 8.33

[2] literally, a reform of the head and the members.

[3] *The Collected Works of St. John of the Cross*, p.709, Kieran Kavanaugh, O.C.D. and Otilio Rodriguez, O.C.D., ICS Publications, Institute of Carmelite Studies, Washington, D.C., 1979

[4] op. cit.

[5] Acts 10.38

EPILOGUE

In the end, something vital remains to be said about the enduring phenomenon of mystical experience itself. It has little to do with epistemology or metaphysics – which at best are only so many superficial tangents to the sublime experience which, we have seen, remains impenetrable to reason. We are, I think, mistakenly inclined to see this deeply personal and profoundly religious experience as somehow confined to the lives of a few remarkable individuals who by and large have been saints in a strictly canonical sense. We are intimidated by what we perceive to be the austerity of the lives they had lived, and tend to see them as persons quite apart from ourselves – and quite fortunately so. Very likely we are acquainted with one narrative or another detailing the severity of the lives they had lived – accounts sometimes

embellished, as all hagiography to some extent is –
with the great trials and hardships they endured in
an adamantine faith that appears quite impossible to
most of us. They are figures who loom largely in
unforgettable but nevertheless dusty tomes from an
age of faith as distant from us as the alchemist's art.

As a consequence, we tend to consign the
experience that shaped and ultimately defined their
lives to the same reliquary to which we reverently,
but no less resolutely, shelf these abstruse
speculative systems together with the devout
biographies that accompany them – for it no longer
seems viable in our age or even possible in our
lives. In short, the great mystical enterprise; indeed,
the mystical phenomenon itself, tends to be
perceived essentially as an *historical* phenomenon.
This, I think, is due in large part to the emphasis
placed upon the medieval mystics who, not
surprisingly, had flourished in an age of faith, an
age in which the Church predominated and whose
every institution to some extent understood itself in
relation to God. It was, moreover, the medieval

mystics who had succeeded in systematically formulating this ancient doctrine into a viable Christian synthesis around which, at least implicitly, entire contemplative communities were subsequently formed. The goal, after all, of every contemplative is contemplation – and perfect contemplation culminates in union. These most conspicuous figures in the history of mysticism, confined to a fixed and distant era, seem – with few notable exceptions since – to have formed the terminus of a tradition whose impulse had somehow withered with the dawn of the Renaissance. But this, of course, is not true. The many Discalced Carmelite monasteries throughout the world – which have not merely survived, but have flourished – are extraordinary testimonies to the vibrant continuity of this tradition. They, and other contemplative orders – to say nothing of the lives of many individuals living contemplatively within the world at large – are reminders in this postmodern era that the ancient mystical impulse is indomitable, incessant, irrepressible – even eternal.

In the end, I think that the invitation to union is far more common than we suppose. I further think that the basic intuition underlying the experience of this invitation is, however indistinctly – and however reluctant we are to concede it – perceived as God. I am equally persuaded, however, that it is a perception we are likely to distort, resist, or even arrogantly dismiss. The reasons for this, to be sure, are many and varied. But I also think that this invitation leaves an indelible impression. However successful we are in explaining it away, this unmistakable invitation, I am convinced, is etched into the heart by God Himself, and continues to beckon us, despite the disdain, even the reproach of reason, to something beyond ourselves, something infinitely greater than our selves. And our reluctance to respond to this invitation seems, in the end, to be rooted in fear; the fear that, in the words of Archbishop Fulton Sheen, "if we give Him our finger, He will take our whole hand." In an age that blenches before any absolute commitment whatever, many of us simply are not prepared to make a commitment as absolute as the invitation requires. For ultimately, we realize, it entails far more than our hand, or even our heart, embracing, as it does, the totality of our being in the totality of His love.

CONCLUSION

For all our speculative efforts to arrive at some rational tangent between epistemological accountability and the phenomenon of ecstatic union, we have achieved nothing more than a logical excursus into a deeply and profoundly preterlogical reality. The rigorously austere terms of logic only yield a pronouncement on form, prescinding from substance. To understand consonance in form is extrinsic to the subject of which it is predicated – except in purely relational terms. That the terms putatively inherent in phenomena accord with logic tells us nothing of the phenomena. Either they accord with logic or reason or they do not. No more. Logic makes no existential statements.

So what does this mean? It means that this tedious discourse has merely presumed to demonstrate that no conflict obtains between the canons of reason and the phenomena of ecstatic union. It gives us absolutely no insight into the experience itself – only the relational consonance inherent within it.

Perhaps a final, even apposite, metaphor remains: for those who have known nothing of conjugal union, the nature, the form, the method – all the physiological mechanics – of consummating that union are clearly understood. But however exhaustive, however extensive, however comprehensively they are apprehended, they yield nothing, absolutely nothing, of the nature of the experience itself. However rich their vocabulary, however profound their knowledge, not only will both be obviated by that union, but within that union both will become utterly superfluous to it.

Ecstatic union? Every *other* union is the merest, the most tenuous *metaphor* – for this sublime union of the soul with God.

It is the *ultimate intimacy* between the soul and God, the Bride and the Groom; the inexpressible consummation of love that demurs from the intrusion of reason, the prurience of language, the invasiveness of words, and none may intrude upon it in a futile and ultimately officious attempt to *understand* what can only be *consummated*.

A curtain is drawn that only the Lover may know the Beloved.

END

About the Author

The author studied philosophy in the Bachelor's, Master's, and Doctoral programs at Boston University. The Metaphysics received the *Imprimatur* and *Nihil Obstat* from the *Censor Librorum* of the Archdiocese of Boston in an earlier redaction. The author is a contributing editor to the <u>Boston Catholic Journal</u>.

Made in United States
North Haven, CT
26 June 2022

20638304R00393